IMAGES
of America

NEWPORT
THE SIN CITY YEARS

On the Cover: Speakeasies were illegal nightclubs that offered illicit alcohol during the Roaring Twenties. Taverns such as this one, located on the outskirts of Newport, survived Prohibition by going underground. (Kenton County Public Library.)

IMAGES
of America

NEWPORT
THE SIN CITY YEARS

Robin Caraway

ARCADIA
PUBLISHING

ISBN 978-0-7385-8692-2

Published by Arcadia Publishing
Charleston, South Carolina

Printed in the United States of America

Library of Congress Control Number: 2010930735

For all general information, please contact Arcadia Publishing:
Telephone 843-853-2070
Fax 843-853-0044
E-mail sales@arcadiapublishing.com
For customer service and orders:
Toll-Free 1-888-313-2665

Visit us on the Internet at www.arcadiapublishing.com

This book is dedicated to my children, Cody, Kira, Sheridan, and Caden, who I hope inherit my love for local history and genealogy.

Contents

ACKNOWLEDGMENTS

Many wonderful people gave their time, assistance, and pictures to make this book possible, and I am indebted to them. A big thank-you goes to the Kenton County Public Library: Elaine Kuhn, Tim Herrmann, Jan Mueller, Lisa Chipman, Charles King, Verna Bond-Broderick, Nicole Frilling, and the wonderful library staff members. Their dedication to providing photographs and resources for those interested in local history is astonishing. I would like to thank Dave Horn, who was gracious enough to share his knowledge and his collection of Northern Kentucky gambling memorabilia. His contributions are a large part of this book.

Thank you to Bernie Spencer at www.nkyviews.com for allowing me to share some of the pictures posted on his Web site. I must also thank the members of the Campbell County Historical Society for contributing pictures and information, especially Mike Stull and Buck Siebert for assisting me with the scanning process.

I wish to thank Mike Sweeney for proofreading the manuscript and sharing his knowledge of Newport's history. I am grateful to Arcadia Publishing and my editor, Luke Cunningham, for his guidance throughout the writing of this book.

Special thanks are owed to my family and friends for their support and assistance throughout this endeavor.

INTRODUCTION

Newport, Kentucky, is a small city with a big reputation. Incorporated in 1795, the city began as a pioneer settlement. By 1805, its economic growth and development increased dramatically after the U.S. Army purchased five acres of land located at the mouth of the Licking River. There they established a military post known as the Newport Barracks.

The Barracks was bustling with activity during the Civil War largely because the Union army used it as a recruiting station. Numerous saloons, brothels, and pool halls began springing up in the city to offer entertainment to the soldiers as a reprieve from their tedious garrison life. One saloon, Eicher's, even offered a shooting gallery for added amusement. Drinking, gambling, and women quickly became a pleasurable pastime for troops when granted a break from the Barracks. This era planted the seeds of vice that sprouted during Prohibition and grew into a massive problem for the city.

During Prohibition, the black market for alcohol flourished. Moonshine stills began popping up throughout the city, and many legal businesses developed into speakeasies. Federal Prohibition agents were given the task of enforcing the law, but local criminals were intent on breaking it. Drinking establishments proved unable to sustain the revelry of the era and began looking for other ways to amuse their patrons. Illegal slot machines and dice games appeared in the bars to amuse and occupy customers. Some offered prostitution as another alternative. Crime, corruption, and illegal activity became commonplace and took a strong hold on the city.

The Cleveland Syndicate set up gambling operations in the wide-open community, and the underworld established its powerful presence in the city by operating numerous Vegas-style casinos. Day and night houses of prostitution began to surface. Officials turned their heads and pretended not to notice. Many were paid not to notice. Newport clubs operated in open defiance of the law and became a breeding ground for crime and violence. People living across the river found the city enticing, and heavy traffic flowed across the bridge into Newport, gaining the city the nickname "Cincinnati's Playground." Others referred to it as "Little Mexico" or "Sin City."

Casinos were so blasé about the possibility of interference with their operations that they advertised openly in the local newspapers and distributed flyers promoting attractions at the clubs. A reform administration gained control of the city government in January 1950. Local businessmen formed the Committee of 500 to oust corrupt city officials and to promote a citywide cleanup campaign. The committee eventually grew to include several thousand members. It would take many years for Newport to shed its tarnished image and emerge as the respected and revitalized community it is today.

One

MOONSHINE AND MONEY

Newport was home to the largest brewery in Northern Kentucky, the George Wiedemann Brewing Company. Federal banning of the sale and consumption of alcohol had a profound effect on the city and its local economy. In 1919, the Wiedemann Brewery closed, leaving 300 employees and 200 field agents unemployed. The Food Administration Act forbade the use of grain to brew beer after December 1, 1918. The brewery tried to survive by manufacturing a near beer labeled Quizz. Near beer was a cereal beverage that was brewed by the same process as regular beer but by legal limit contained less than 1 percent alcohol. The use of the word "beer" on the beverage labels caused controversy and sparked the first of several investigations of the brewery by federal agents.

The brewery continued to distill bonded liquor for industrial and medicinal purposes. Permits were needed to withdraw liquor, and many permits were forged or counterfeited.

George Remus quickly became one of Wiedemann's biggest customers. Remus was a criminal defense lawyer and former pharmacist who settled in Cincinnati because of its close proximity to 80 percent of America's bonded whiskey producers. Remus bought distilleries and pharmacies as a ruse to obtain permits giving him access to liquor for medicinal purposes. This illegal liquor launched Remus's lucrative bootlegging empire and propelled him into the status of "King of the Bootleggers."

He bribed hundreds of police, judges, and government officials, including the U.S. attorney general. This large-scale operation was the foundation for the crime and corruption that found its way across the river into Newport.

With no liquor available and the want in high demand, some took advantage of the opportunity and made their own homemade brew. Many built moonshine stills and bottled and sold their product. Since the manufacture of home brew was not regulated, poor quality sometimes caused extreme illness or death.

The black market for alcohol flourished and fueled the enterprise of organized crime.

Violence was often used to settle differences. In 1927 alone, Newport experienced 31 murders. As Prohibition lingered, many bootleggers and rumrunners became wealthy. There was money to be made in Newport, and the Syndicate wanted a piece of the action.

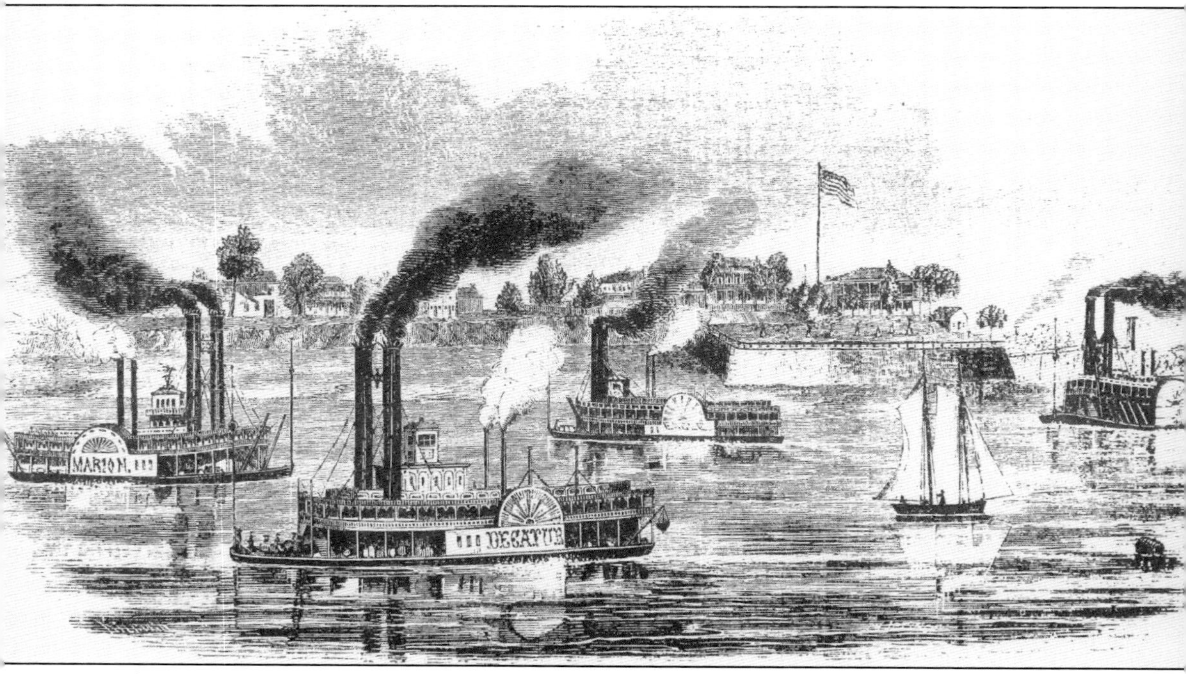

The Newport Barracks was a military installation located at the confluence of the Licking and Ohio Rivers. The post was a Union recruiting station during the Civil War. The taverns in the city provided the soldiers with entertainment and recreation. (Kenton County Public Library.)

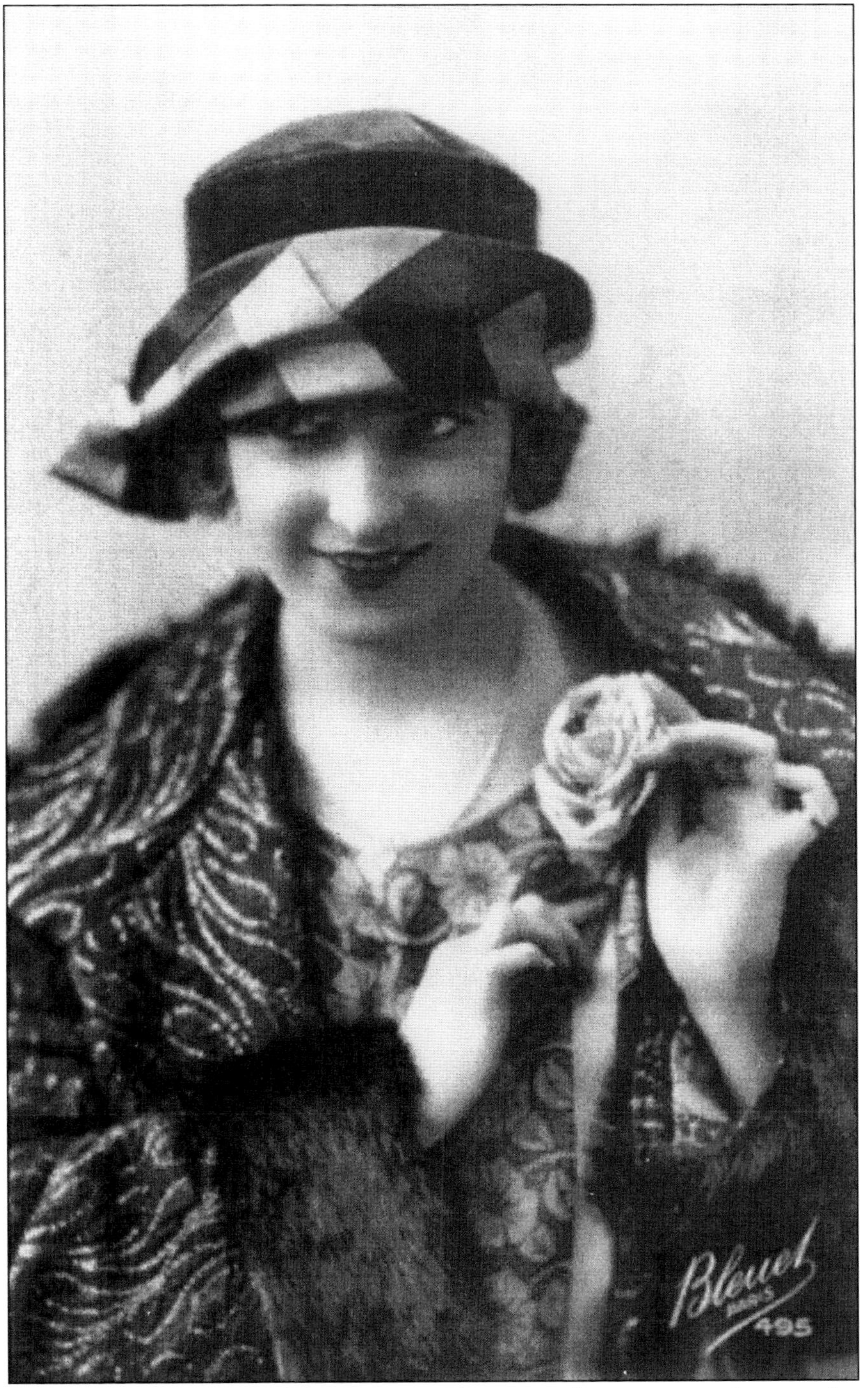

Newport in the 1920s experienced the jazz age, and some residents were caught up in the popular fads of the time. Some women started dressing in the flapper style and bobbing their hair like the woman in this photograph. Since Prohibition closed legal saloons and cabarets, speakeasies sprang up around town, and many Newportians continued to enjoy their alcohol as well as other popular fads of the era such as jazz music and marathon dancing. "I have to go see a man about a dog" often meant going to buy whiskey, and Newport was not in short supply. (Author's collection.)

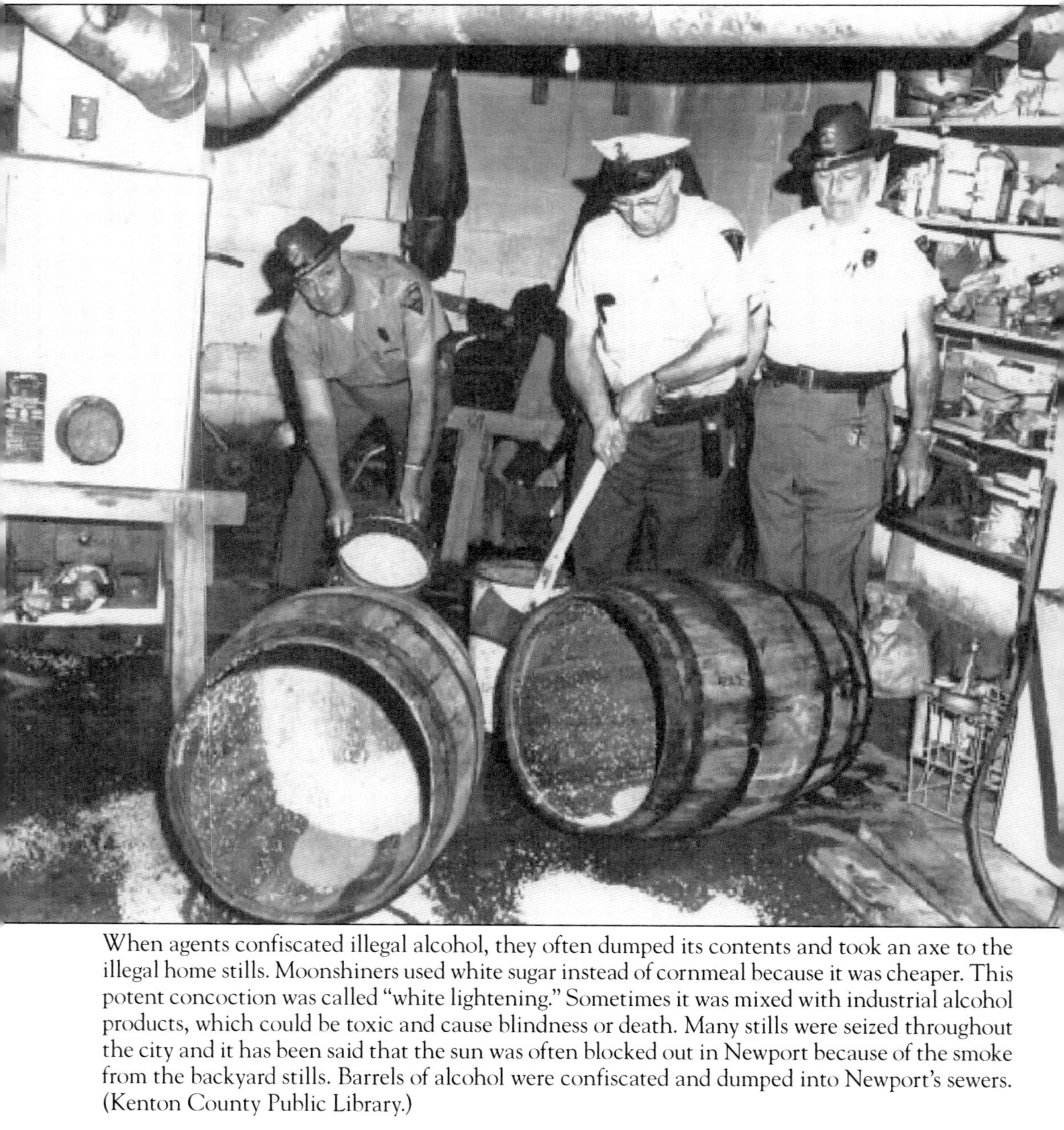

When agents confiscated illegal alcohol, they often dumped its contents and took an axe to the illegal home stills. Moonshiners used white sugar instead of cornmeal because it was cheaper. This potent concoction was called "white lightening." Sometimes it was mixed with industrial alcohol products, which could be toxic and cause blindness or death. Many stills were seized throughout the city and it has been said that the sun was often blocked out in Newport because of the smoke from the backyard stills. Barrels of alcohol were confiscated and dumped into Newport's sewers. (Kenton County Public Library.)

Brig. Gen. John T. Thompson (right) was born in Newport on December 31, 1860, at the historic Southgate House (below), which had been his family's homestead for generations. Thompson graduated from the U.S. Military Academy at West Point in 1882. He was then assigned duty at the Newport Barracks as a second lieutenant to the 2nd Artillery. Thompson attended engineering and artillery schools that enabled him to specialize in improving small weapons. Inspired by the trench warfare of World War I, Thompson set out to develop a one-man hand-held machine gun. Named the Thompson submachine gun, the weapon was commonly referred to as the "Tommy Gun." The gun became popular with gangsters and law enforcement officials during the Prohibition era. Thompson died in 1940. (Campbell County Historical Society.)

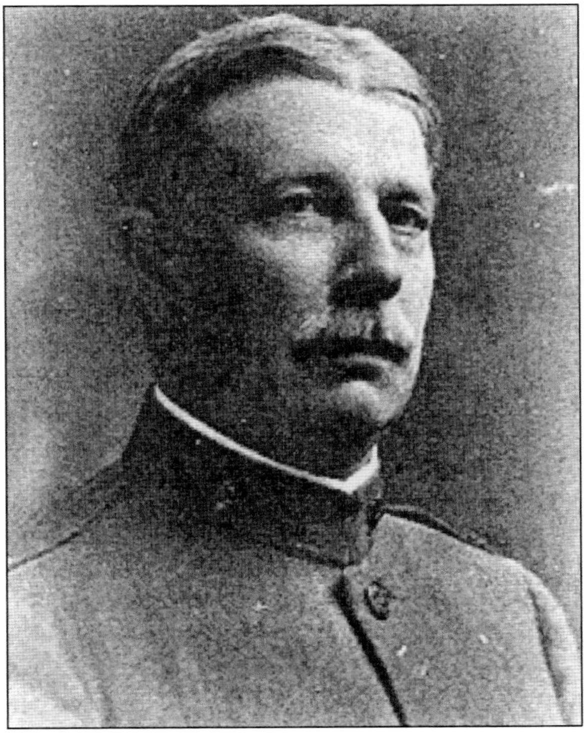

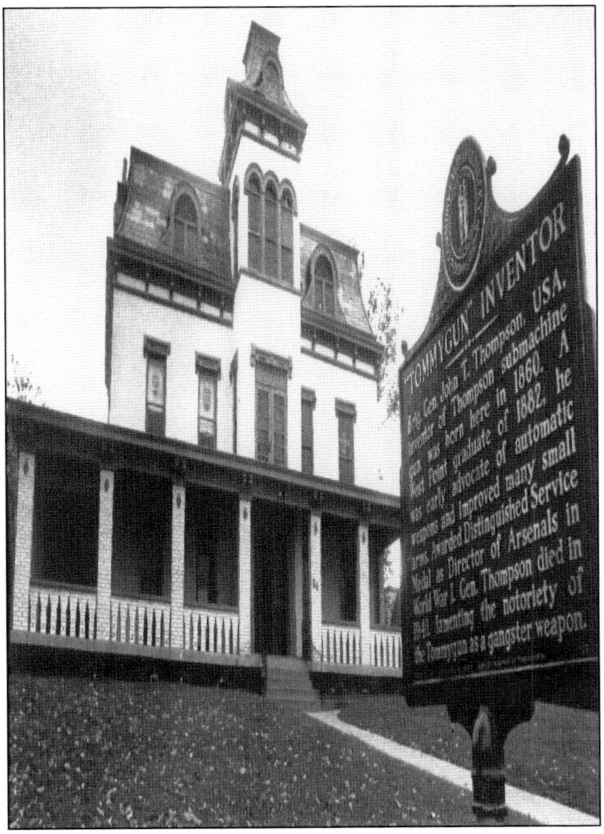

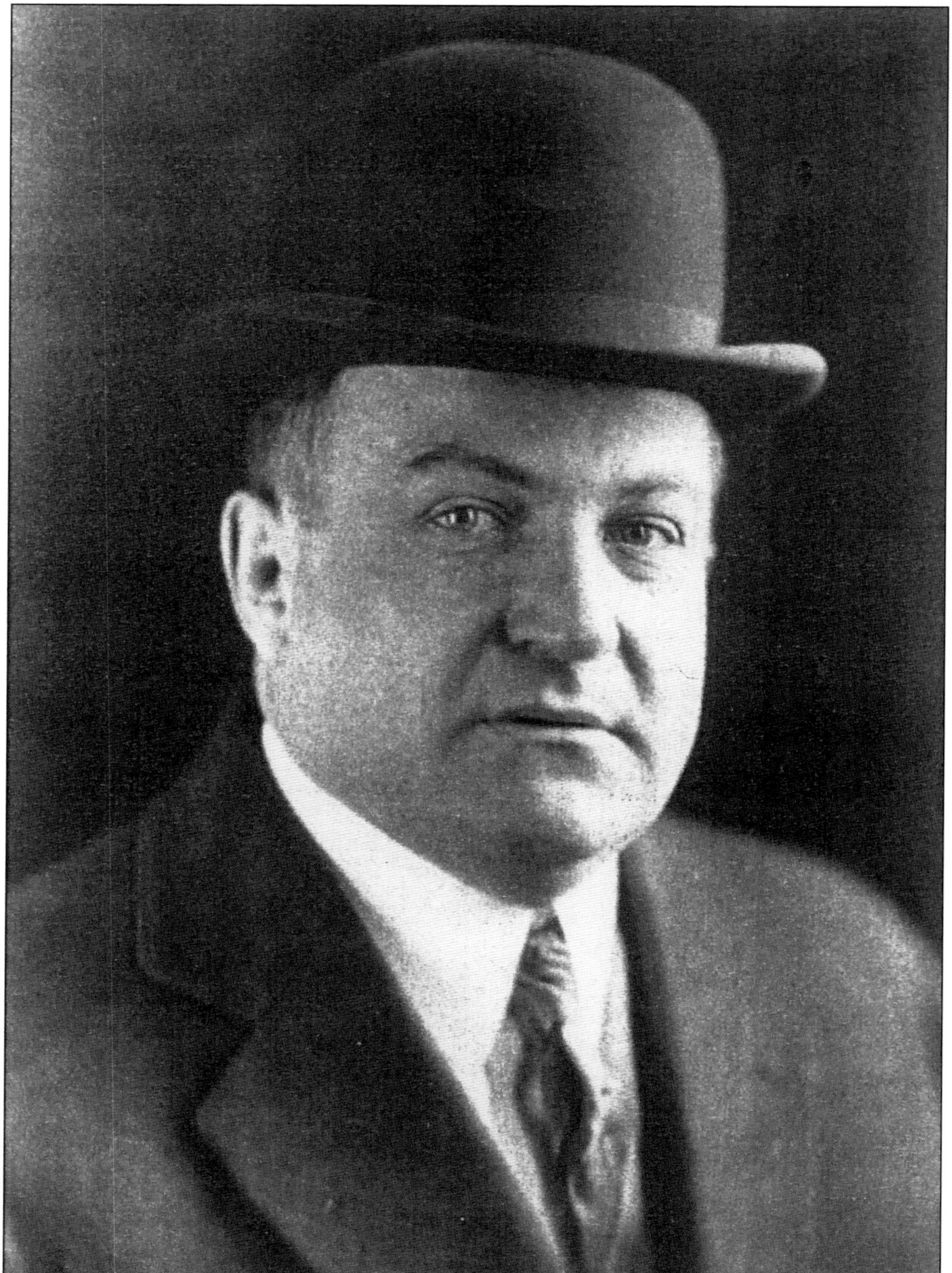

George Remus was born in Germany in 1876. George supported his family by working at a pharmacy, and by age 23, he owned two of them. He quickly grew tedious of the pharmacy business and entered law school in Chicago. In 1900, he became a lawyer specializing in criminal defense. He studied the Volstead Act to find loopholes in the law and made a fortune selling contraband liquor, earning him the nickname "King of the Bootleggers." (Author's collection.)

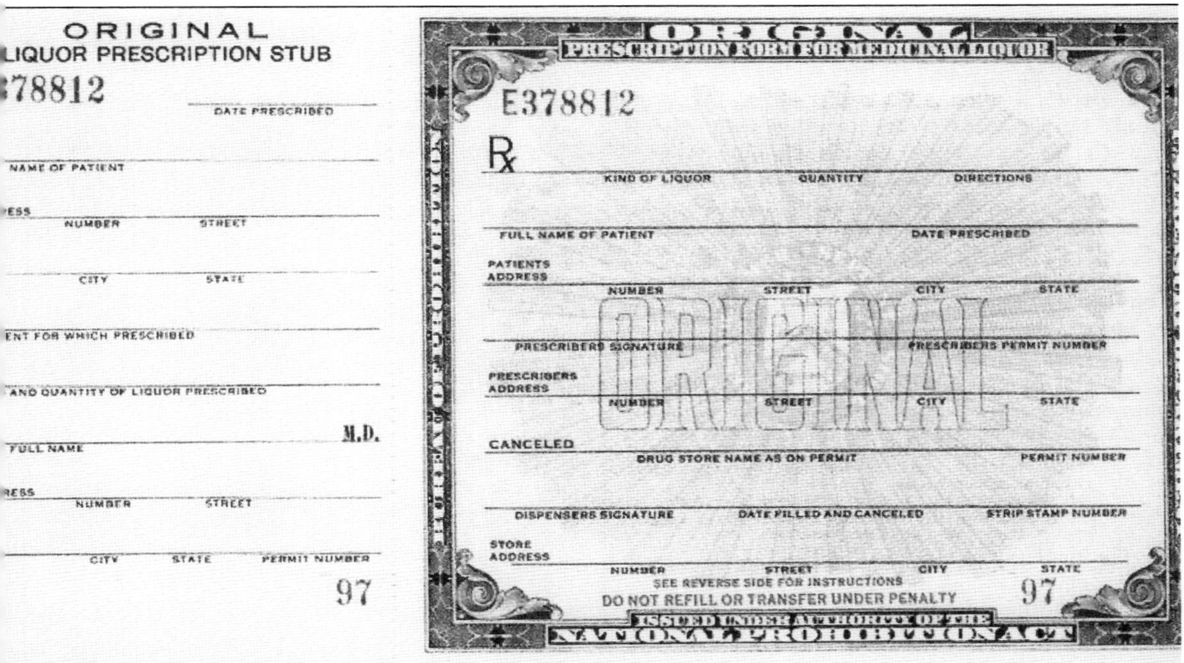
ORIGINAL
LIQUOR PRESCRIPTION STUB
78812
DATE PRESCRIBED
NAME OF PATIENT
ESS
NUMBER STREET
CITY STATE
ENT FOR WHICH PRESCRIBED
AND QUANTITY OF LIQUOR PRESCRIBED
M.D.
FULL NAME
RESS
NUMBER STREET
CITY STATE PERMIT NUMBER
97

PRESCRIPTION FORM FOR MEDICINAL LIQUOR
E378812
℞
KIND OF LIQUOR QUANTITY DIRECTIONS
FULL NAME OF PATIENT DATE PRESCRIBED
PATIENTS ADDRESS
NUMBER STREET CITY STATE
ORIGINAL
PRESCRIBERS SIGNATURE PRESCRIBERS PERMIT NUMBER
PRESCRIBERS ADDRESS
NUMBER STREET CITY STATE
CANCELED
DRUG STORE NAME AS ON PERMIT PERMIT NUMBER
DISPENSERS SIGNATURE DATE FILLED AND CANCELED STRIP STAMP NUMBER
STORE ADDRESS
NUMBER STREET CITY STATE
SEE REVERSE SIDE FOR INSTRUCTIONS
DO NOT REFILL OR TRANSFER UNDER PENALTY
97
ISSUED UNDER AUTHORITY OF THE
NATIONAL PROHIBITION ACT

The Prohibition commissioner controlled all withdrawals from bonded warehouses containing liquor for medicinal purposes. He also controlled the issuance of prescriptions for liquor by physicians. Often these permits were counterfeited, and a great deal of liquor was illegally drawn. George Remus, a former pharmacist, bought distilleries and pharmacies so he could buy alcohol from himself for medicinal purposes. He bribed hundreds of police, judges, and government officials and sold the liquor. (Author's collection.)

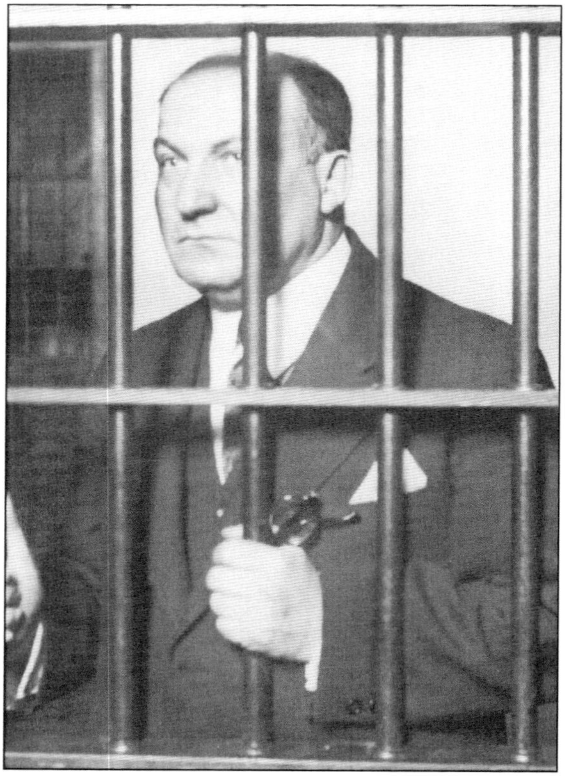

Remus spent six months at the State Hospital for the Criminal Insane at Lima, Ohio. In June 1928, by a 4-3 vote, the Ohio Supreme Court ordered his release. He returned to Cincinnati and opened a real estate business and eventually remarried. He suffered a stroke on August 9, 1950, at his home in Covington. George Remus died on January 20, 1952. (Author's collection.)

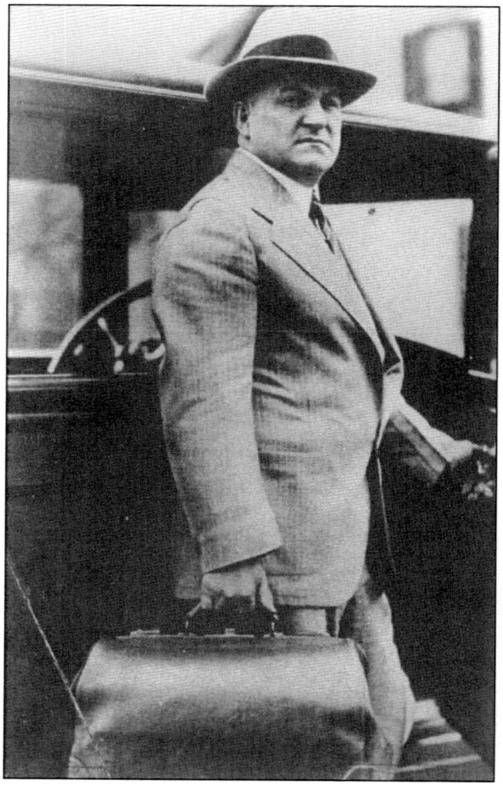

George Remus was a frequent visitor to the grand Seelbach Hotel in Louisville, Kentucky, where he stayed for business and pleasure. Gangsters Lucky Luciano and Dutch Schultz were also known to visit the hotel. It was there Remus met writer F. Scott Fitzgerald. Supposedly Fitzgerald was so taken with Remus's charisma and power that he used George Remus as the inspiration for the character of Jay Gatsby in *The Great Gatsby*. (Author's collection.)

George Wiedemann Sr. was born in Germany in 1833. He came to the United States in 1855 and moved to Newport in 1870. That year, he entered into a partnership with John Butcher and together they operated the Jefferson Street Brewery. When Wiedemann became sole owner of the plant, he also purchased the Costans Brewery on Monmouth Street in 1882 and operated both breweries as the George Wiedemann Brewing Company. Wiedemann died in 1890. (www.nkyviews.com.)

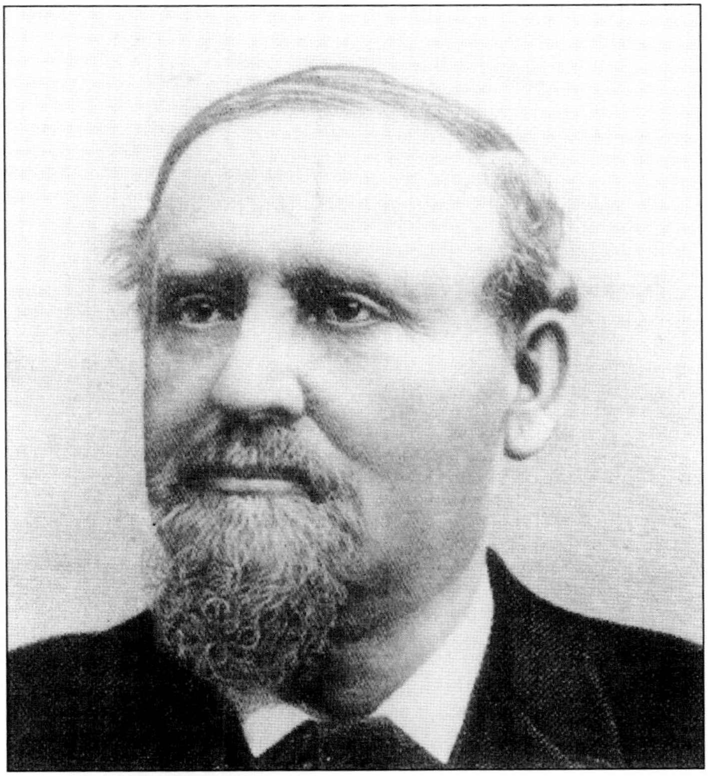

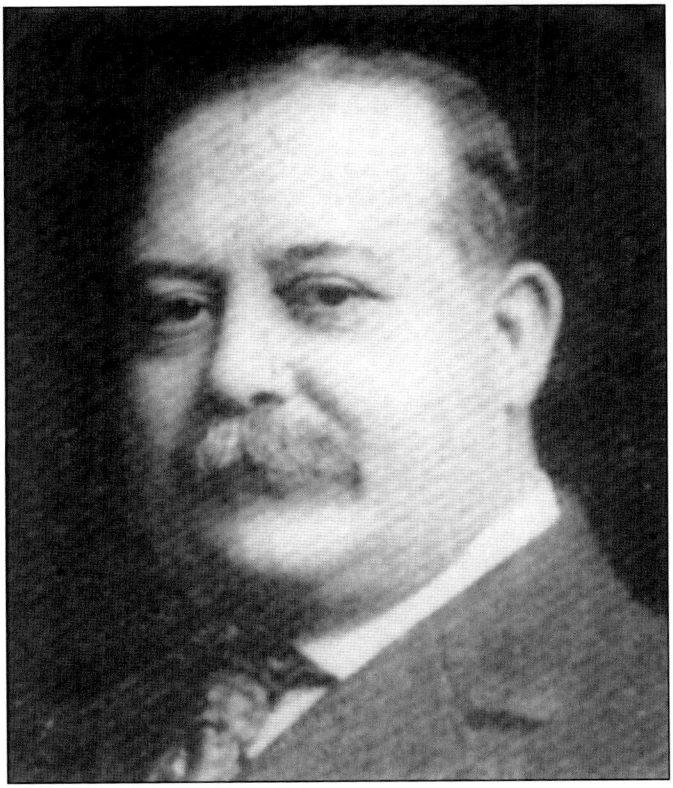

After the death of its founder, Wiedemann Brewery continued to operate under the guidance of Wiedemann's two sons, George Jr. and Charles Wiedemann (left). Charles became the president of the company, and George became vice president. Charles managed the business affairs of the brewery until federal agents shut down its operations and charged Wiedemann with violating Prohibition laws. (www.nkyviews.com.)

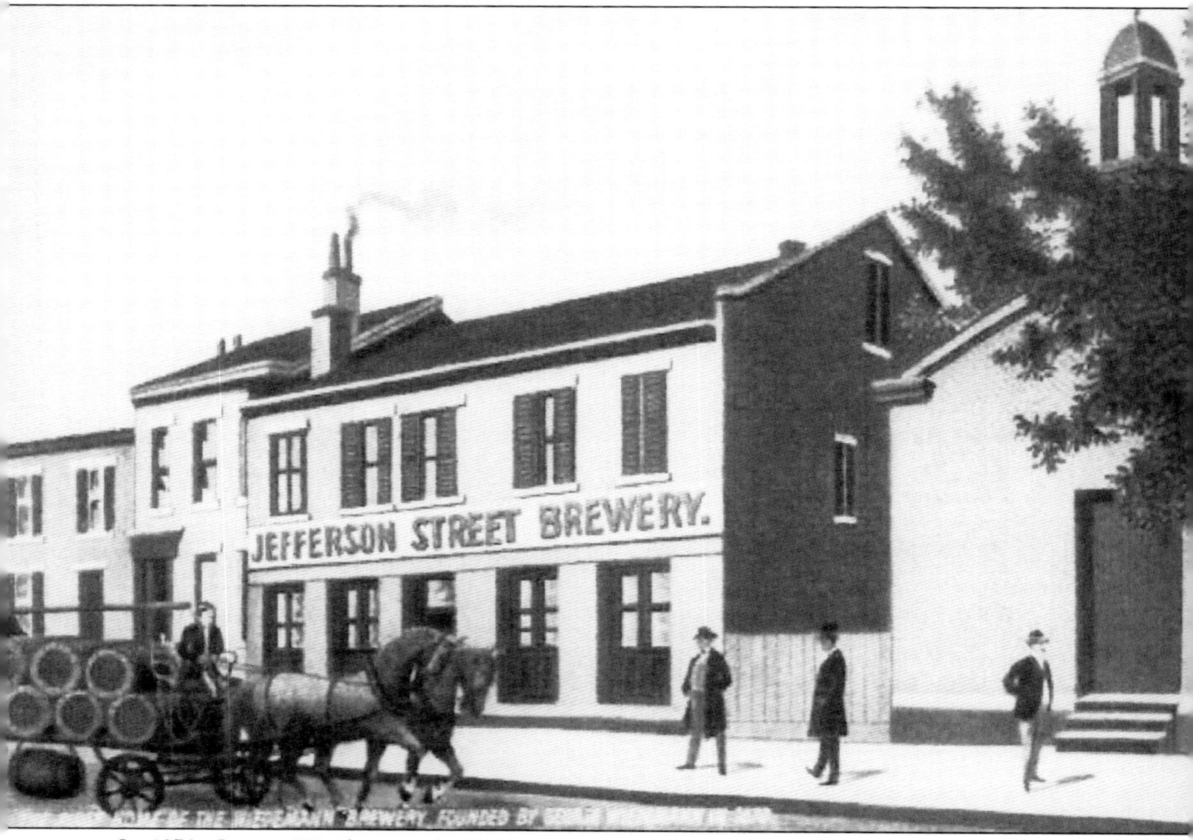

In 1870, George Wiedemann became partners with John Butcher in the operation of Newport's Jefferson Street Brewery. Wiedemann became sole owner of the brewery in 1878 and renamed it the George Wiedemann Brewing Company. As business increased, a malt house, grain elevator, and bottling house were added to the brewing empire. (www.nkyviews.com.)

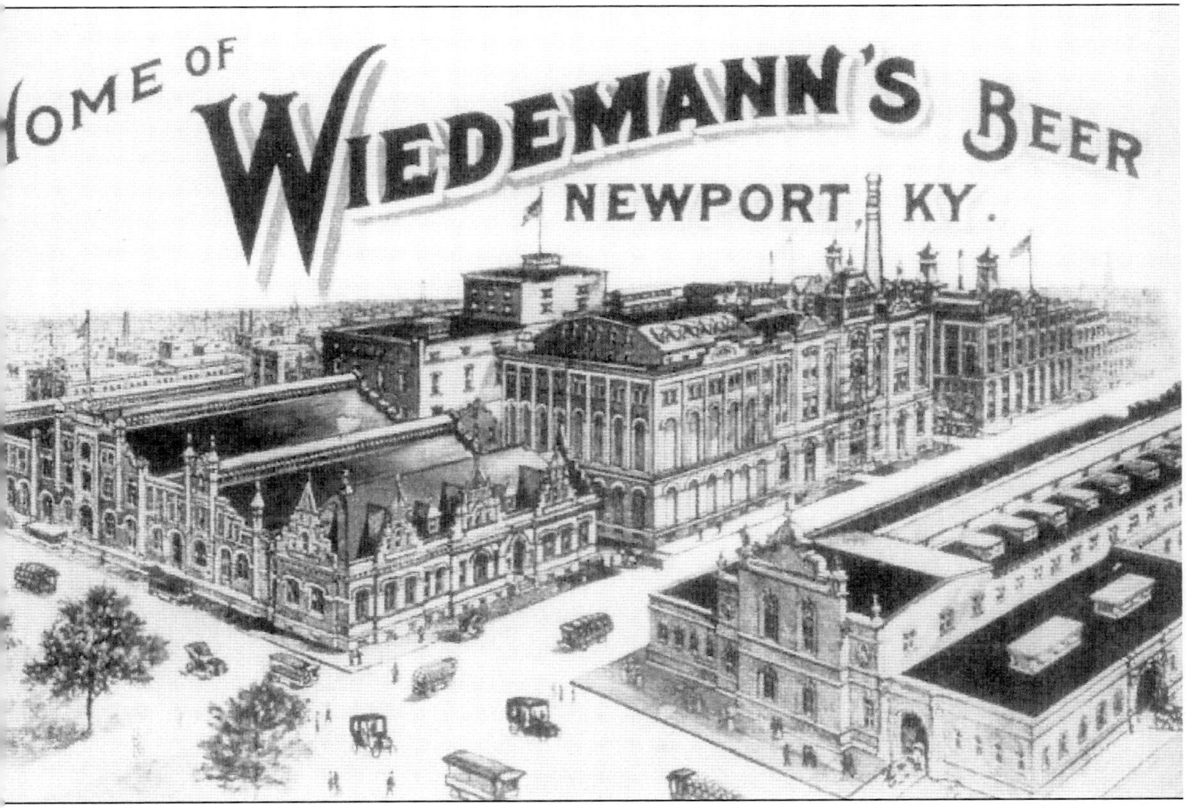

The George Wiedemann Brewing Company was the largest brewery in Northern Kentucky. Wiedemann's beer was sold throughout the United States and as far away as the Philippines and Cuba. The company boasted that it used the best malts and hops prepared in the finest German tradition. "The Standard Lager," "Extra Pale Lager," "Bohemian," and the "Muenchener Export" were several of the brands carried by Wiedemann Brewery. (www.nkyviews.com.)

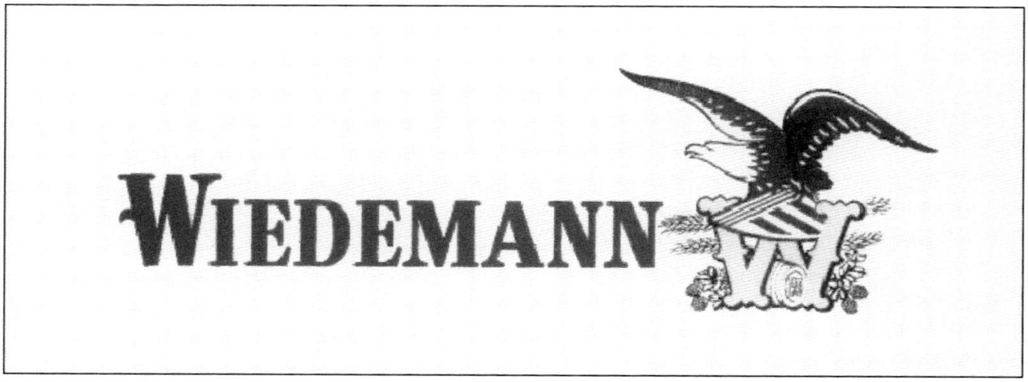

George Wiedemann Jr., son of the original proprietor, created the famous Wiedemann label with the popular "W" and eagle symbol. Wiedemann Jr. studied at the famous Munich Practical Brewing Academy in Bavaria, Germany. Wiedemann's skills as a brewmaster contributed to the company's success, and advertising made the Wiedemann brand mark familiar across the nation. (www.nkyviews.com.)

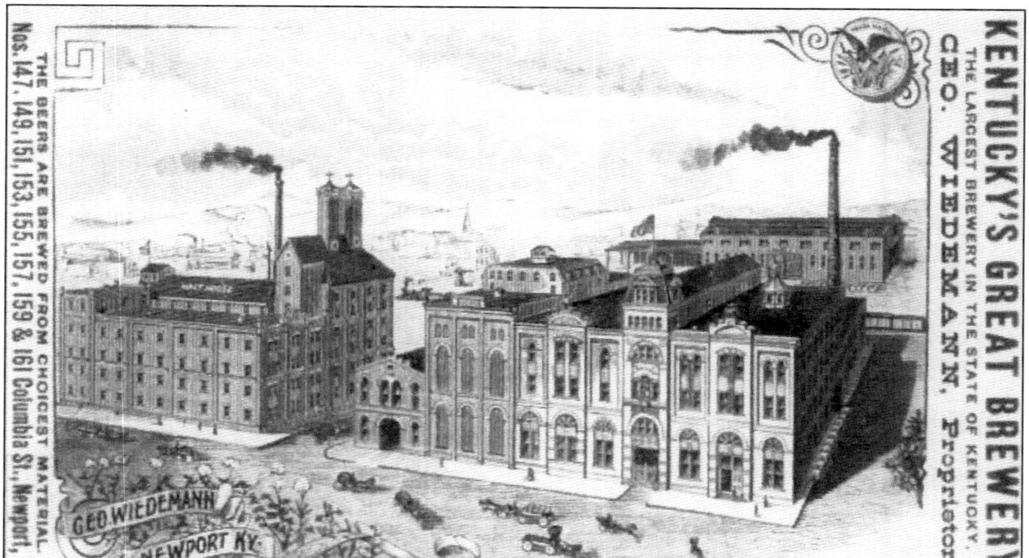

During Prohibition, the Wiedemann Brewery continued to distill bonded alcohol for industrial and medicinal uses. Many of the permits needed to withdraw liquor were forged or counterfeited. Distillery robberies became common, and in December 1918, Wiedemann's was robbed. In 1928, Wiedemann Brewery was charged with producing more than 1.5 million gallons of illegal alcohol. Wiedemann was found guilty of 23 violations of the Volstead Act. (www.nkyviews.com.)

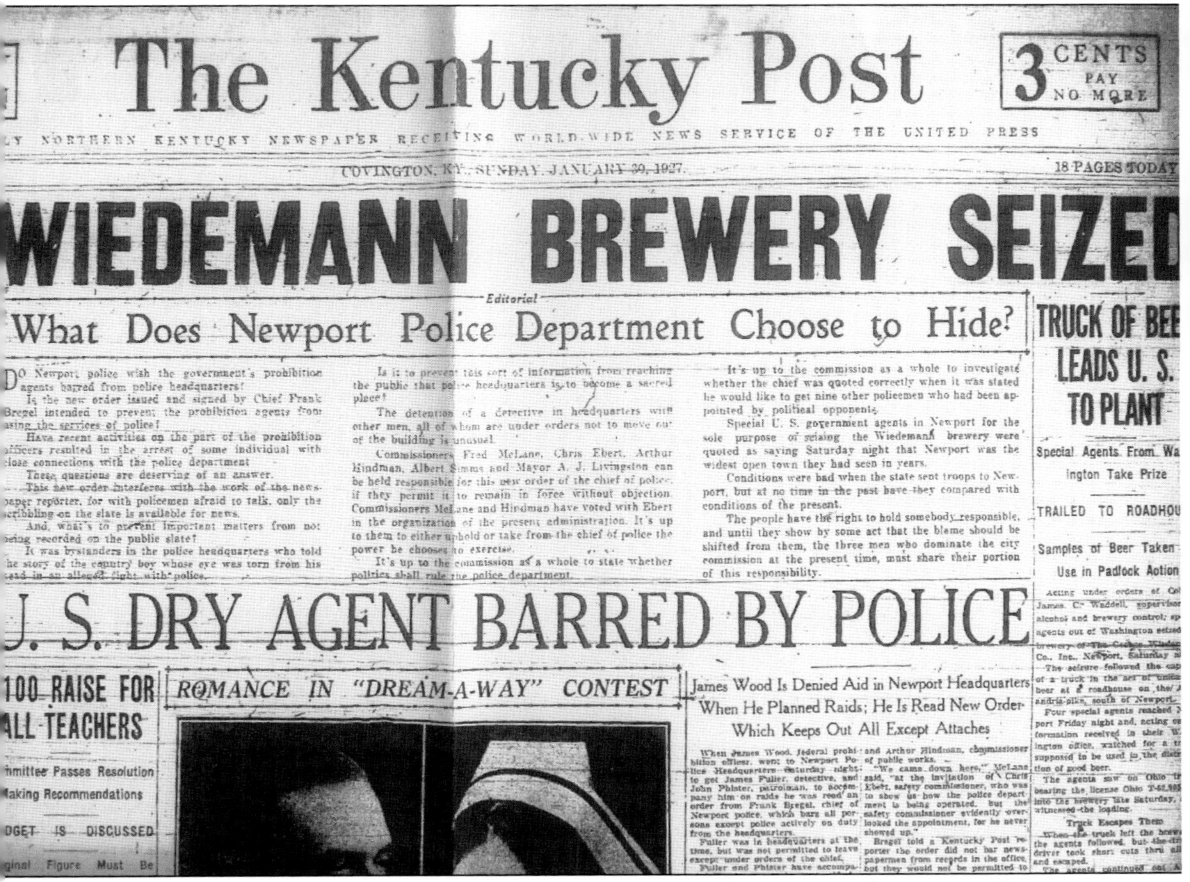

The Kentucky Post

3 CENTS PAY NO MORE

Y NORTHERN KENTUCKY NEWSPAPER RECEIVING WORLD-WIDE NEWS SERVICE OF THE UNITED PRESS

COVINGTON, KY., SUNDAY, JANUARY 30, 1927.

18 PAGES TODAY

WIEDEMANN BREWERY SEIZED

Editorial

What Does Newport Police Department Choose to Hide?

DO Newport police wish the government's prohibition agents barred from police headquarters?

Is the new order issued and signed by Chief Frank Bregel intended to prevent the prohibition agents from using the services of police?

Have recent activities on the part of the prohibition officers resulted in the arrest of some individual with close connections with the police department

These questions are deserving of an answer.

This new order interferes with the work of the newspaper reporter, for with policemen afraid to talk, only the scribbling on the slate is available for news.

And, what's to prevent important matters from not being recorded on the public slate?

It was bystanders in the police headquarters who told the story of the country boy whose eye was torn from his head in an alleged fight with police.

Is it to prevent this sort of information from reaching the public that police headquarters is to become a sacred place?

The detention of a detective in headquarters with other men, all of whom are under orders not to move out of the building is unusual.

Commissioners Fred McLane, Chris Ebert, Arthur Hindman, Albert Simms and Mayor A. J. Livingston can be held responsible for this new order of the chief of police, if they permit it to remain in force without objection. Commissioners McLane and Hindman have voted with Ebert in the organization of the present administration. It's up to them to either uphold or take from the chief of police the power he chooses to exercise.

It's up to the commission as a whole to state whether politics shall rule the police department.

It's up to the commission as a whole to investigate whether the chief was quoted correctly when it was stated he would like to get nine other policemen who had been appointed by political opponents.

Special U. S. government agents in Newport for the sole purpose of seizing the Wiedemann brewery were quoted as saying Saturday night that Newport was the widest open town they had seen in years.

Conditions were bad when the state sent troops to Newport, but at no time in the past have they compared with conditions of the present.

The people have the right to hold somebody responsible, and until they show by some act that the blame should be shifted from them, the three men who dominate the city commission at the present time, must share their portion of this responsibility.

TRUCK OF BEE
LEADS U. S.
TO PLANT

Special Agents From Wa
ington Take Prize

TRAILED TO ROADHOU

Samples of Beer Taken
Use in Padlock Aotion

Acting under orders of Col James C. Waddell, supervisor alcohol and brewery control; sp agents out of Washington seized brewery of The George Wiedem Co., Inc., Newport, Saturday n

The seizure followed the cap of a truck in the act of unloa beer at a roadhouse on the A andria pike, south of Newport.

Four special agents reached N port Friday night and, acting on formation received in their W ington office, watched for a tr supposed to be used in the distr tion of good beer.

The agents saw an Ohio tr bearing the license Ohio T-62,985 into the brewery late Saturday, witnessed the loading.

Truck Escapes Them

When the truck left the brew the agents followed, but the dri driver took short cuts thru al and escaped.

The agents continued out A

U. S. DRY AGENT BARRED BY POLICE

100 RAISE FOR
ALL TEACHERS

mmittee Passes Resolution
Making Recommendations

DGET IS DISCUSSED

ginal Figure Must Be

ROMANCE IN "DREAM-A-WAY" CONTEST

James Wood Is Denied Aid in Newport Headquarters When He Planned Raids; He Is Read New Order Which Keeps Out All Except Attaches

When James Wood, federal prohibition officer, went to Newport Police Headquarters Saturday night to get James Fuller, detective, and John Phister, patrolman, to accompany him on raids he was read an order from Frank Bregel, chief of Newport police, which bars all persons except police actively on duty from the headquarters.

Fuller was in headquarters at the time, but was not permitted to leave except under orders of the chief.

Fuller and Phister have accompa-

and Arthur Hindman, commissioner of public works.

"We came down here," McLane said, "at the invitation of Chris Ebert, safety commissioner, who was to show us how the police department is being operated, but the safety commissioner evidently overlooked the appointment, for he never showed up."

Bregel told a Kentucky Post reporter the order did not bar newspapermen from records in the office, but they would not be permitted to

On January 29, 1927, four special Prohibition officers out of Washington acted on a tip and came to Newport to observe the activity surrounding the Wiedemann Brewery. The agents witnessed a truck enter the brewery and observed it being loaded with 16 barrels. The agents followed the truck to a roadhouse on Alexandria Pike, where the driver proceeded to unload the barrels. The agents were able to confiscate the contraband and seize the brewery for manufacturing beer with alcohol content exceeding the legal limits. (*Kentucky Post*.)

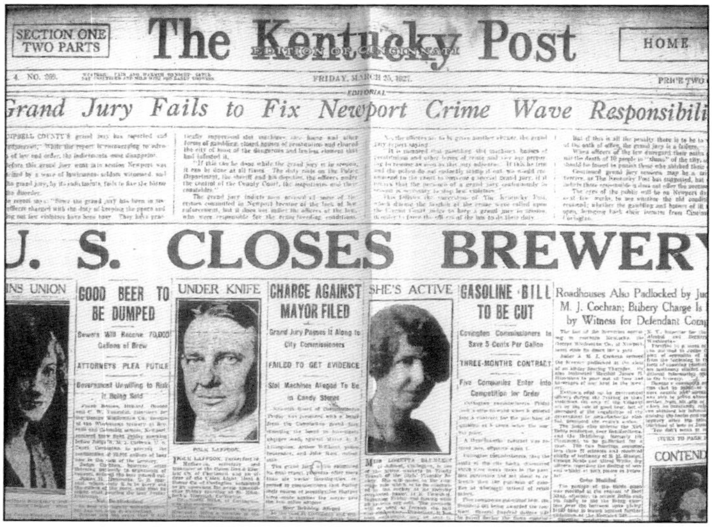

SECTION ONE TWO PARTS

The Kentucky Post

EDITION OF CINCINNATI

HOME

FRIDAY, MARCH 25, 1927.

EDITORIAL

Grand Jury Fails to Fix Newport Crime Wave Responsibili

U. S. CLOSES BREWERY

GOOD BEER TO BE DUMPED

UNDER KNIFE

CHARGE AGAINST MAYOR FILED

SHE'S ACTIVE

GASOLINE BILL TO BE CUT

Roadhouses Also Padlocked by Judge M. J. Cochran; Bribery Charge Is by Witness for Defendant Comp

CONTEND

On March 24, 1927, Judge A. Cochran ordered the brewery be closed for one year and demanded the 70,000 gallons of beer be poured out. Wiedemann's lawyers argued that dumping the beer would be like pouring money into the sewer. The judge refused to let the brewery dealcoholize and keep its inventory of near beer. He stated, "Anyone who buys near beer isn't satisfied with it and they invariably spike it." (*Kentucky Post*.)

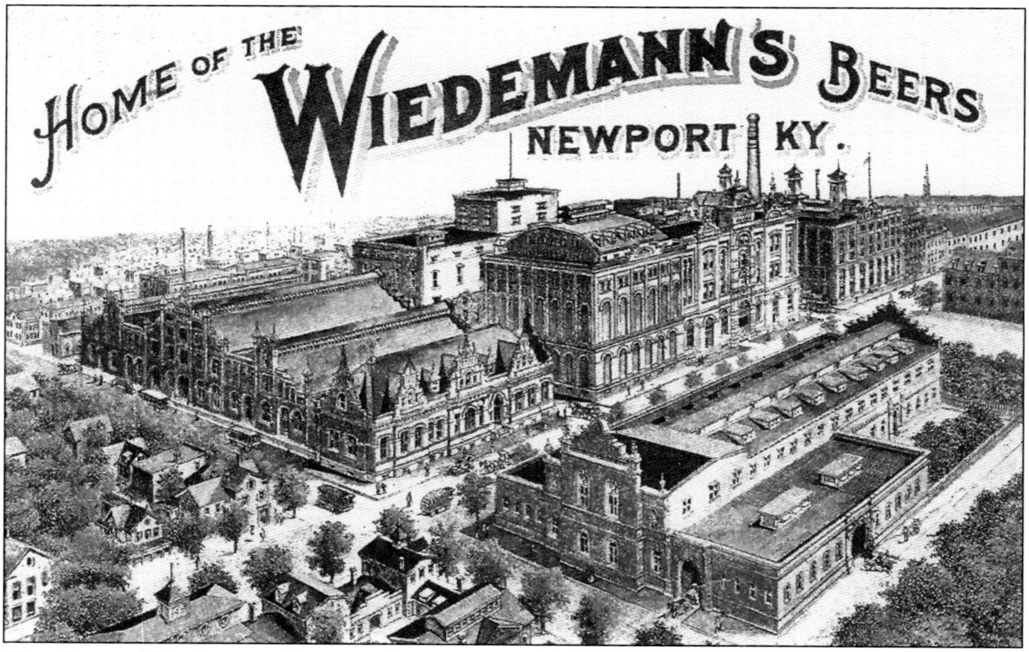

The George Wiedemann Brewing Company was reopened after the repeal of Prohibition. On December 16, 1933, the brewery rolled out its first half barrel of beer. Production continued until 1967, when Wiedemann merged with G. Heileman Brewing Company of La Crosse, Wisconsin. Heileman Brewing decided to cease operations in Newport and closed the brewery in May 1983, but continued to offer Wiedemann's primary brands. Today the beer is brewed under license by the Pittsburgh Brewing Company. (www.nkyviews.com.)

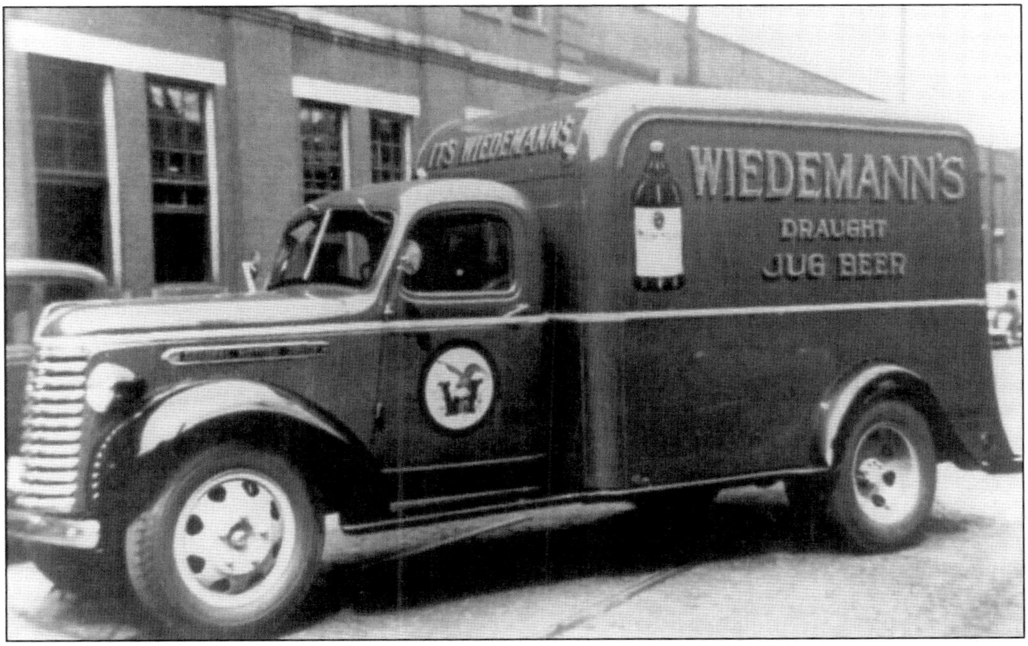

During World War I, Wiedemann Brewery encountered a severe shortage of gasoline and tires for its vehicles thanks to wartime rationing. As a solution to their problem, the brewery revived the old tradition of horse-drawn wagon deliveries around town and relieved some of the restrictions placed upon the brewery by the war. The Wiedemann stables held 150 horses used to pull wagons that delivered kegs of beer to the local restaurants and taverns. (Both images, Campbell County Historical Society.)

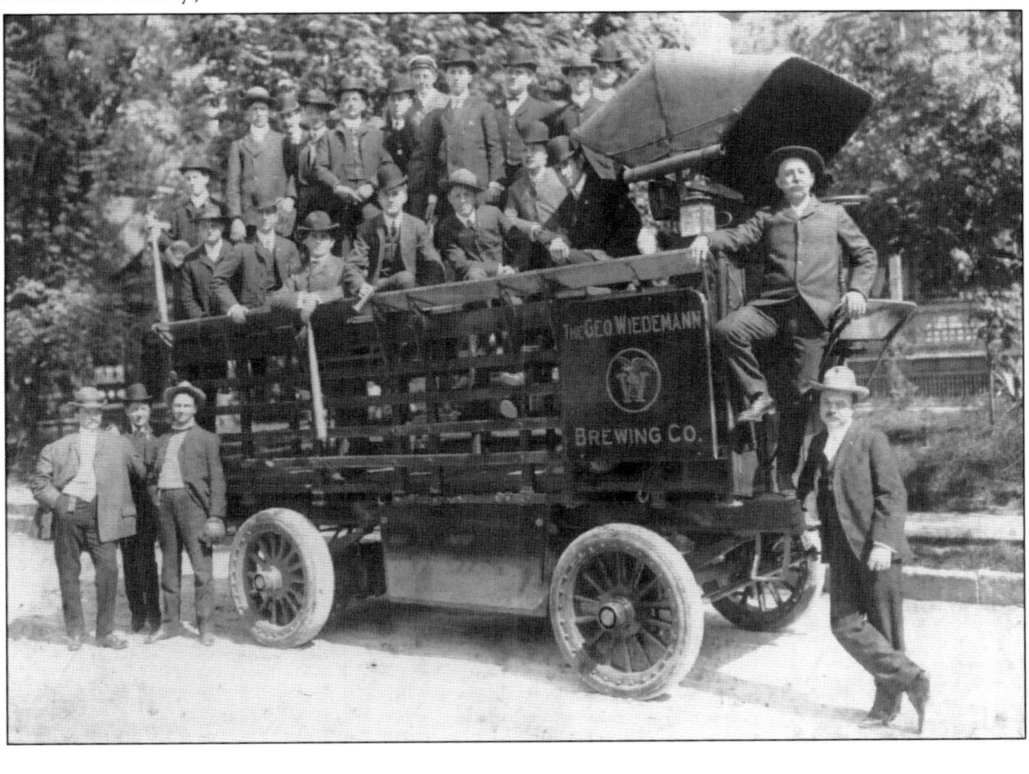

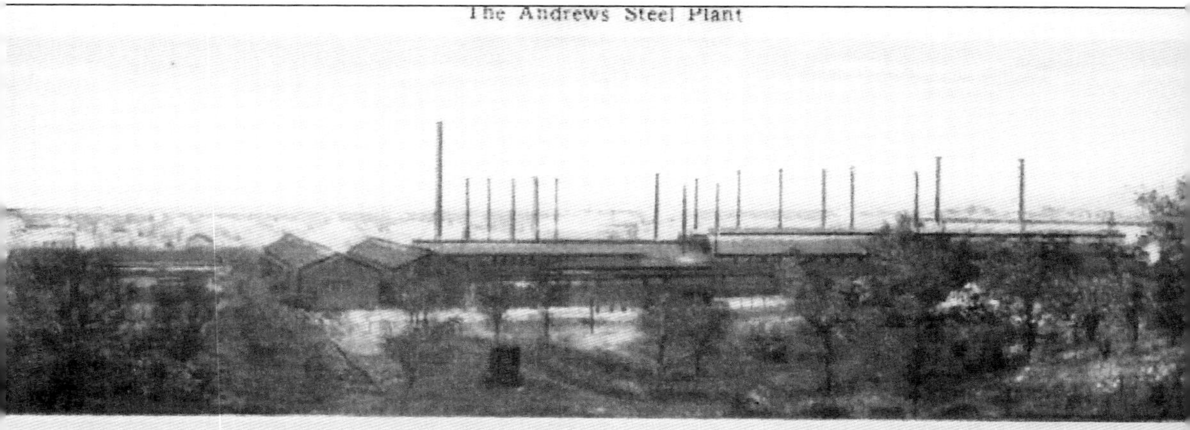

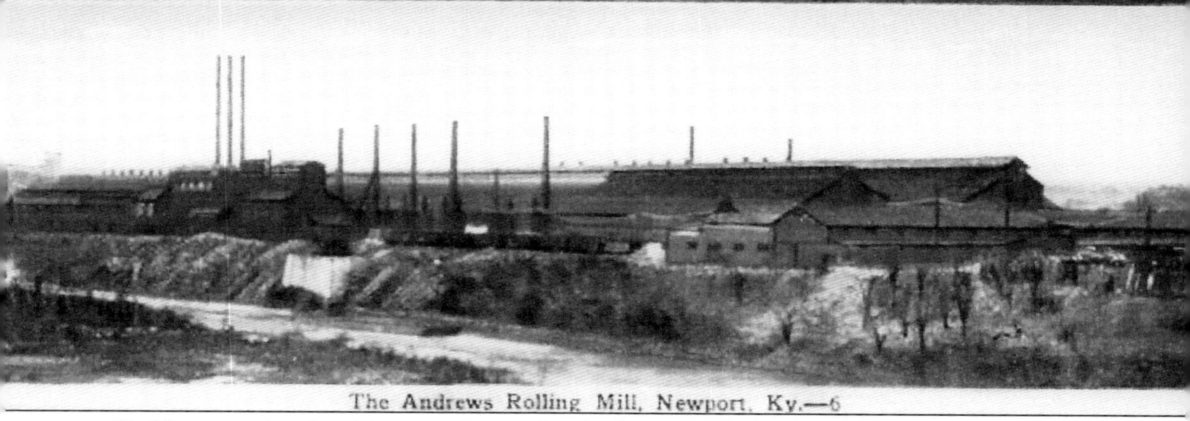

Problems escalated in Newport during the Andrews Steel Plant strike in November 1921. Faced with a pay cut, more than 2,000 employees walked out. When the company threatened to hire new non-union workers, violence ensued and gunfire broke out between the strikers and officials of the plant. On December 24, 1921, Gov. Edwin Morrow sent Col. H. H. Denhardt and 200 National Guardsmen to Newport to quell the violence. The disgruntled strikers began shooting at the troops, and Newport's west end resembled a war zone. Col. H. H. Denhardt ordered his troops to shoot and kill if necessary, and Newport was placed under martial law. (Kenton County Public Library.)

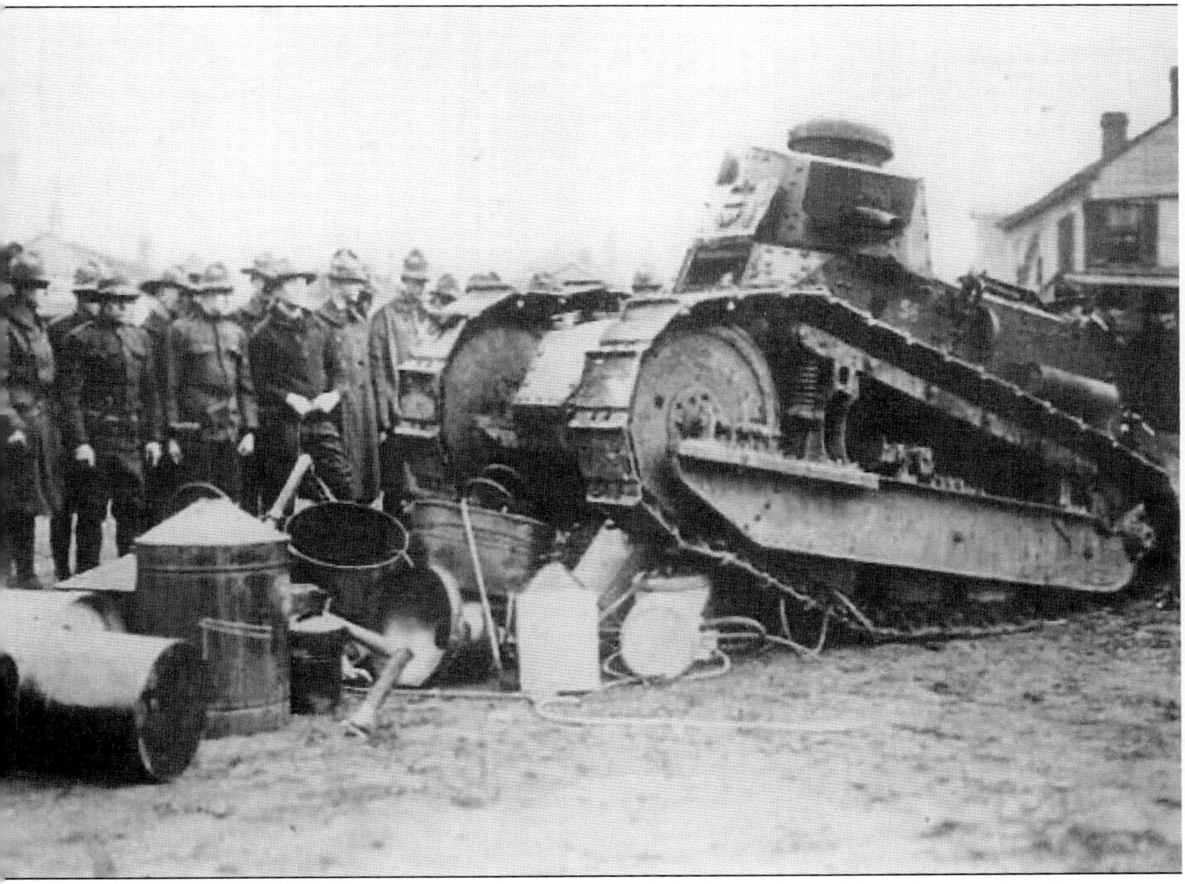

While in Newport, the troops found evidence of illegal alcohol and gambling. Over 200 raids occurred, and Newport officials were accused of not doing their duty to suppress lawlessness. On February 16, 1922, Colonel Denhardt arrested Newport's mayor, chief of police, county attorney, and several patrolmen for conspiring to violate the National Prohibition Act. The militia found hundreds of gallons of moonshine and whiskey. In this picture, the troops are destroying moonshine stills. (www.nkyviews.com.)

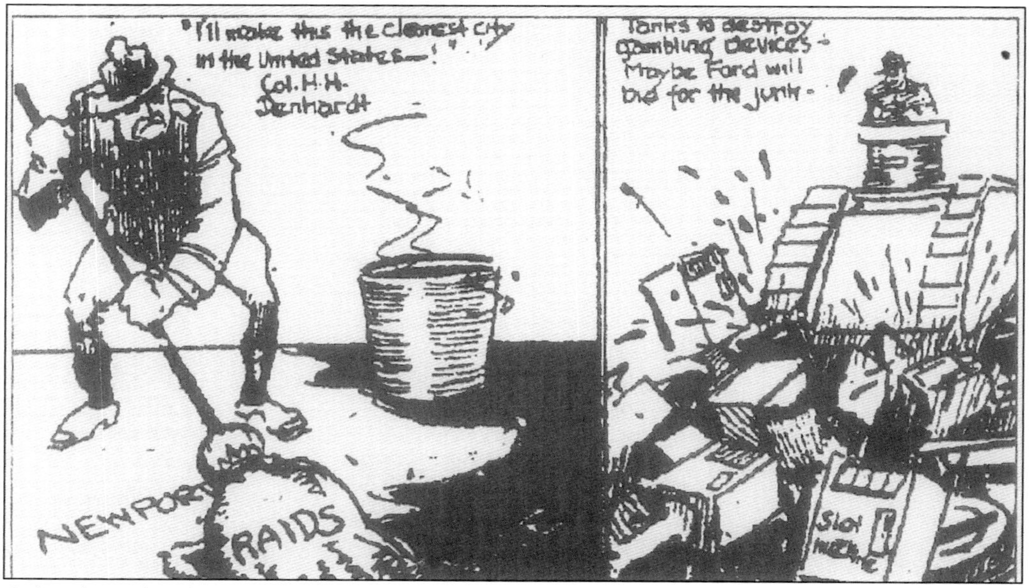

Colonel Denhardt warned that the guardsmen meant business and promised to rid the city of undesirables. The *Kentucky Post* ran the cartoon above, depicting Denhardt cleaning up Newport and destroying slot machines. (Dave Horn Collection.)

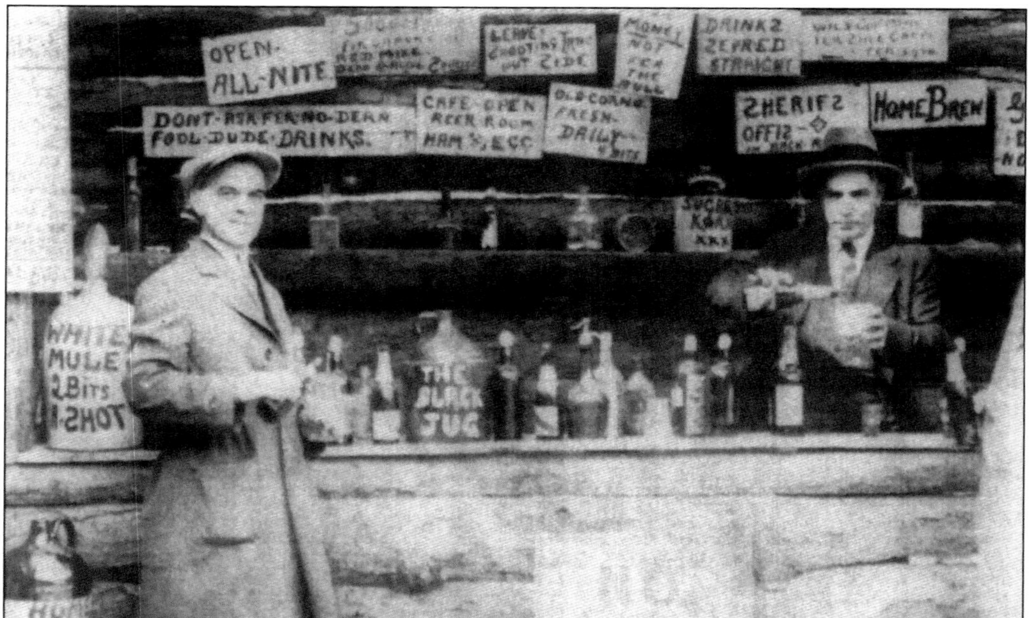

Local bootlegger Pat Fitters (left) lived at 619 Isabella Street in Newport. In 1926, Fitters became embroiled in an altercation with local gangster Red Masterson and several of his henchmen. An argument between the men took place in front of Doc Boesinger's saloon on the corner of Seventh and Columbia Streets. As Fitters attempted to leave, Masterson and his gang drew their guns and fired upon Fitters's automobile. More than 25 shots were discharged, riddling the car with bullet holes but only hitting Fitters once in the hand. Fitters managed to return fire, killing one of the men. After pleading self defense, he was acquitted of murder charges. In 1930, Fitters was arrested after federal agents found a 75-gallon still in his basement. (Susannah Fitters.)

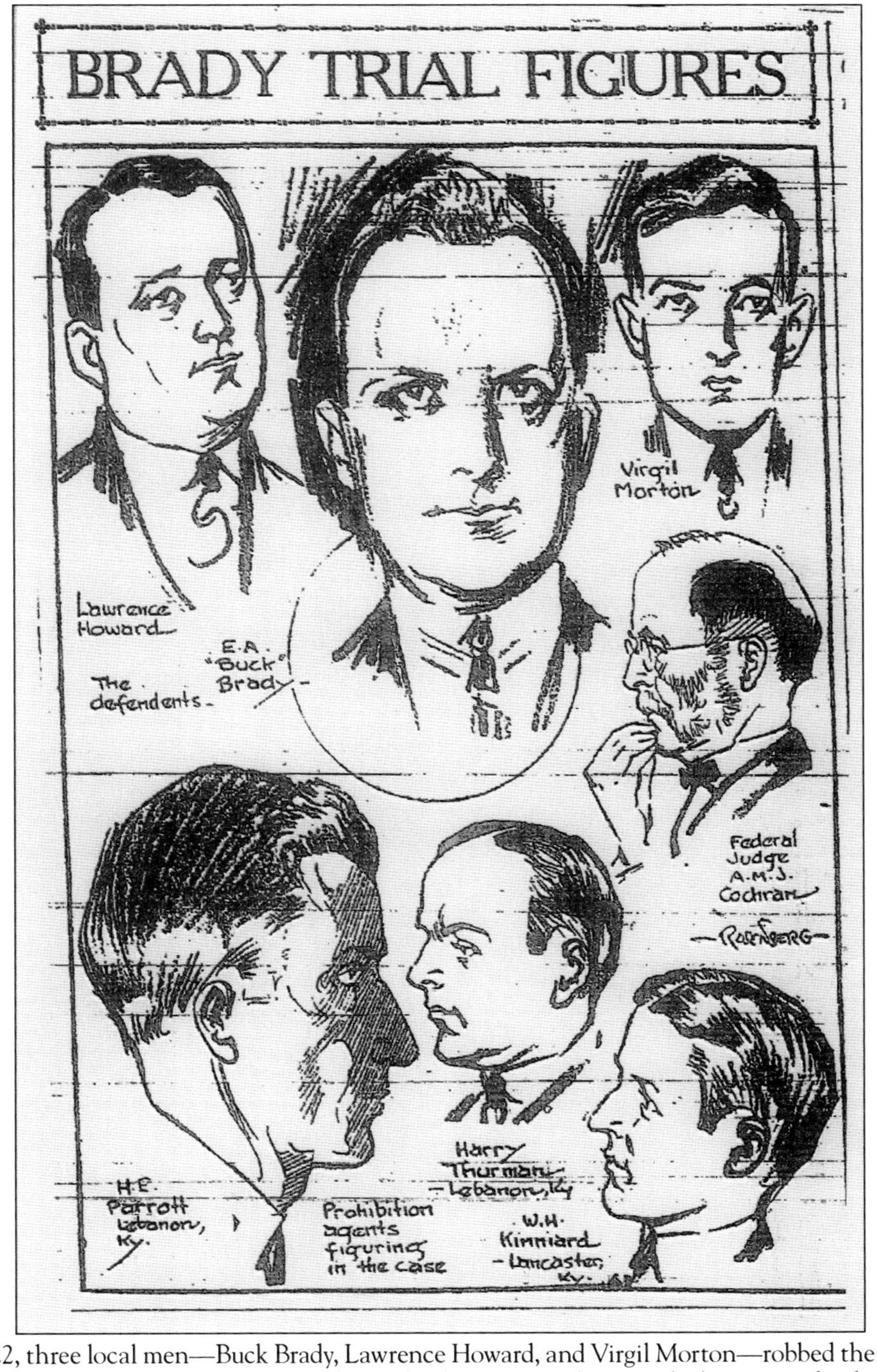

In 1922, three local men—Buck Brady, Lawrence Howard, and Virgil Morton—robbed the Burk's Springs Distillery in Lebanon, Kentucky. Federal agents caught up with the trio, and a shoot-out known as "the Battle of Perryville" took place. The agents confiscated 410 gallons of whiskey. Each man was sentenced to two years in the Atlanta Federal Penitentiary. Buck Brady was a rumrunner who worked for George Remus and later operated a popular restaurant and casino on the outskirts of Newport known as the Primrose. An artist's rendering of the trial figures appeared in the local newspaper. (*Kentucky Post.*)

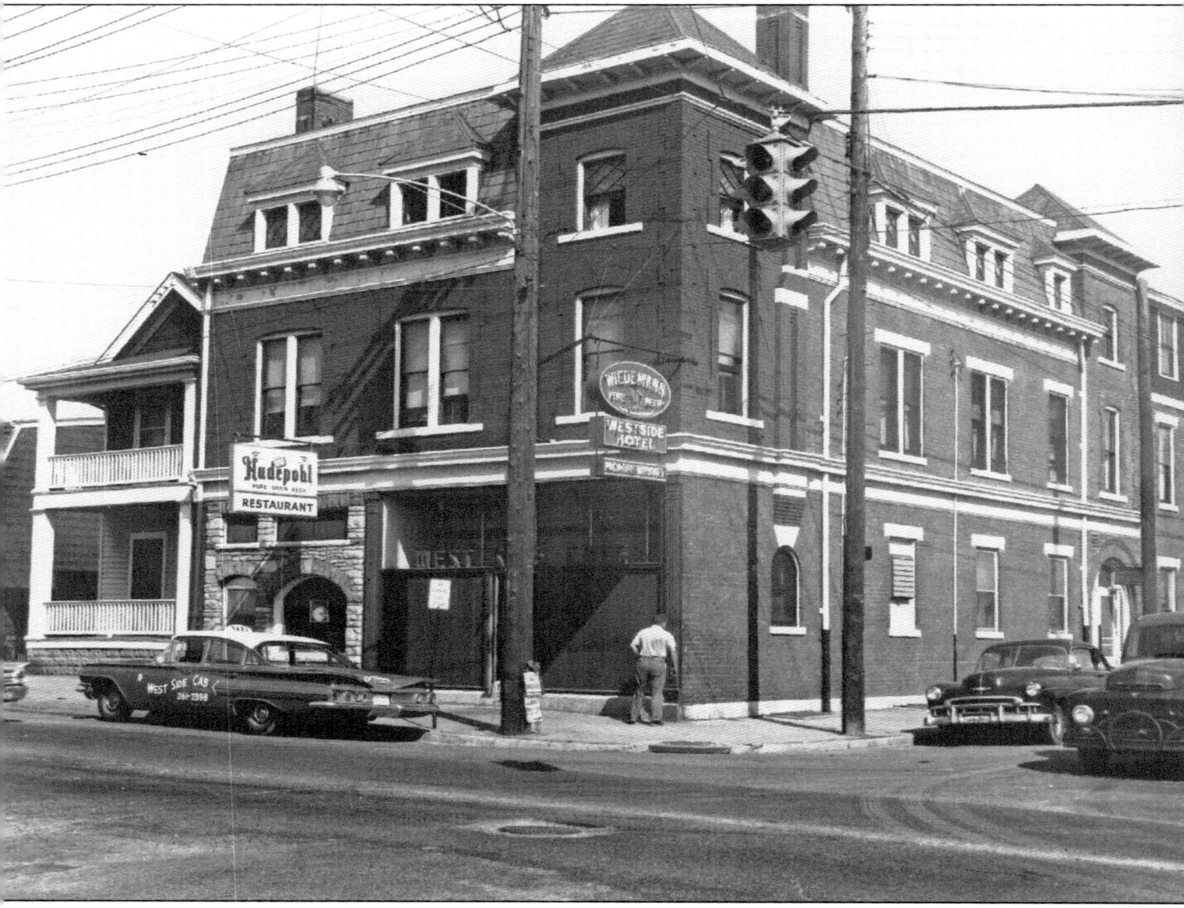

The West Side Café is located at 438 West Eleventh Street. It started out as a restaurant, bar, and hotel. In 1932, Prohibition agents raided the bar, arrested the proprietors for serving illegal alcohol, and ordered the building padlocked. The business is still in operation with a bar and restaurant, but the hotel is no longer in service. The rooms are now rented as apartments. (Campbell County Historical Society.)

Two

The Syndicate Comes to Town

One of the most powerful syndicates in the nation was the Cleveland Syndicate. It was composed of four leaders—Moe Dalitz, Morris Kleinman, Louis Rothkopf, and Sam Tucker—who shared equal partnership in all ventures. They were business partners and allies with Meyer Lansky and Bugsy Siegel in several projects in New York. During Prohibition, they were involved with rum-running and distributed some of their illegal hooch in Newport. After repeal, the syndicate transferred its activities to the even more lucrative field of gambling. When notorious gangster Dutch Schultz was assassinated, the group took over the operations of his Coney Island Racetrack in Cincinnati and renamed it River Downs. They also acquired a horse track outside of Newport named the Latonia Park (now Turfway Park). The syndicate was involved in many local gambling dens in Cincinnati until law officials chased them away. After visiting Campbell County and witnessing the wide-open gambling, the syndicate decided to muscle in on the casinos and penetrate Newport's gambling operations. Through force and intimidation, the syndicate acquired such clubs as the Beverly Hills Club, Primrose, Look-Out House, Yorkshire Club, Merchants Club, Flamingo Club, Latin Quarter, the Stardust, and the Tropicana.

Police and county officials were put on the syndicate's payroll to pretend such illegal conditions did not exist. Besides the Cleveland faction, many small-time gangsters invaded the city, set up shop, and took advantage of Newport's open policy on vice. When fed-up citizens cried out for reform, the syndicate funded a reform campaign and created the Newport Civic Association. This enabled the syndicate to put their own candidates in office to ensure their protection. In 1958, a group of local clergyman made an attempt at campaigning for reform and organized the Social Action Committee. It would take a group of local businessmen and citizens known as the Committee of 500 to orchestrate a successful reform movement.

When it became clear the syndicate would not be able to continue its usual business in Newport, the members of the Cleveland Four invested their interests in casinos in the newly developed city of Las Vegas, Nevada.

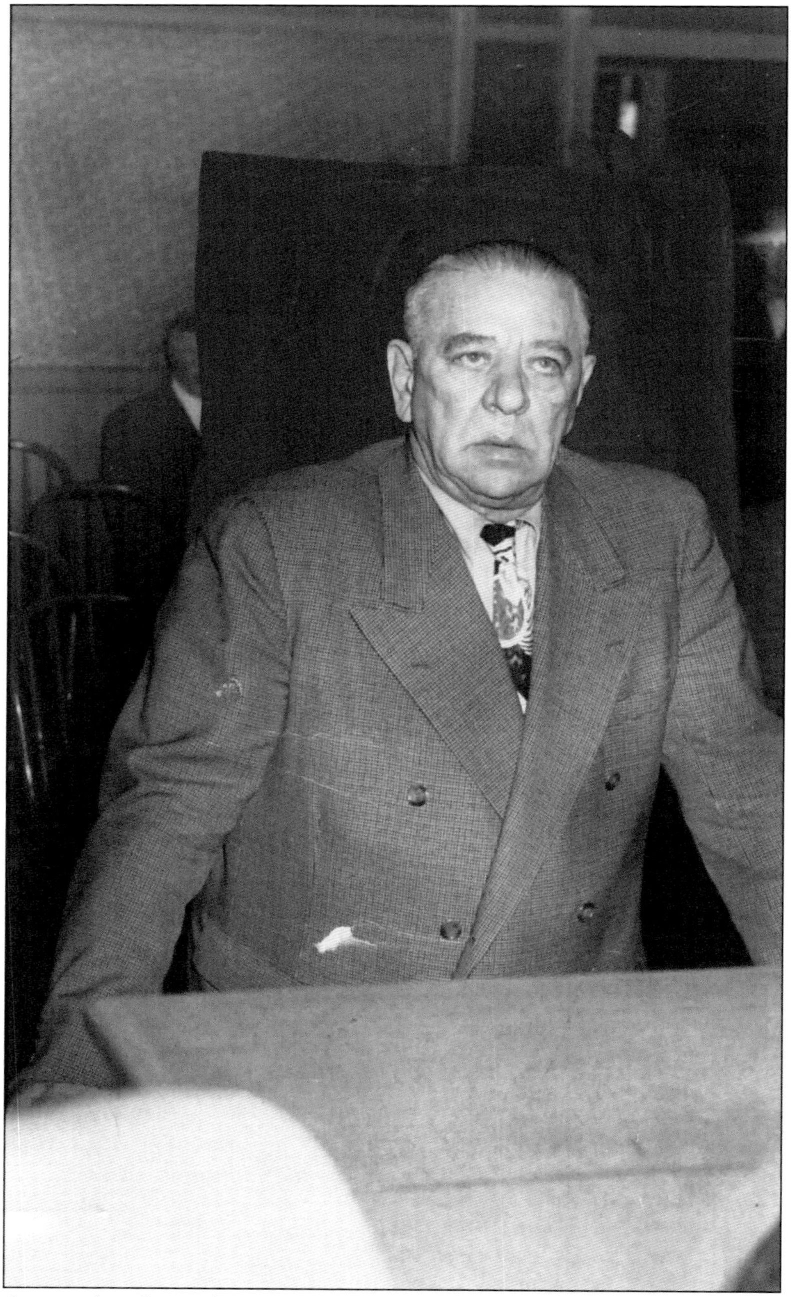

Pete Schmidt was a key figure during Newport's sin city era. Schmidt was affiliated with George Remus during Prohibition, becoming a rumrunner in Remus's bootlegging operation. Schmidt used the money he made during that venture to buy the first of his many Newport gambling clubs. He owned the Glenn Hotel, the Beverly Hills Country Club, the Glenn Rendezvous, and the Glenn Schmidt Playtorium. Most of his clubs were named after his son. Pete Schmidt had visions of owning a grand casino and tried several times to make his dream come true. The syndicate made sure Schmidt did not become too successful since they did not like any competition. Schmidt endured years of harassment by the syndicate, but remained an independent club operator. (Kenton County Public Library.)

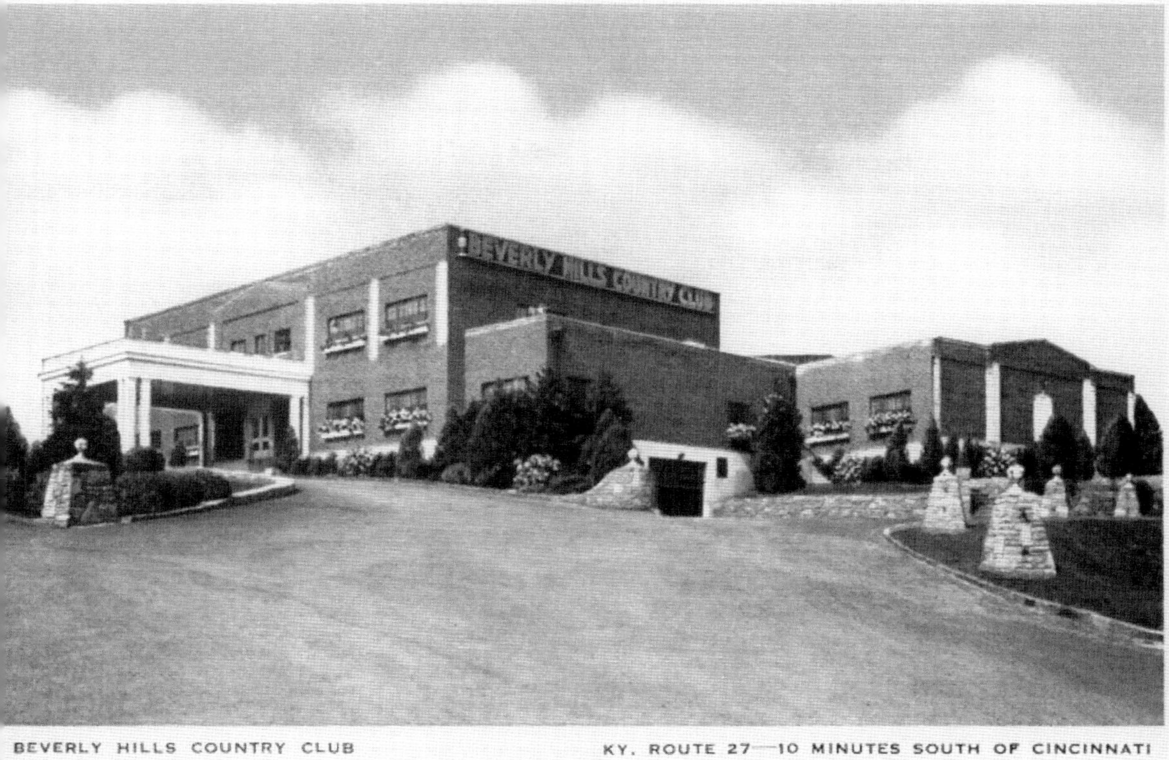

In 1935, Pete Schmidt's vision of owning a grand casino became reality when he opened the Beverly Hills Club. It was a luxurious restaurant and casino located atop a hill on the outskirts of Newport. The success of the Beverly Hills Club garnered the attention of the Cleveland Syndicate, who offered to buy the club and make Schmidt a partner, but Schmidt declined their proposal. After a suspicious fire in 1936, Schmidt rebuilt the club on an elaborate scale and renamed it the Beverly Hills Country Club. Red Masterson and Dave Whitfield, two known associates of the Cleveland Syndicate, were suspected of setting the fire, which killed the property caretaker's young niece. (Kenton County Public Library.)

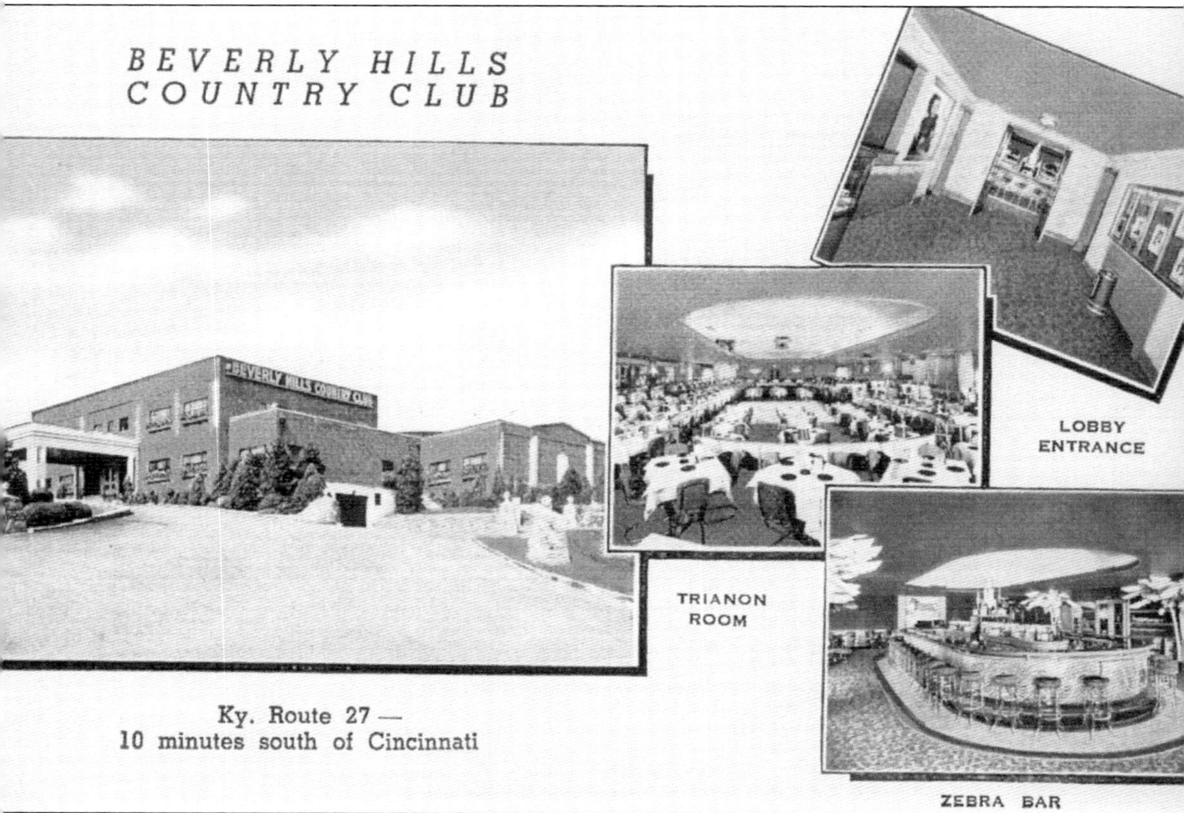

The newly rebuilt Beverly Hills Country Club was a huge sensation. Governors and politicians from several states attended its grand opening in 1937. The club had all of the glitz and glamour of a Vegas-style casino, including showgirls and top name entertainment. The syndicate began harassing and intimidating Schmidt. They were tired of asking him to hand over the club and threatened to take it on their own terms. Schmidt finally relinquished control of the club in 1940. (Kenton County Public Library.)

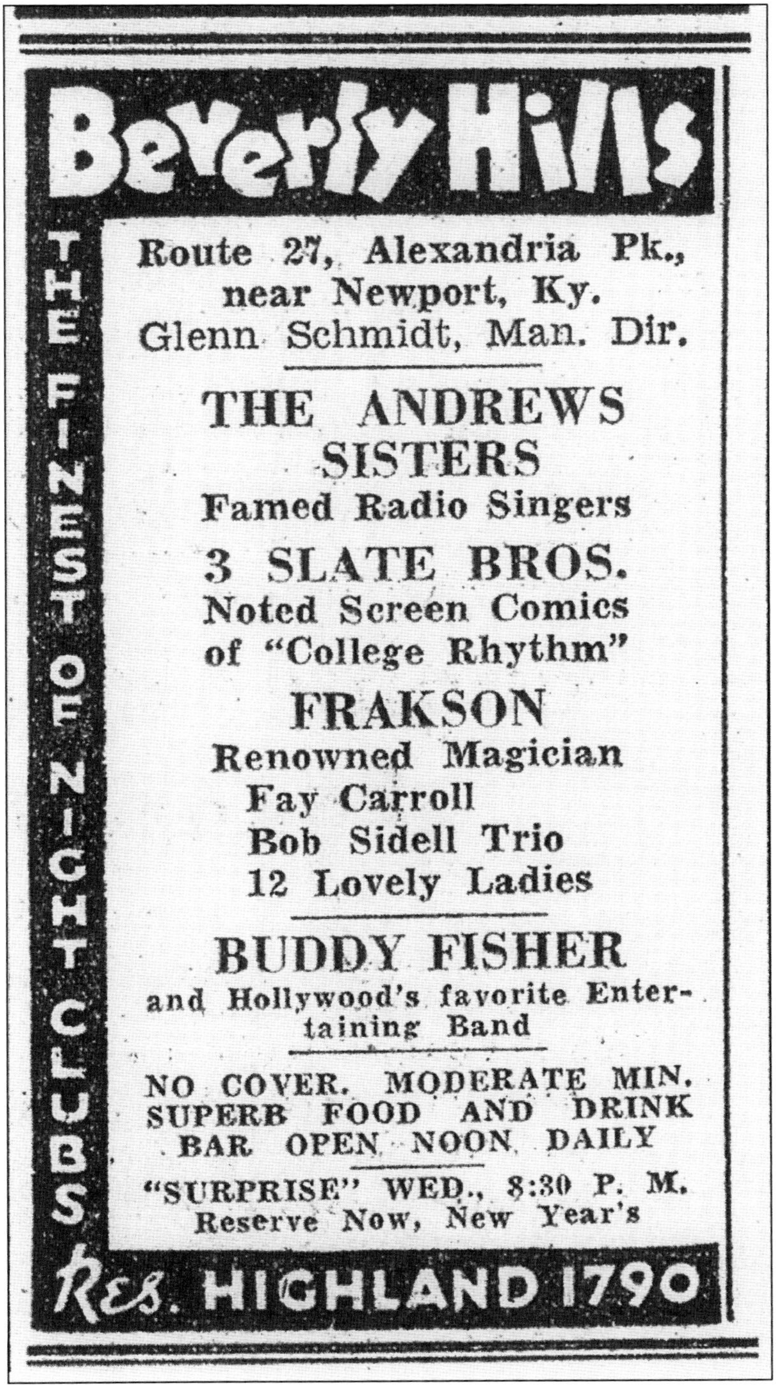

The advertisement pictured here appeared in the *Cincinnati Times-Star* in December 1938. The club was advertising a show by the famous Andrews Sisters. Also on the venue was the Bob Sidell Trio. Bob Sidell was a friend of Schmidt's who played regularly at the club. He later managed Schmidt's Snax Bar casino. Schmidt encouraged Sidell to run for mayor of Newport so Schmidt would have a close friend in city government protecting his interests. Sidell won and served as the mayor of Newport from 1952 to 1956. (Dave Horn Collection.)

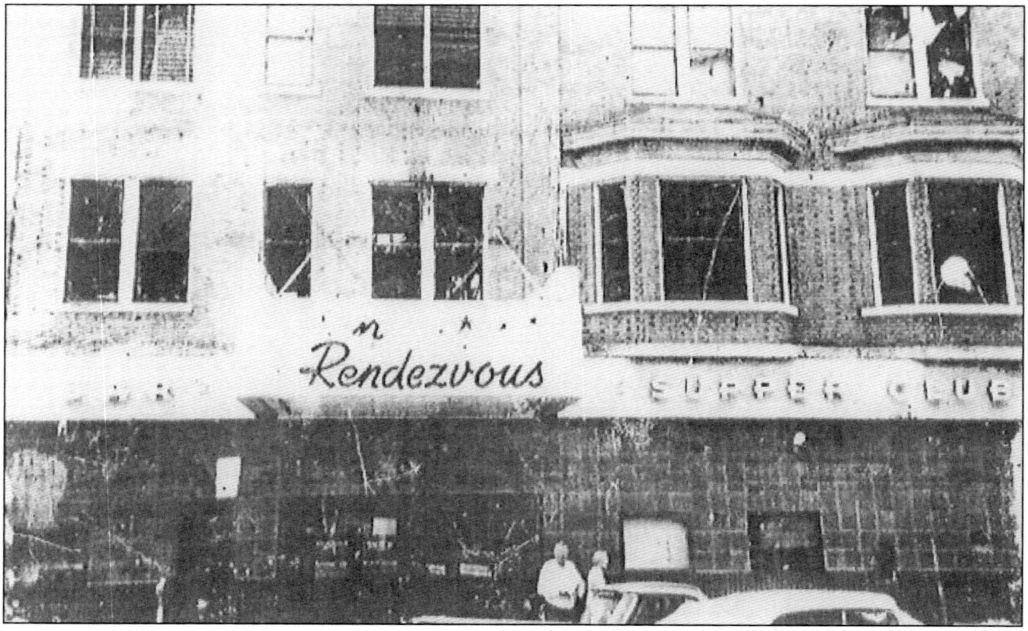

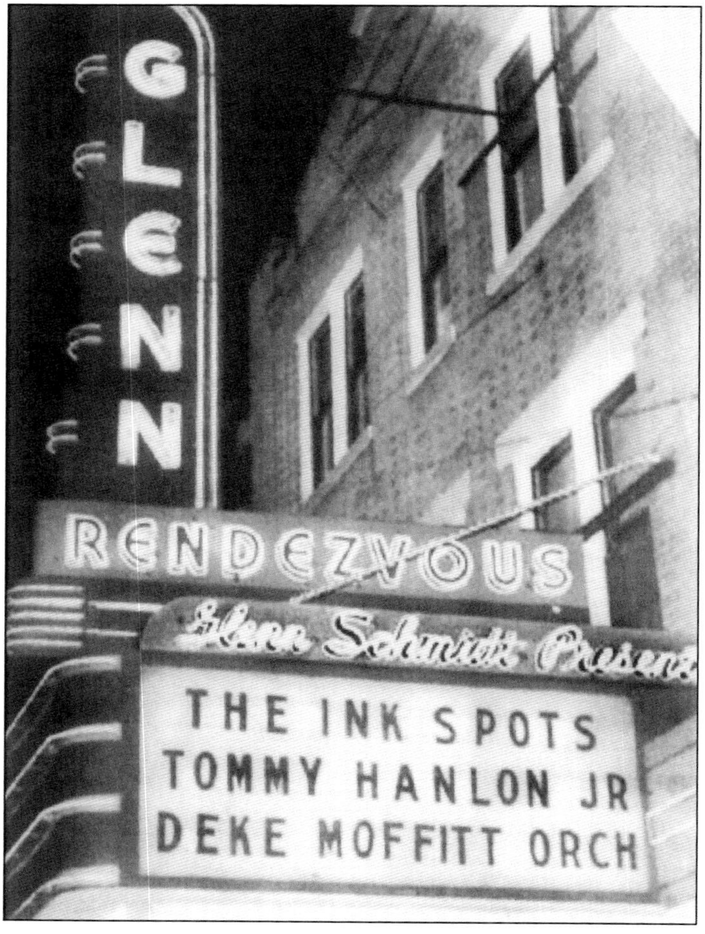

After the syndicate forced him out of the Beverly Hills Country Club, Pete Schmidt focused on renovating a hotel he owned at 928 Monmouth Street in Newport. In 1943, Schmidt remodeled his Glenn Hotel and expanded the casino. He renamed it the Glenn Rendezvous. It contained a large casino and bookmaking operation. The syndicate viewed the venue as competition and started to hassle Schmidt. Syndicate associates began publicly urinating in the lobby of his club. This tactic was known as "ding donging." Fearing another syndicate takeover, Schmidt sold the hotel to the Levinson brothers. Ed, Mike, and "Sleep-out Louie" Levinson were associated with Meyer Lansky and the New York Syndicate. (Both images, Dave Horn Collection.)

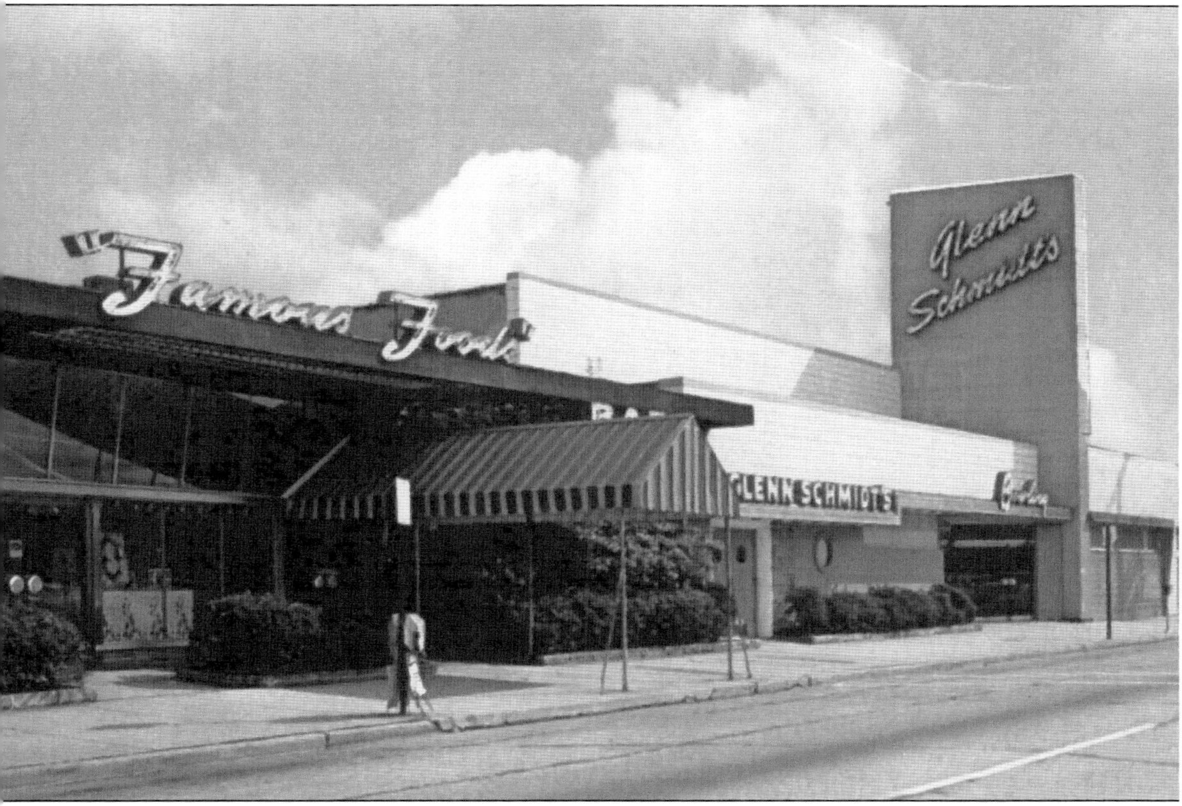

In 1951, Pete Schmidt opened a new establishment known as the Glenn Schmidt Playtorium. Located at 18 East Fifth Street, the building housed a restaurant, bar, bowling alley, and casino. It was so successful that Schmidt decided to move the casino next door into a separate club that he named the Snax Bar. After Schmidt's death in 1958, his son Glenn continued to operate the bowling alley for many years. In 1995, a local redeveloper bought the building and turned it into an up-scale restaurant aptly named the Syndicate. (Kenton County Public Library.)

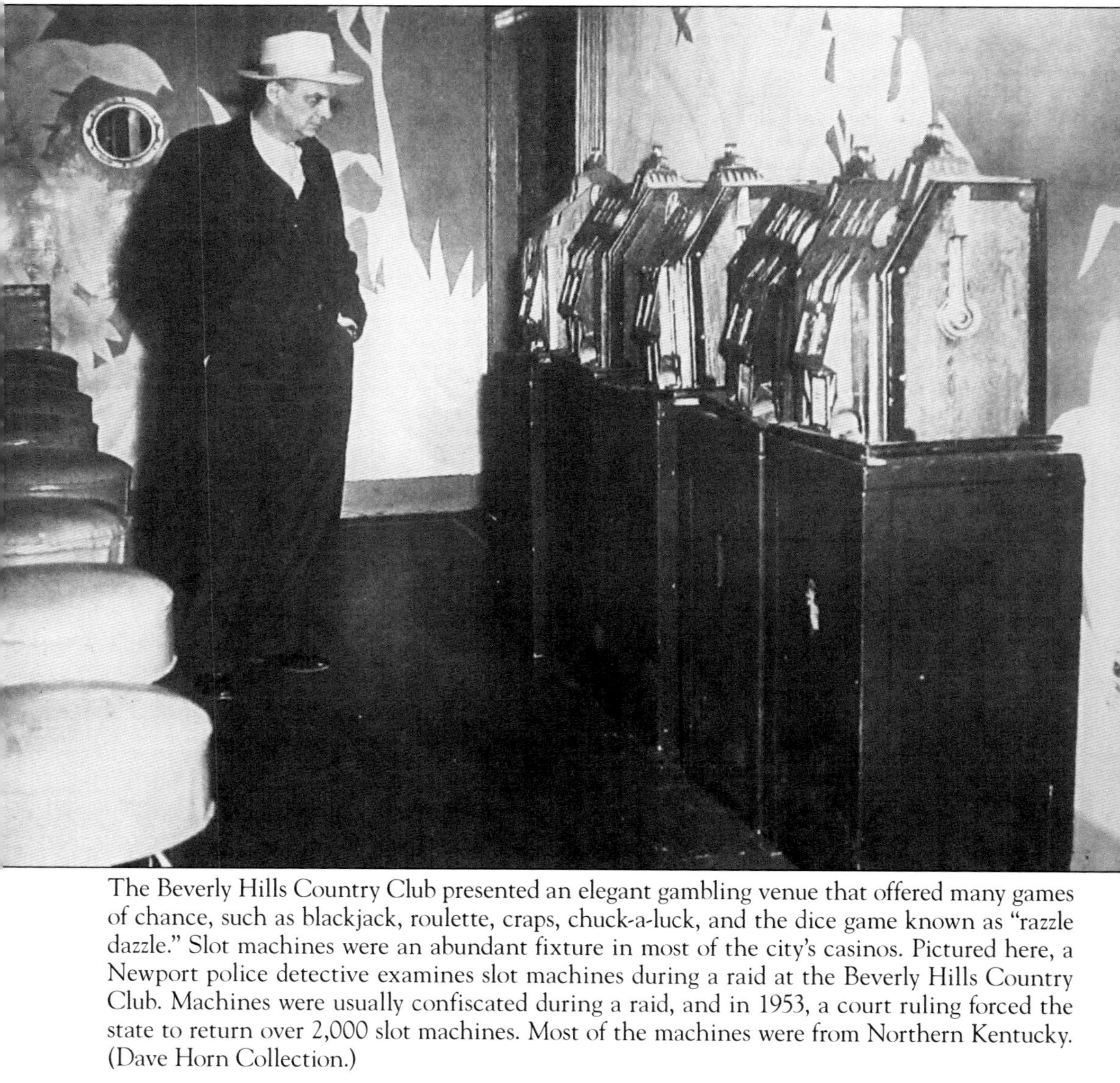

The Beverly Hills Country Club presented an elegant gambling venue that offered many games of chance, such as blackjack, roulette, craps, chuck-a-luck, and the dice game known as "razzle dazzle." Slot machines were an abundant fixture in most of the city's casinos. Pictured here, a Newport police detective examines slot machines during a raid at the Beverly Hills Country Club. Machines were usually confiscated during a raid, and in 1953, a court ruling forced the state to return over 2,000 slot machines. Most of the machines were from Northern Kentucky. (Dave Horn Collection.)

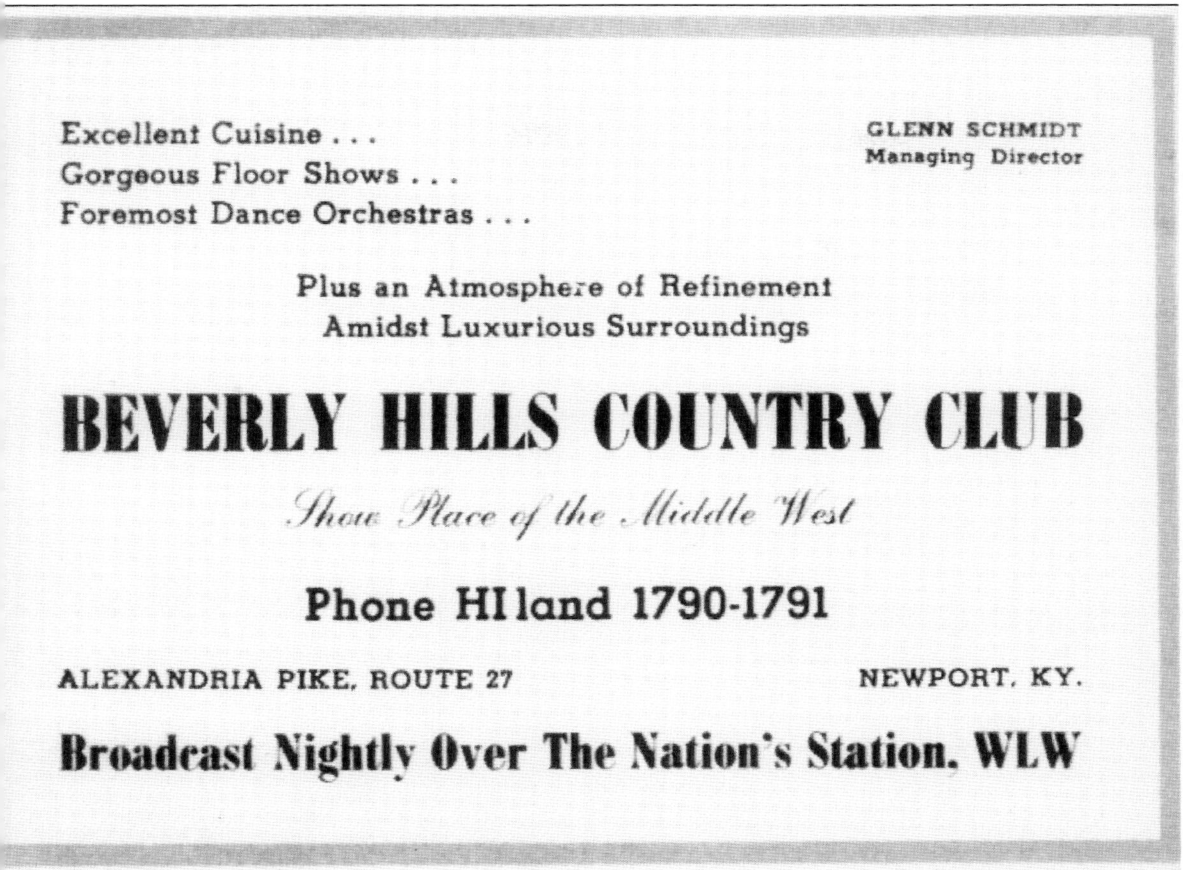

This promotional advertisement for the Beverly Hills Country Club advertises the club's excellent cuisine, gorgeous floor shows, and outstanding dance orchestras. The entertainment at the Beverly Hills Country Club was broadcast nightly over Cincinnati's radio station WLW. The Andrews Sisters, the Mills Brothers, Eydie Gormet, Shecky Green, the De Castro Sisters, Myron Cohen, Ted Lewis, Guy Lombardo, Gypsy Rose Lee, Buddy Hackett, Pearl Bailey, Liberace, Ozzie and Harriet, Joey Bishop, Dean Martin, Frank Sinatra, Marilyn Monroe, and many other famous performers graced the stage at the club. Allegedly, Frank Sinatra lost a lot of money in the casino while in town. (Dave Horn Collection.)

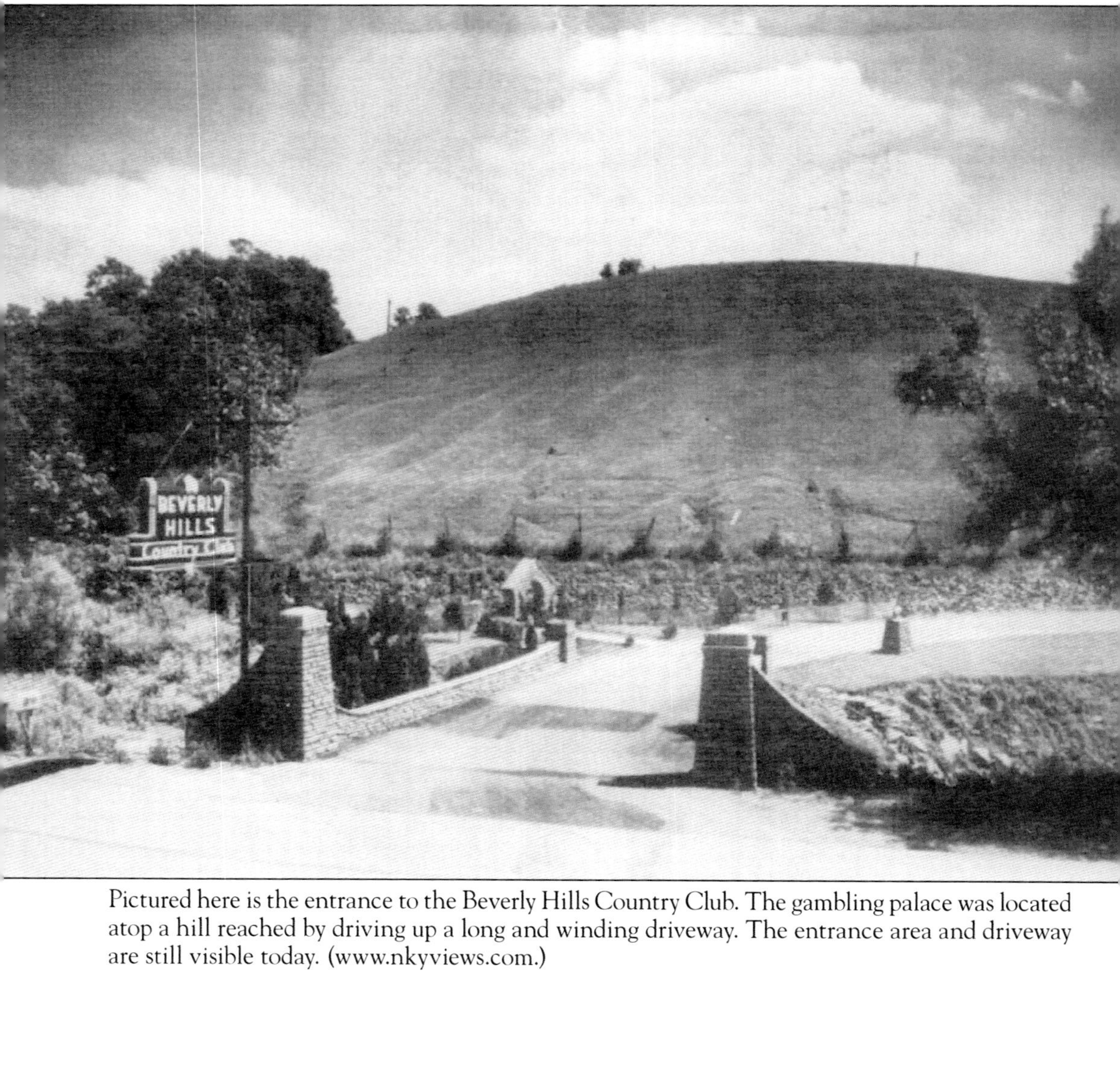

Pictured here is the entrance to the Beverly Hills Country Club. The gambling palace was located atop a hill reached by driving up a long and winding driveway. The entrance area and driveway are still visible today. (www.nkyviews.com.)

The Beverly Hills Country Club was elegant and lavish. The cocktail area contained a circular bar called the Rendezvous Bar. The dining and showroom was known as the Trianon Room. It included a large dance floor so diners could enjoy the floor show or watch the resident chorus line perform. The casino contained beautiful, hand-carved gaming tables, plush carpeting, gilded gold-leaf wallpaper, and crystal chandeliers. (www.nkyviews.com.)

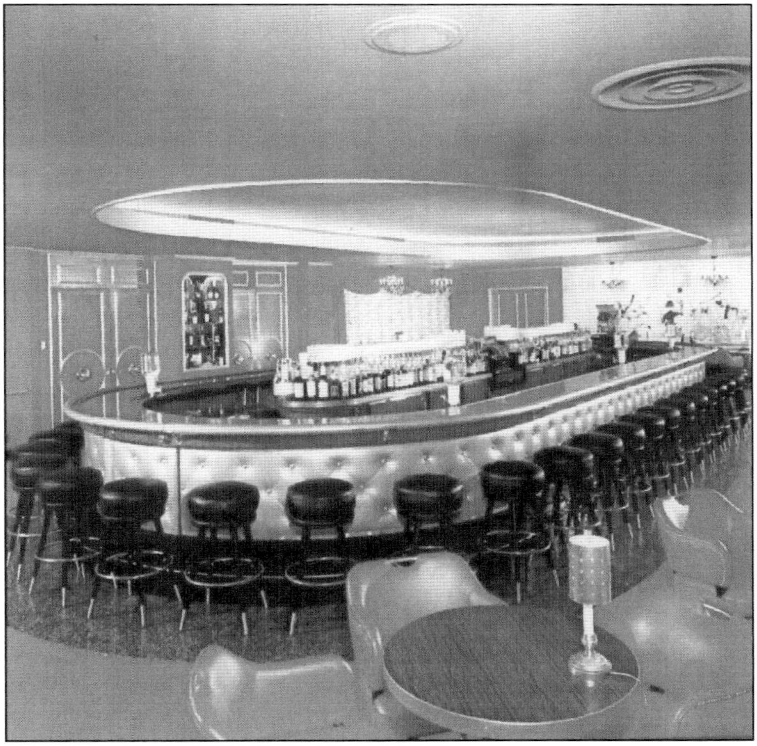

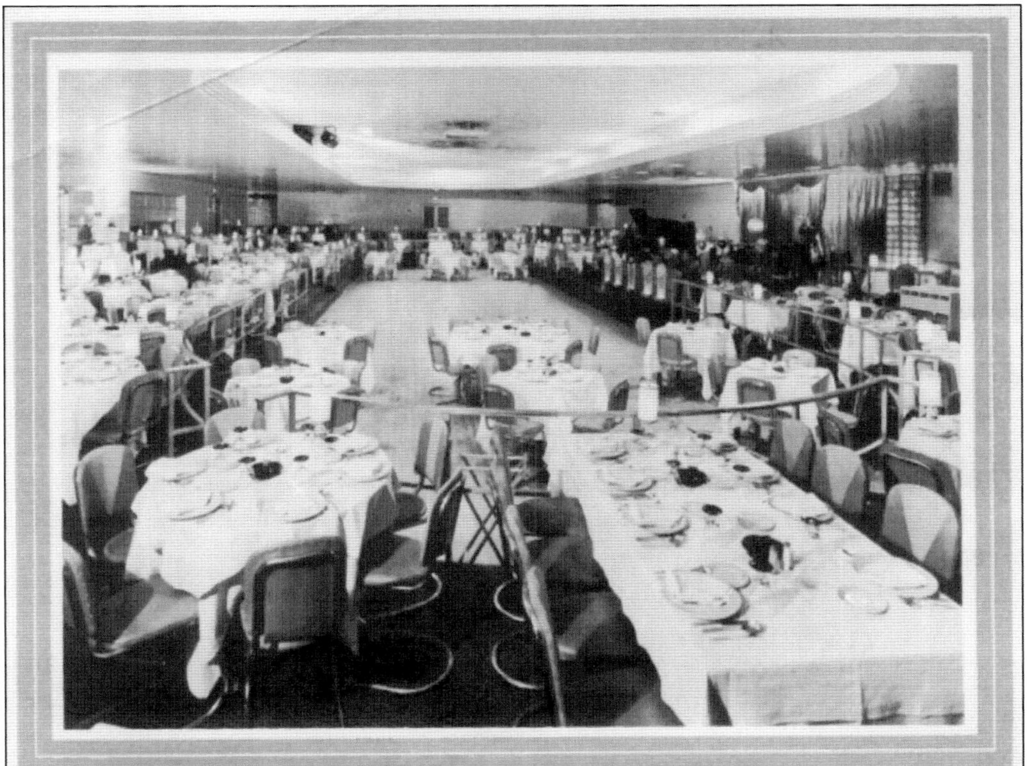

TRIANON ROOM

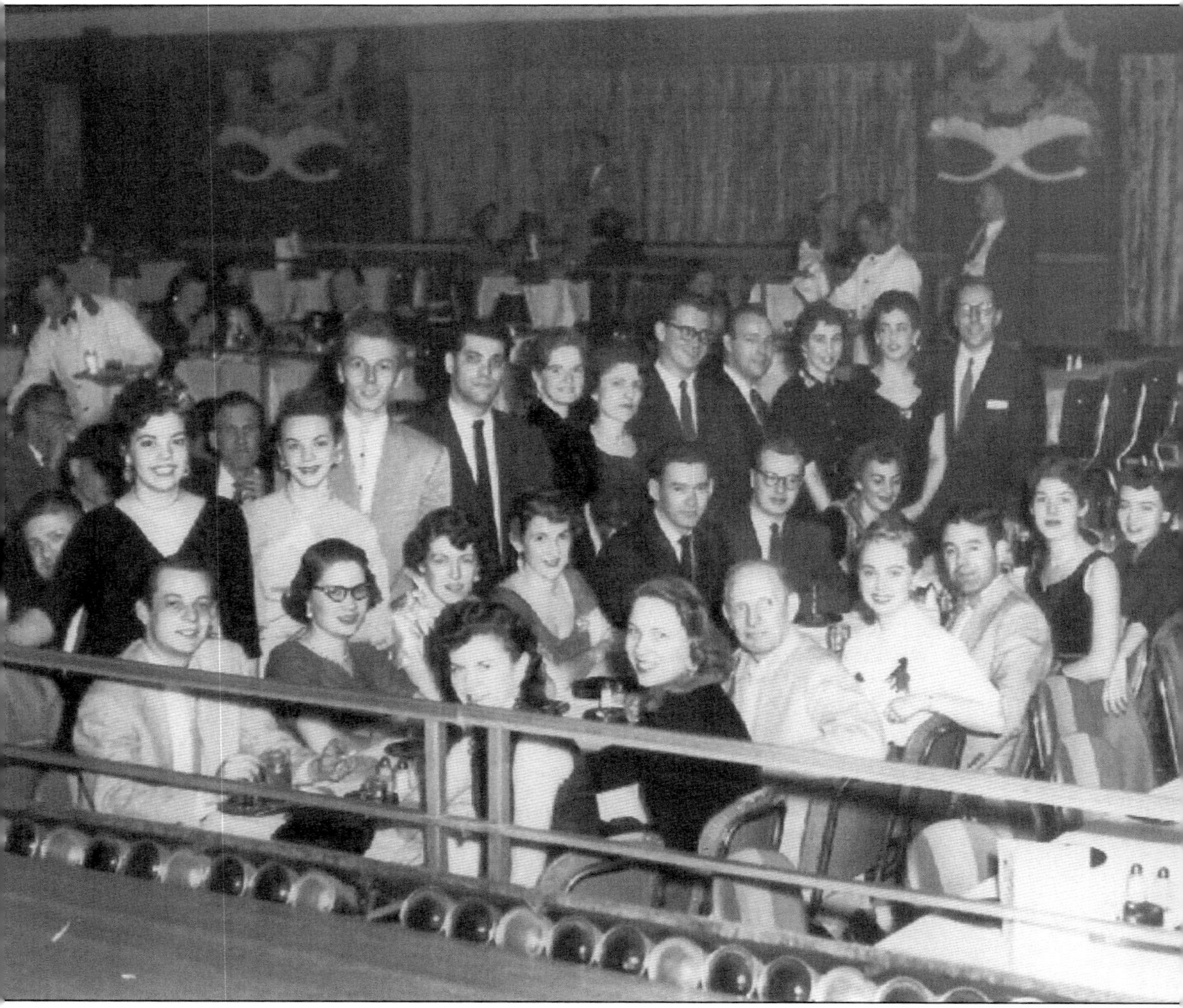

In this photograph taken at the Beverly Hills Country Club, a smiling group of people is enjoying cocktails and waiting for the floor show to begin. The club kept a photographer at hand to capture the memory of their special evening at the club. (Dave Horn Collection.)

Edward Levinson and his brothers "Sleep-out Louie" and Mike were natives of Chicago who came to Newport in the late 1930s. The Levinson brothers seized control of the Flamingo/633 Club from Art Dennert. The club featured a bar, cafeteria, and gambling casino as well as a bookmaking operation in the back. Edward Levinson was a close associate of Meyer Lansky and Bugsy Siegel. Ed left Newport for Las Vegas, where he was involved with the operations of the Desert Inn, the Stardust, and the Freemont Hotel. (Kenton County Public Library.)

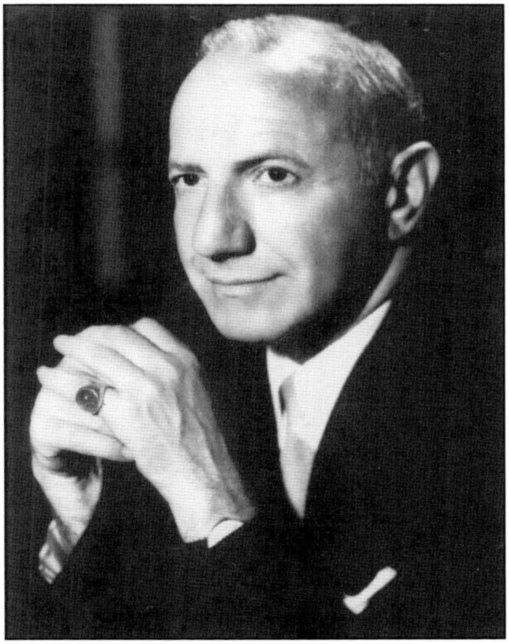

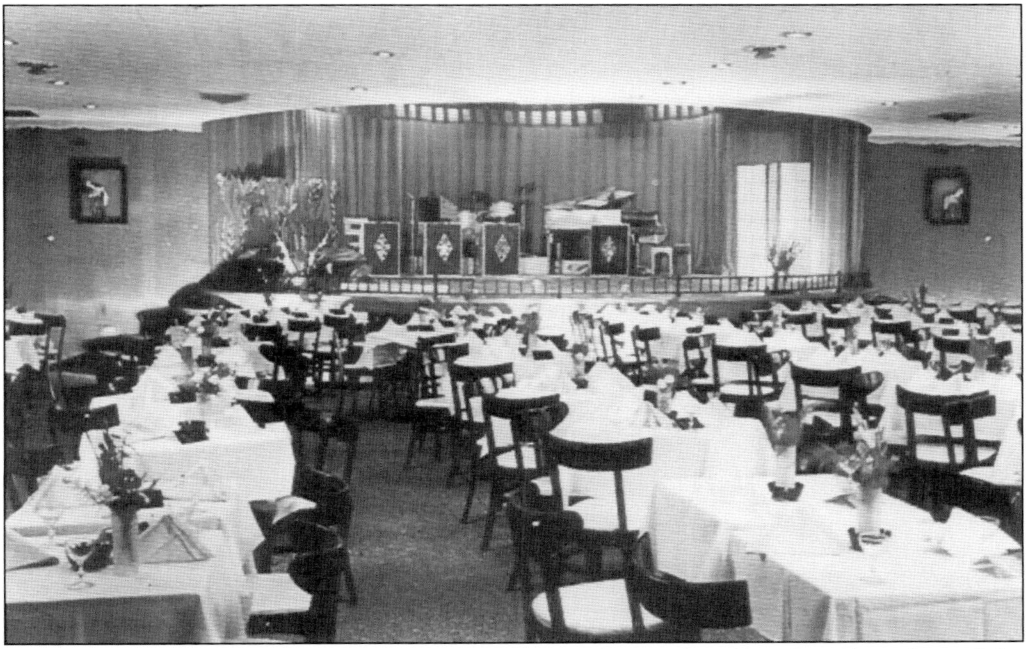

The Silver Slipper, located at 613 Monmouth Street, advertised itself as the "Showplace of the Midwest." It featured fine dining, popular bands, floor shows, and gambling. Cigarette girls carried around trays offering patrons cigarettes and cigars. They also kept a supply of candy and gum on their trays. The club's owner, Jim Harris, went to prison for pandering and turned the club over to the Cleveland Syndicate, who renamed it the Stardust. The venue saw multiple name changes over the years. Besides the Silver Slipper and the Stardust, it was known as the Stork Club, Club Bongo, Frolics, and the Galaxie. After the Galaxie Club burned in 1970, the building was reconstructed and is currently operating as a strip club known as the Brass Mule. (www.nkyviews.com.)

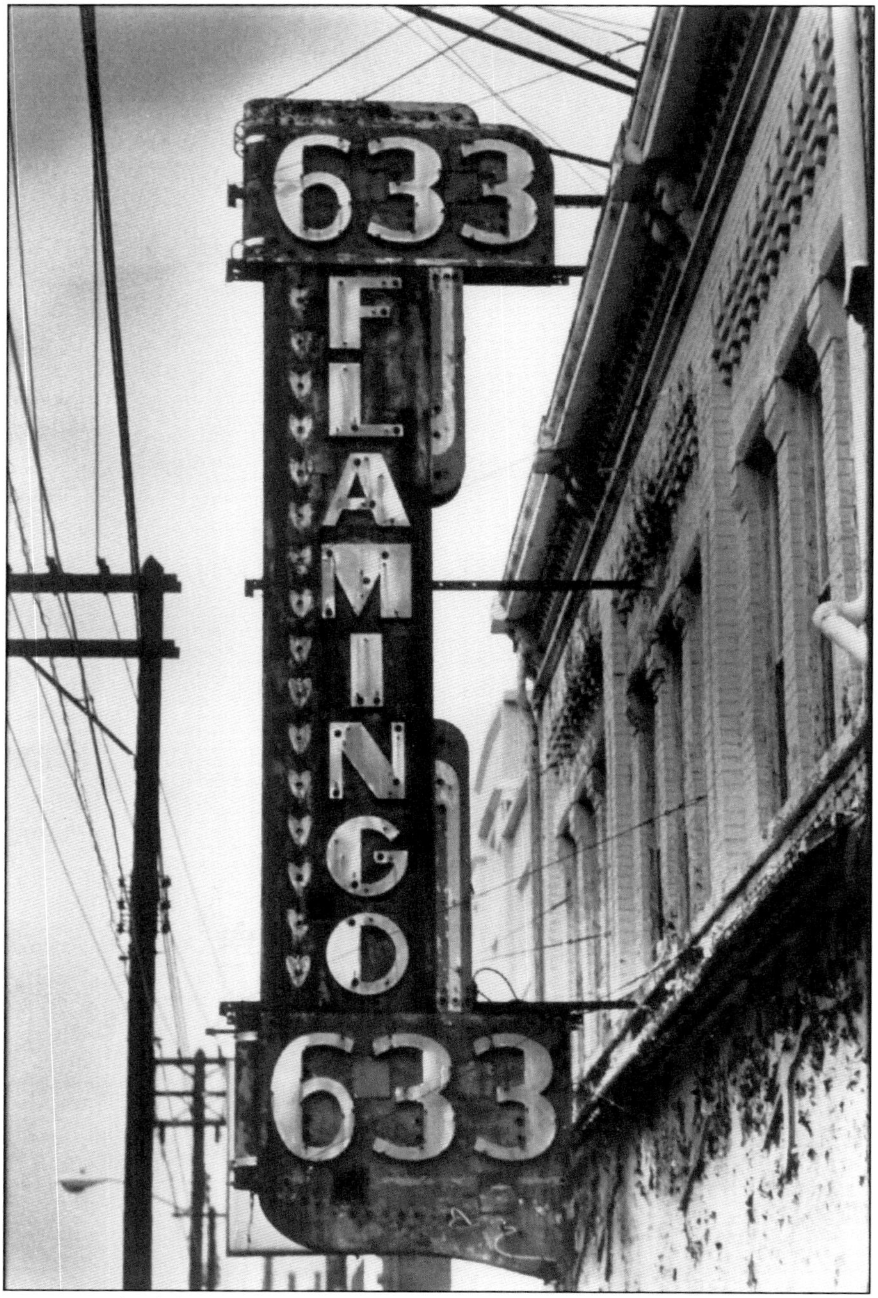

The Flamingo Nightclub and Casino was located at 633 York Street. Art Dennert opened the club in the 1930s but was forced to relinquish control of the club to the Levinson brothers representing the interests of the New York mob. The Cleveland Syndicate tolerated the intrusion into their territory because the Levinsons had close ties to Meyer Lansky, Bugsy Siegel, and "Trigger" Mike Coppola. Dennert was allowed to keep a share of the club, but upon his death, the Cleveland Syndicate claimed his share and became co-managers of the club. The upscale resort featured a bar and cafeteria in the front and a casino and betting parlor in the back. The club was easily identified by the large Vegas-style neon sign (seen above), which hung in front of the building. (Kenton County Public Library.)

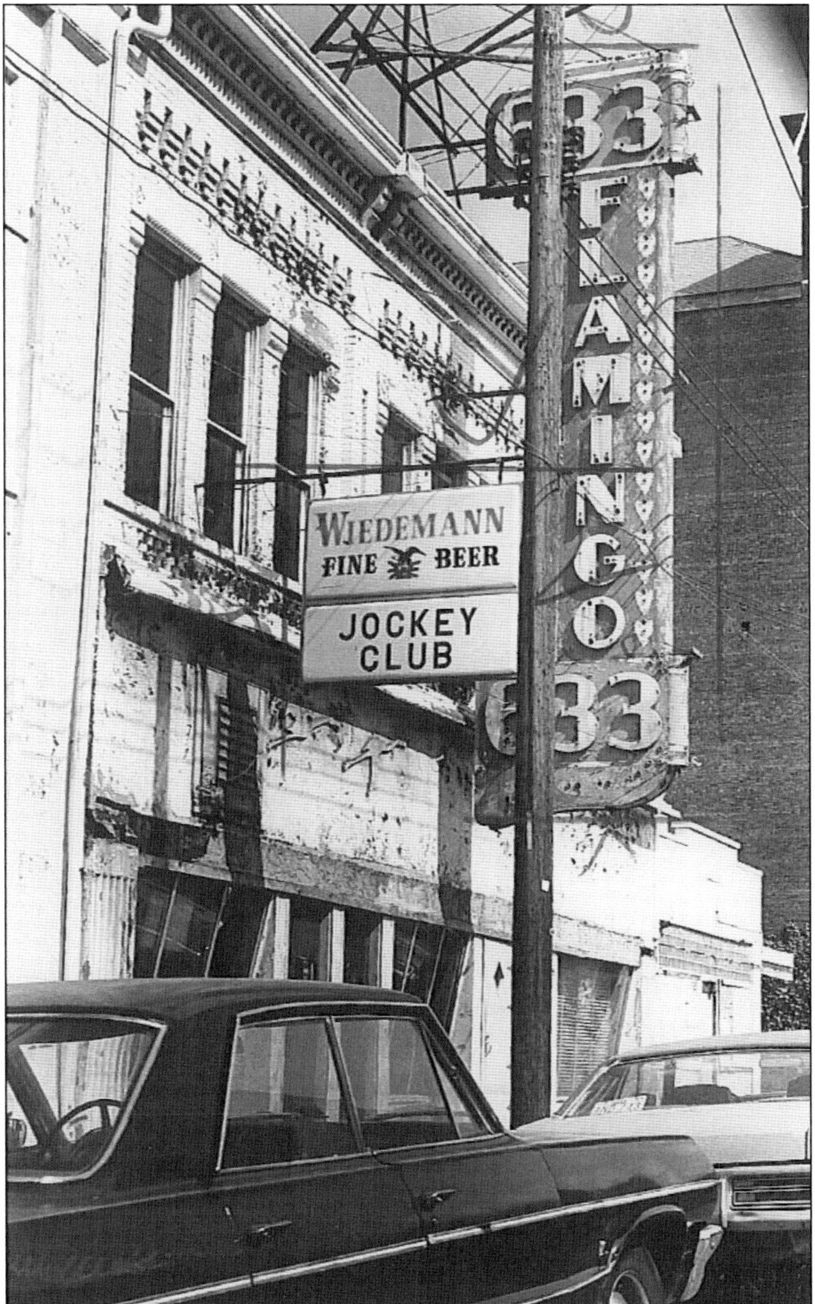

Once the Cleveland Syndicate moved their operations to Vegas, the Flamingo Club was sold to Charles Stegman, who turned it into a rock-and-roll dance haven for teenagers. Many famous acts such as the Isley Brothers, Jerry Lee Lewis, Little Richard and Chuck Berry performed at the club. In 1971, the building was sold to the Mincey brothers, who changed the name to the Jockey Club (seen here). During the 1980s, the club was a popular concert venue featuring infamous punk bands such as the Ramones, the Dead Kennedys, and the Violent Femmes. The large neon Flamingo sign remained in place for many years. The building no longer exists, and the property is now part of the Yellow Cab Company. (Kenton County Public Library.)

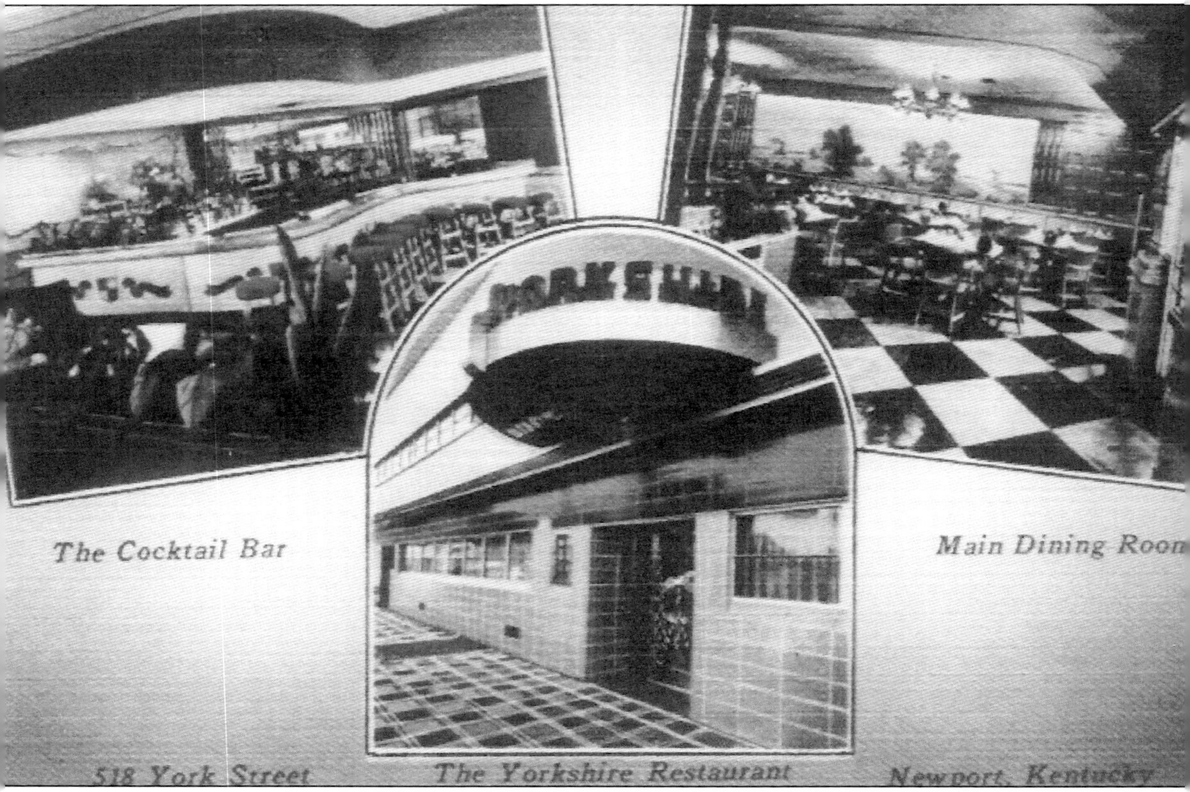

The Yorkshire was located at 518 York Street. The restaurant and casino were managed by Joe and Martin Berman. The Bermans were associates of Meyer Lansky and the New York faction. They managed the club for the syndicate after acquiring it from Jimmy Brink in 1944. Bernhardt's Bakery currently operates in the original building. (www.nkyviews.com.)

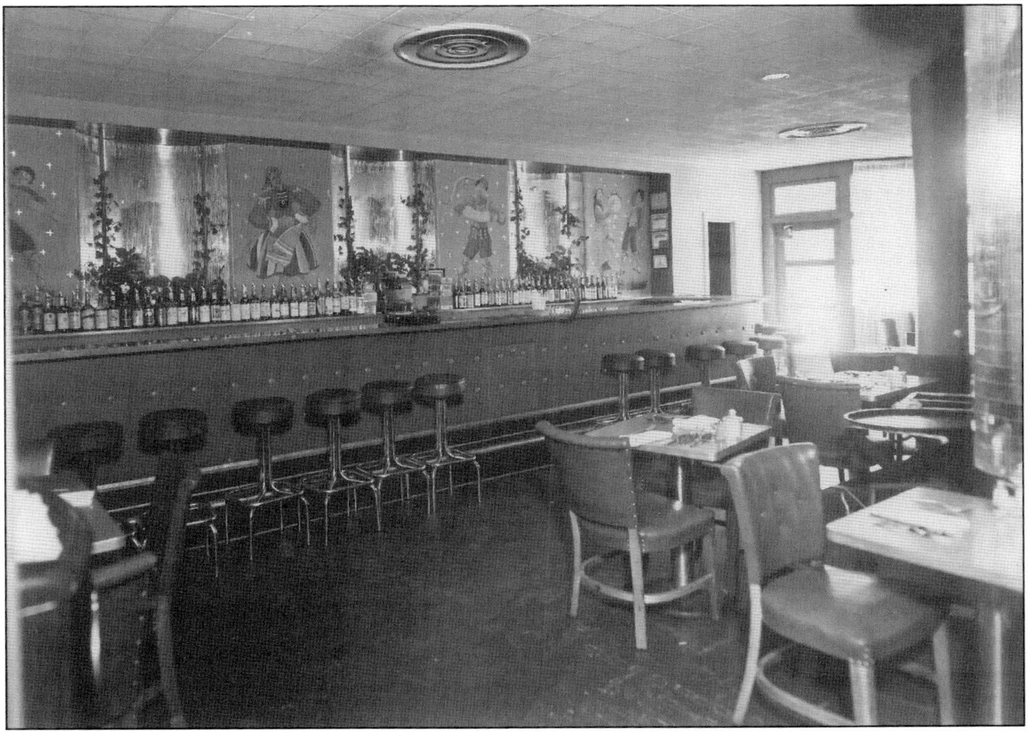

These pictures show the Yorkshire Club's bar and cocktail area. The plush casino was over 7,500 square feet. It offered all the amenities of the other casinos and included a large bookmaking operation in the back. It was estimated by federal officials that the Yorkshire casino grossed wages of $2 million per month. The club was open seven days a week from 11:00 a.m. until the last bet was placed. (Both images, Dave Horn Collection.)

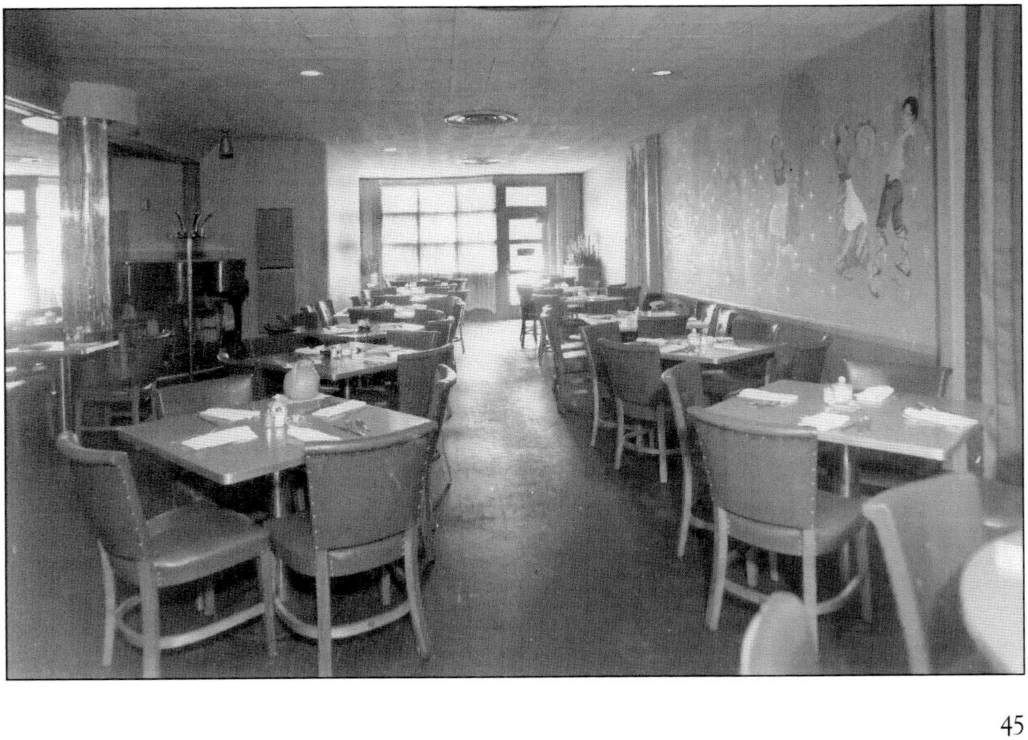

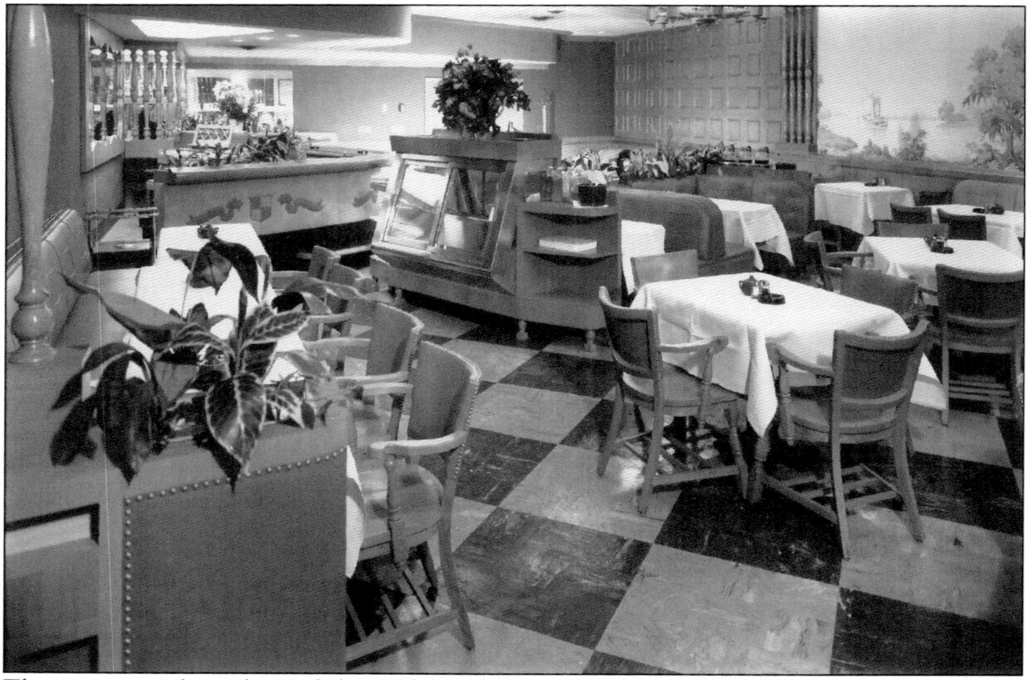

These pictures show the Yorkshire Club cafeteria (above) and the club's elegant dining room (below). The Yorkshire was an upscale venue that served drinks and food at moderate prices. The casino was located down the hall from the dining area. It was concealed by a steel-clad door that was installed at a sharp angle to hamper efforts made by police to bust the door down during raids. (Both images, Dave Horn Collection.)

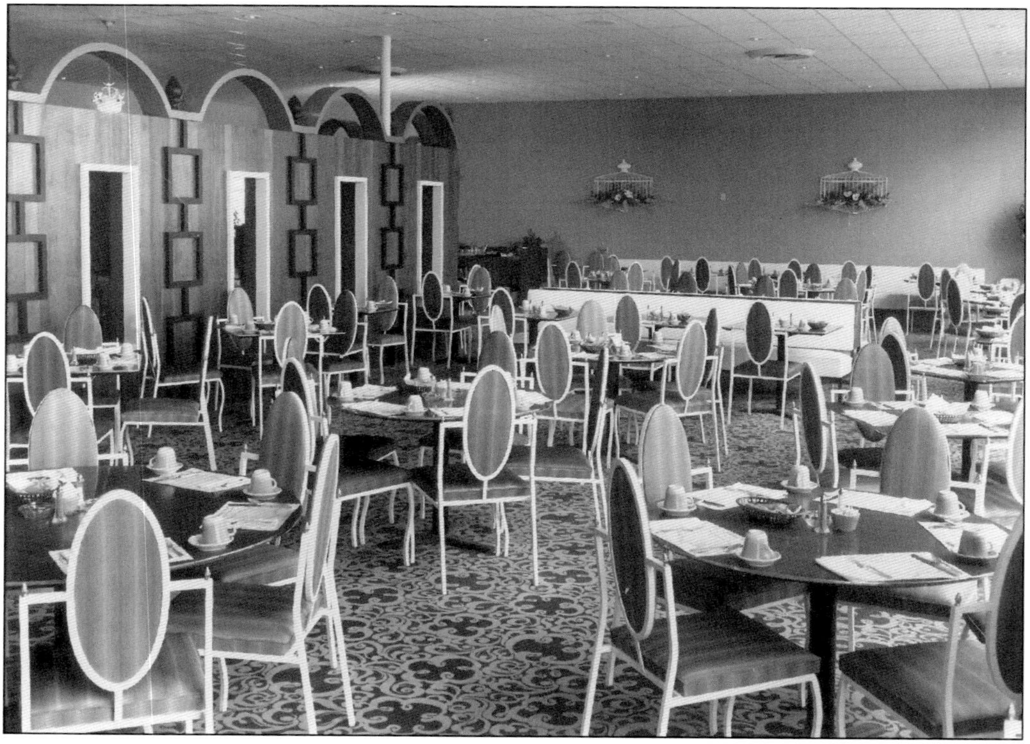

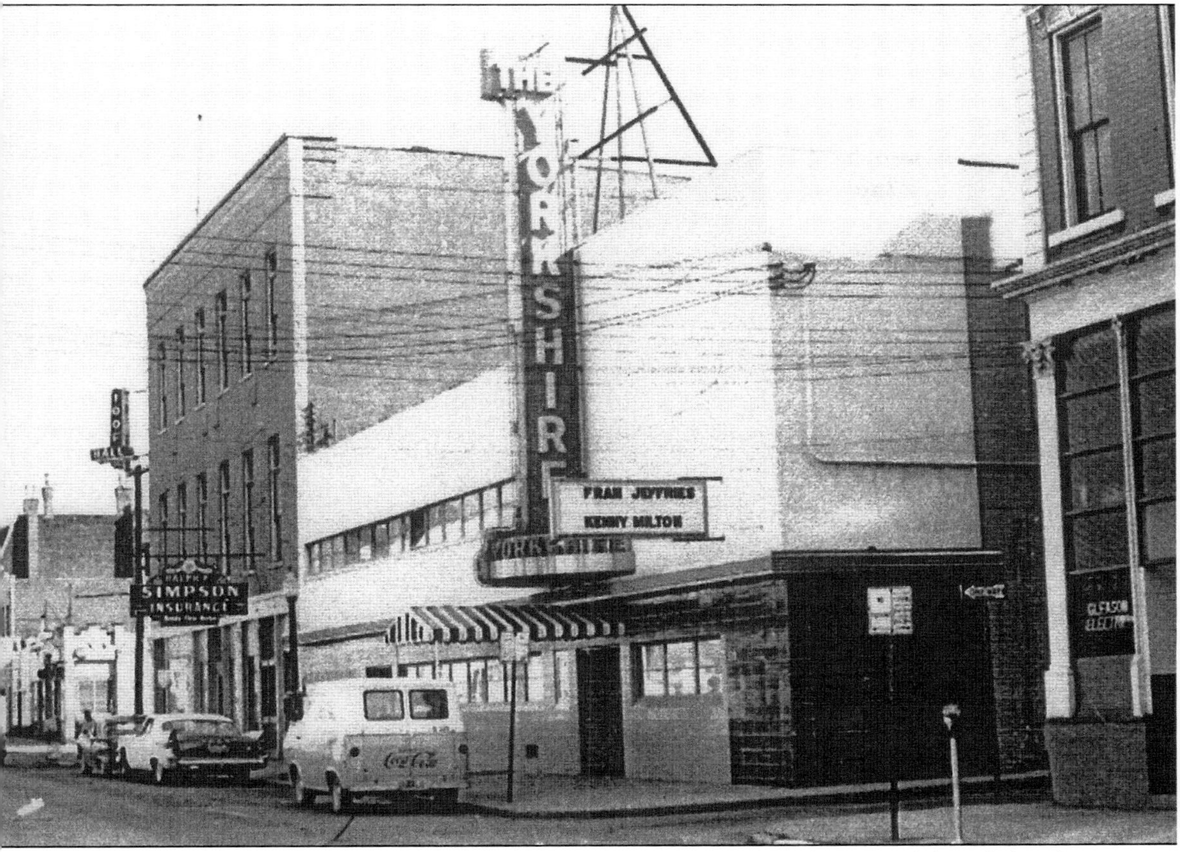

The Yorkshire contained one of Newport's busiest bookie joints. Several racetrack boards lined the rear wall of the casino. Race results poured in constantly from tracks around the country. In February 1953, the club was raided; three men described as "big-shot Cleveland gamblers" were charged in U.S. tax court in Washington, D.C., with hiding $273,000 in profits from the Yorkshire Club. (Dave Horn Collection.)

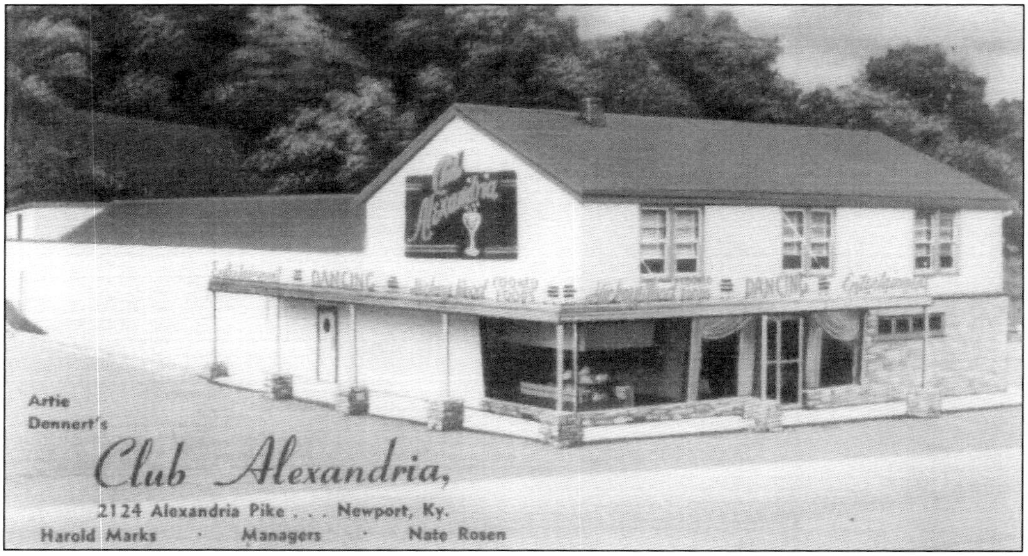

In the 1940s, Artie Dennert opened a swanky cocktail lounge and casino at 2124 Monmouth Street. Club Alexandria got its name from the fact that it was situated where Monmouth Street ends and becomes Alexandria Pike. The spacious casino offered the usual popular games and was capable of holding hundreds of gamblers. Artie Dennert at one time had an interest in the Flamingo Club and the Glenn Rendezvous. Club Alexandria was raided several times in 1956, resulting in slot machines being confiscated and ordered by the court to be destroyed. Today an Advance Auto Parts store sits on the site. (www.nkyviews.com.)

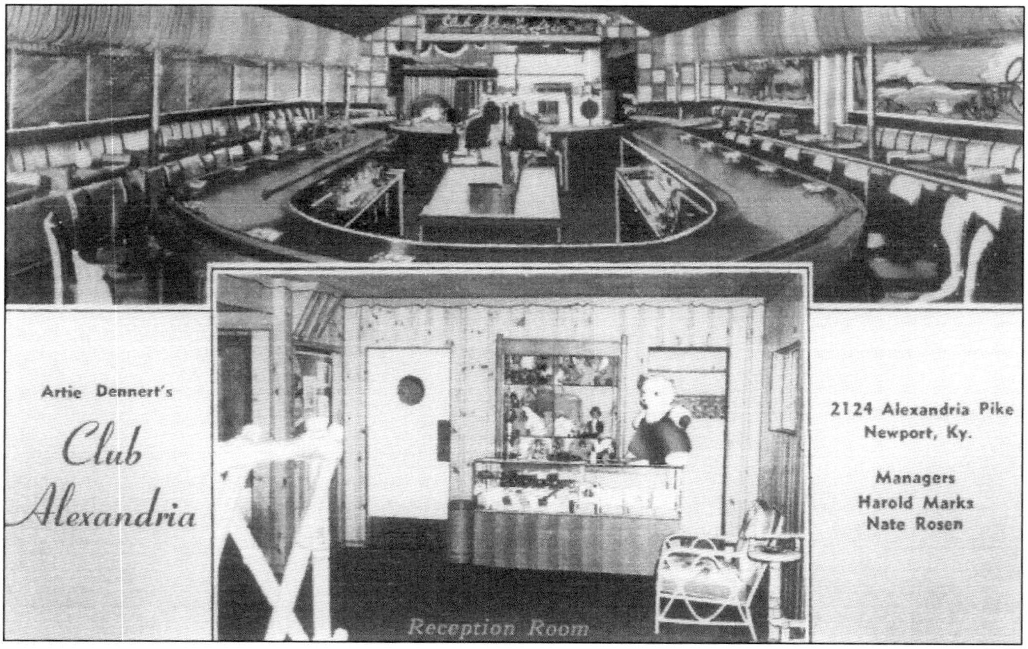

In January 1950, several men pretending to be milkmen making a delivery were admitted into Club Alexandria during closing hours. The men turned out to be bandits who tied up the watchman and robbed the club safe of $24,000. Jack Thiem, head detective of Newport's gangster unit, suspected the robbery was an inside job. He conducted an investigation into the affair, but no arrests were made. (www.nkyviews.com.)

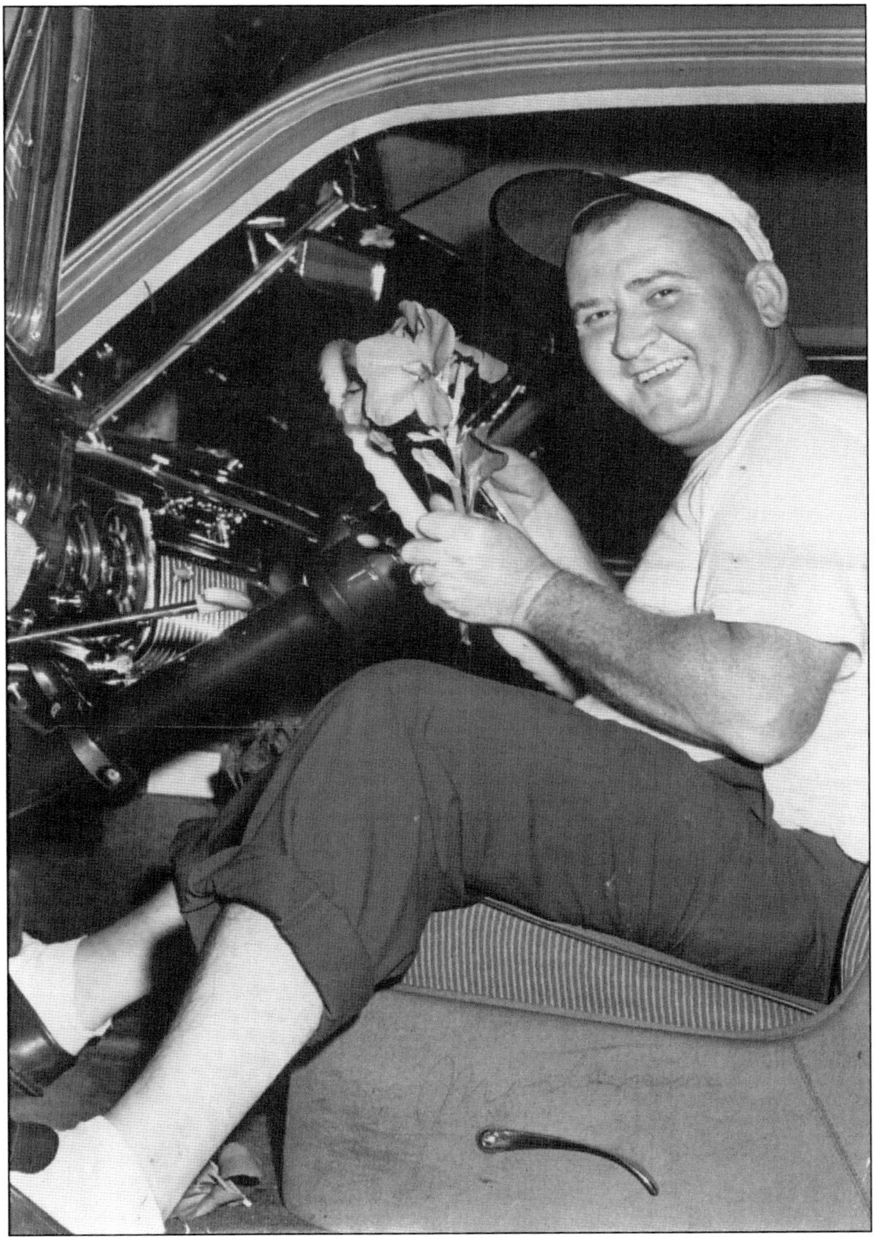

Albert "Red" Masterson was a moonshiner, thief, gambler, and murderer. He had close ties to the Cleveland Syndicate. In 1926, Masterson was involved in a shoot-out with Pat Fitters in front of the Wiedemann Brewery. In the early 1930s, he shot and killed both Elmer McCabe and John Rosen, being acquitted in each instance. Masterson, the "enforcer," protected local syndicate gambling houses. He forced independent club operators such as Pete Schmidt, Buck Brady, and Jimmy Brink to hand their clubs over to the syndicate. In 1936, Masterson was accused of helping set the fire to the Beverly Hills Country Club, which resulted in the death of six-year-old Mary Lou Rardin. In 1946, Masterson was shot while sitting in his car at Third and Monmouth Streets. He survived the ambush, but refused to identify the shooter, Buck Brady. Masterson controlled the syndicate-owned Merchants Club for over 20 years. He died in December 1972. (Campbell County Historical Society.)

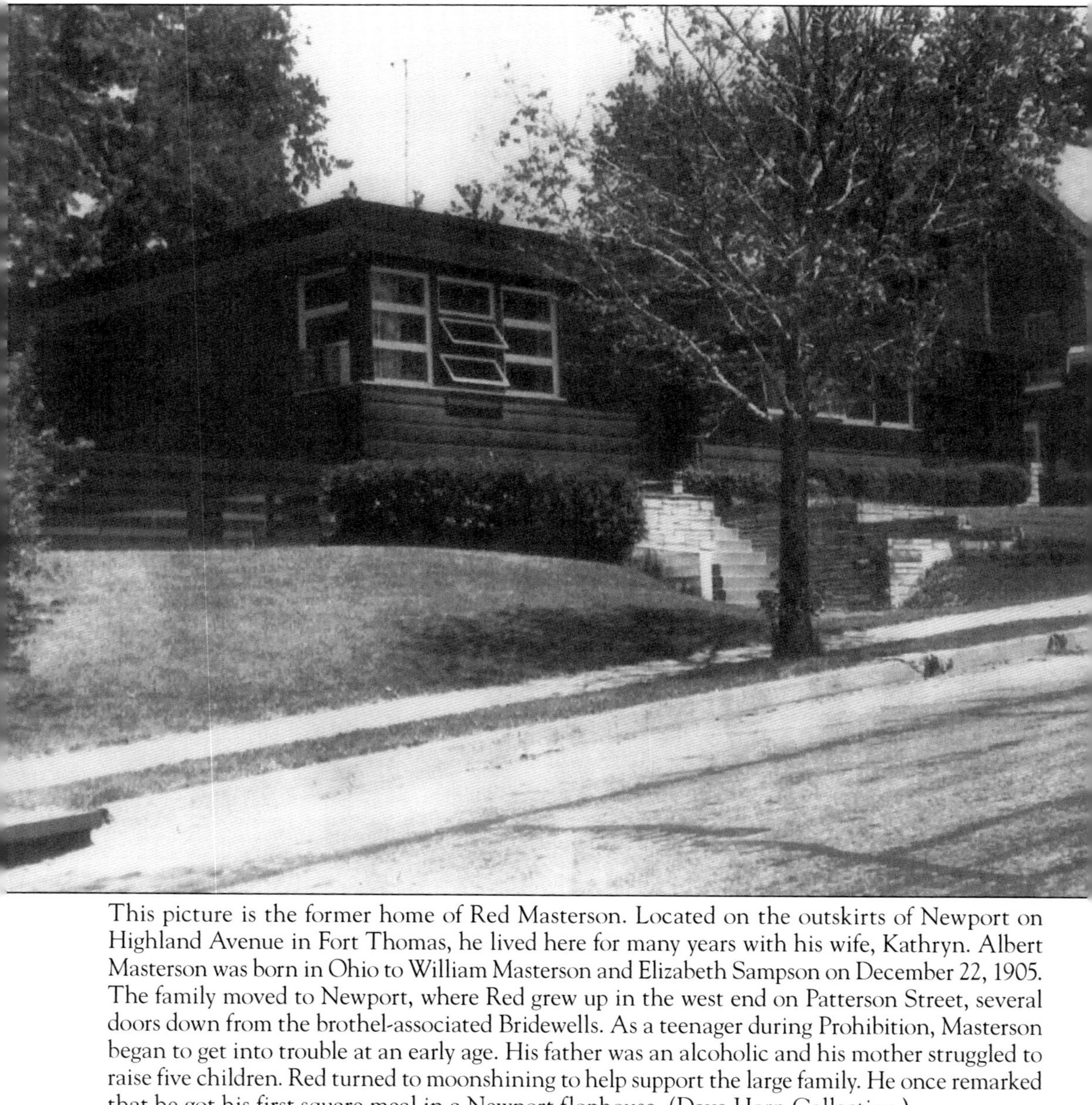

This picture is the former home of Red Masterson. Located on the outskirts of Newport on Highland Avenue in Fort Thomas, he lived here for many years with his wife, Kathryn. Albert Masterson was born in Ohio to William Masterson and Elizabeth Sampson on December 22, 1905. The family moved to Newport, where Red grew up in the west end on Patterson Street, several doors down from the brothel-associated Bridewells. As a teenager during Prohibition, Masterson began to get into trouble at an early age. His father was an alcoholic and his mother struggled to raise five children. Red turned to moonshining to help support the large family. He once remarked that he got his first square meal in a Newport flophouse. (Dave Horn Collection.)

The Merchants Club was located at 15 East Fourth Street. It was a three-story building with a dining room and casino. Red Masterson managed the club for the syndicate for over 20 years. During the Kefauver Committee hearings in 1951, Newport's police chief George Gugel was asked to list the notorious gambling houses operating in his jurisdiction. Gugel named the Merchants Club as one of them. The club was located in close proximity to the police station and courthouse. In 1951, the club was raided and its occupants were marched single file up the street to the police station. Today a Goodyear Auto Service Center sits on the site. (Both images, Dave Horn Collection.)

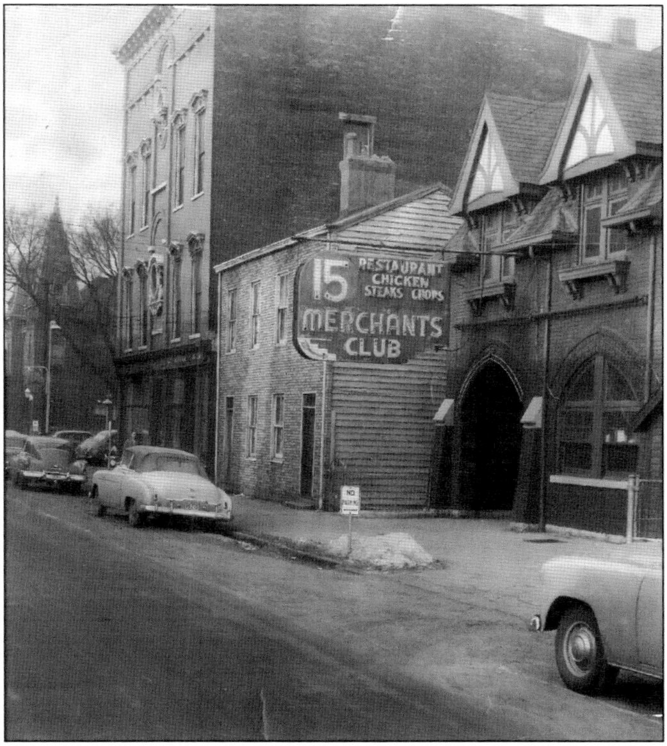

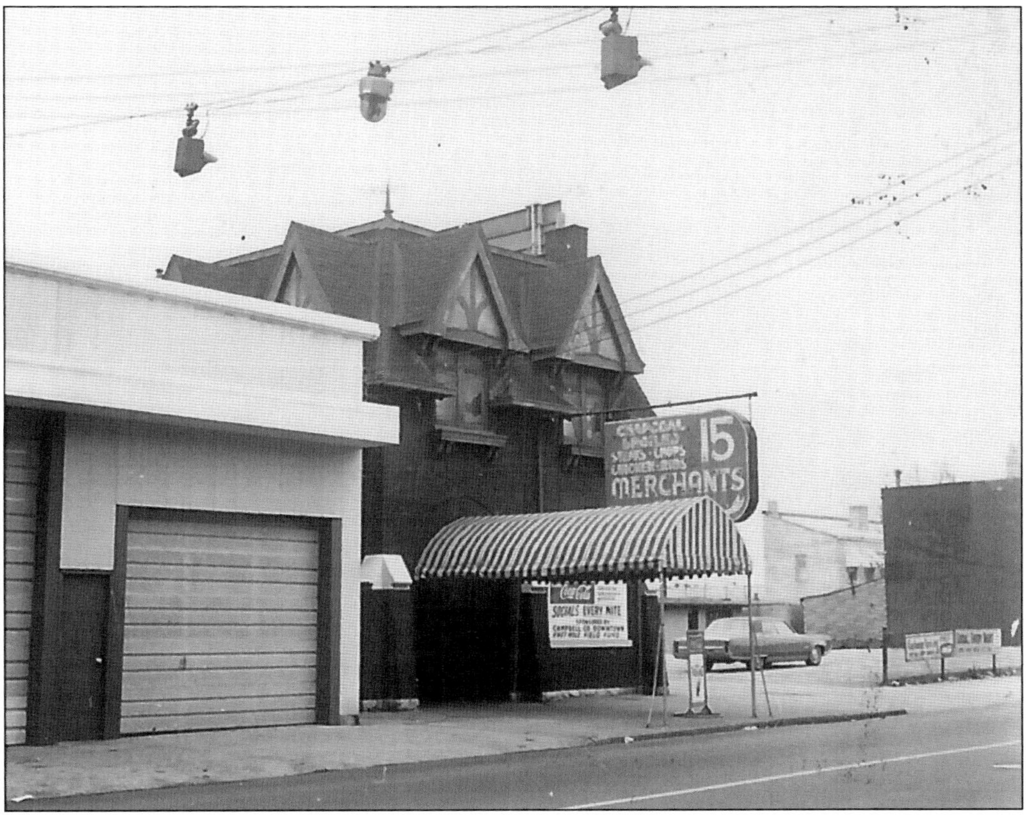

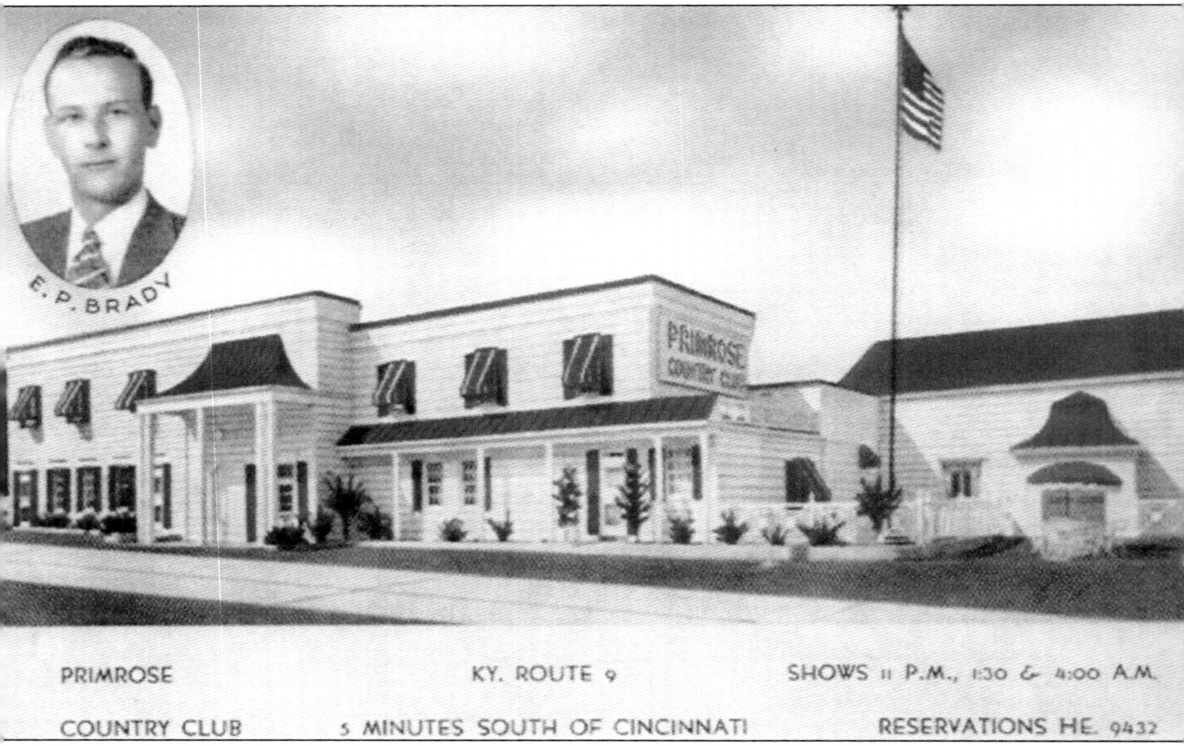

The Primrose Country Club was located on the outskirts of Newport. Owned and operated by Ernest "Buck" Brady, the club was viewed by the syndicate as competition, and they delegated Red Masterson to talk him into selling the club to them. On August 5, 1946, Brady, feeling pressure from a syndicate takeover, shot Masterson in front of the Merchants Club. Masterson survived the attack and threatened to kill Brady, who turned his club over to the Cleveland Syndicate and left town. The syndicate renovated the club and turned it into one of the area's most popular nightspots. It is now Bobby Mackey's Music World, a country-western bar complete with a mechanical bull. (www.nkyviews.com.)

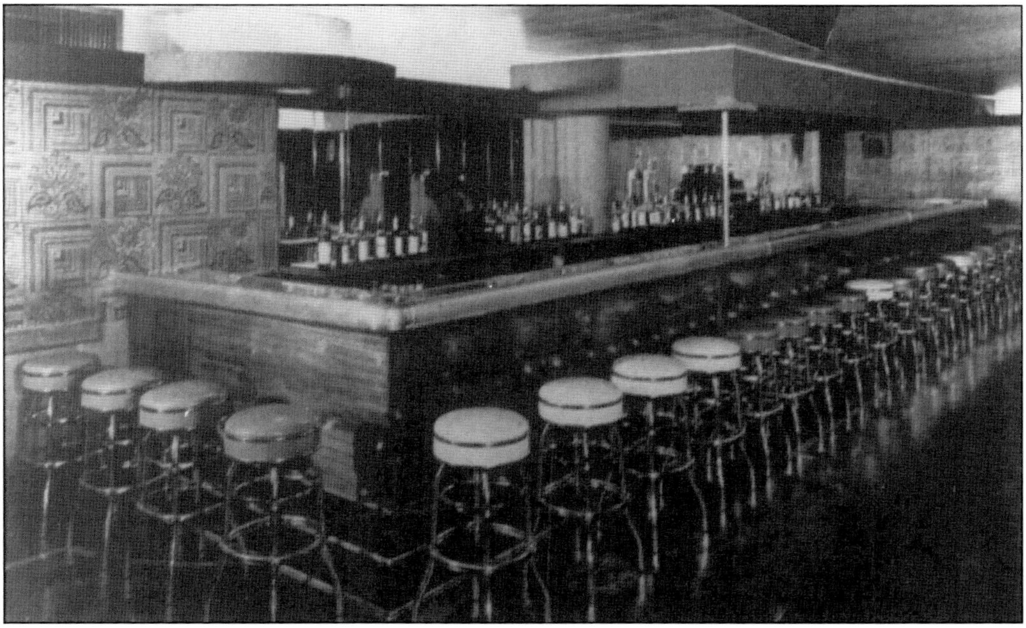

The syndicate remodeled the Primrose and changed its name to the Latin Quarter. It became an upscale restaurant and bar. The casino contained three craps tables, two roulette wheels, blackjack tables, and many slot machines. During one of the gambling raids at the club, the orchestra struck up the song "If I Knew You Were Coming Id've Baked a Cake." The club showcased the most popular entertainers of the time, including Pearl Bailey, Nat King Cole, and Duke Ellington. These pictures show the bar and dining area at the club. (Both images, Kenton County Public Library.)

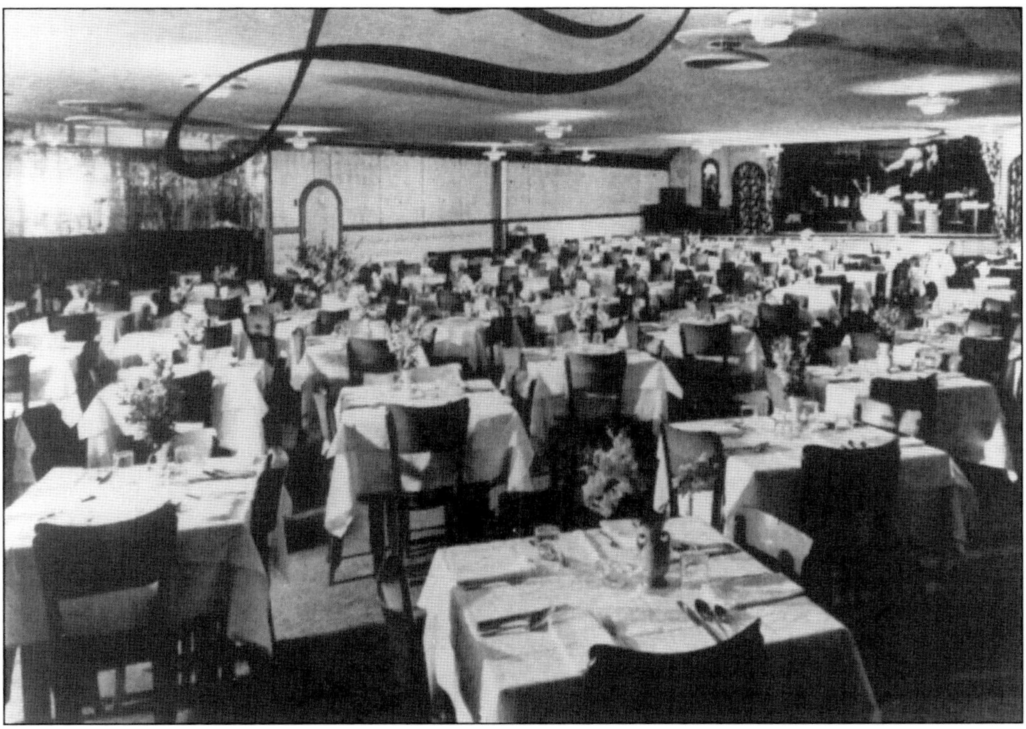

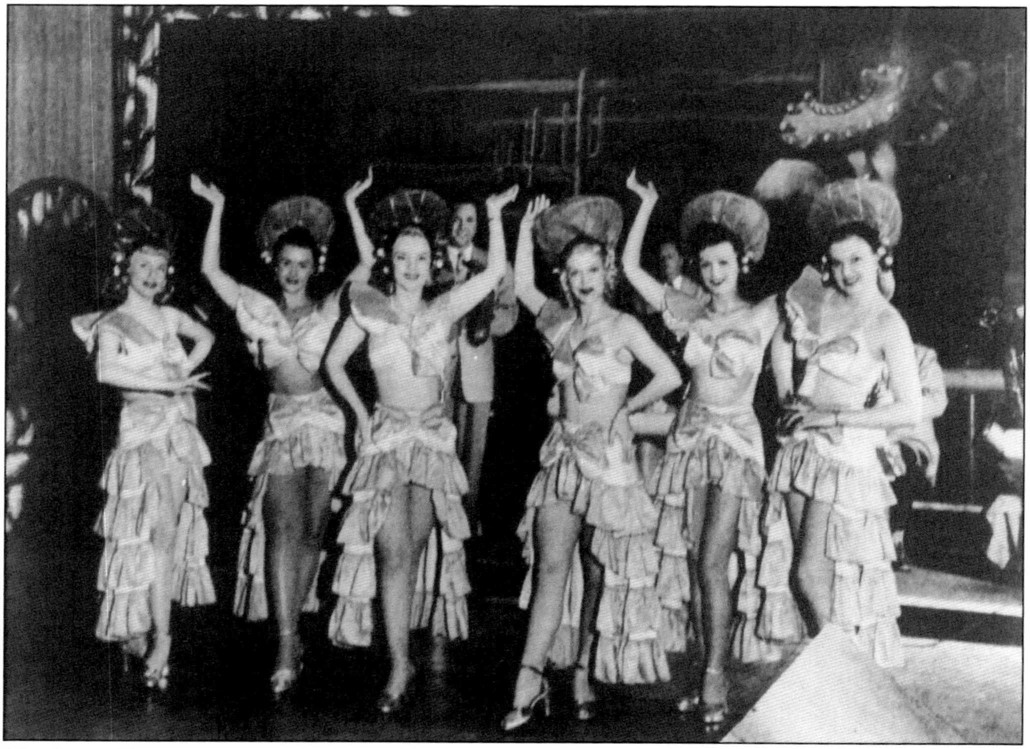

The Latin Quarter was an entertainment hot spot. The venue drew top-name performers in show business. Between acts, the club's resident chorus line (shown above) entertained crowds with their elaborate floor shows. The girls wore glamorous costumes and performed dance routines similar to the ones seen today in Las Vegas. (Kenton County Public Library.)

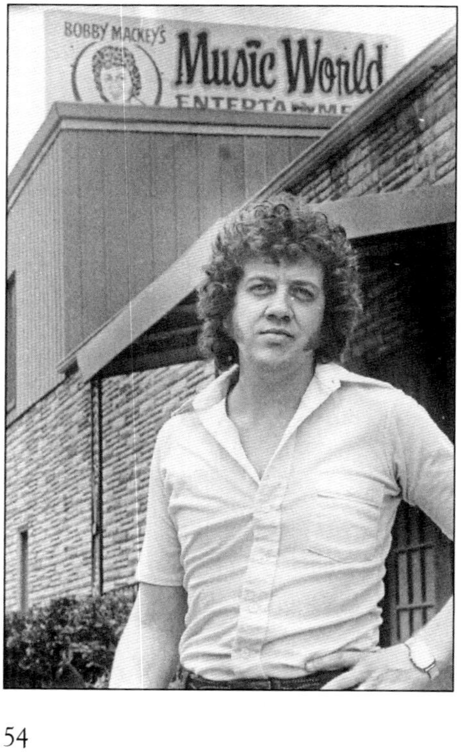

Bobby Mackey's Music World was formerly known as the Primrose and the Latin Quarter. Bobby Mackey (shown at left in front of his club) bought the building in 1976. It is notoriously known for allegedly being haunted. One of the purported spirits is a young girl named Johanna, a cabaret dancer during the club's casino period. She supposedly killed herself after her mobster father murdered her boyfriend, who worked at the club. The ghost of Buck Brady is also rumored to haunt the nightclub as well as numerous other apparitions. (Kenton County Public Library.)

Samson "Sammy" Eisner was a well-known figure in Newport. He had a criminal record, and police suspected him of being involved in organized crime. In July 1972, Eisner was shot and killed at his place of business. (Kenton County Public Library.)

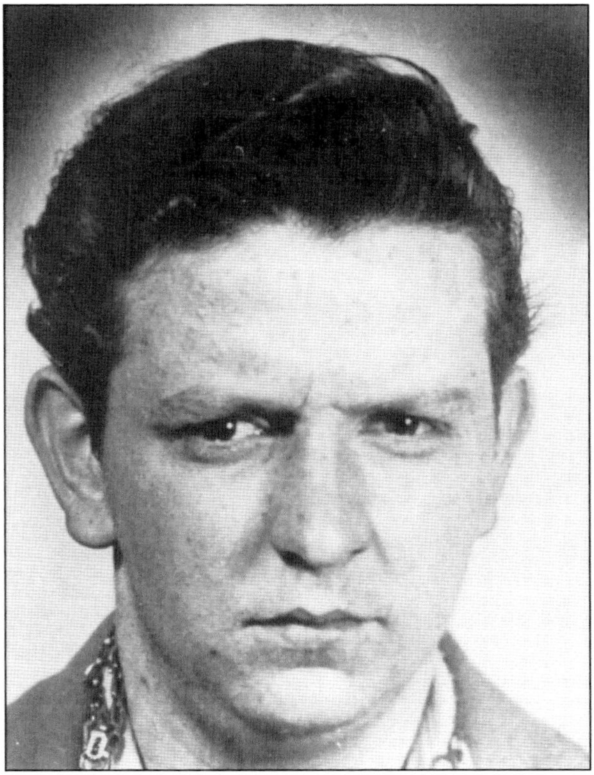

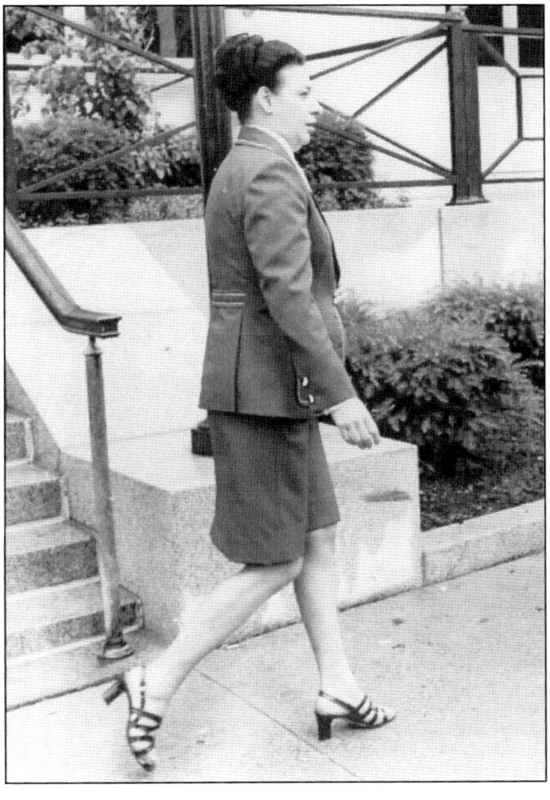

Callie Blain Eisner was a former burlesque dancer who owned several clubs in Illinois before opening the Pink Pussycat Lounge in Newport. She was the wife of Sammy Eisner, who was rumored to have ties to the underworld. (Kenton County Public Library.)

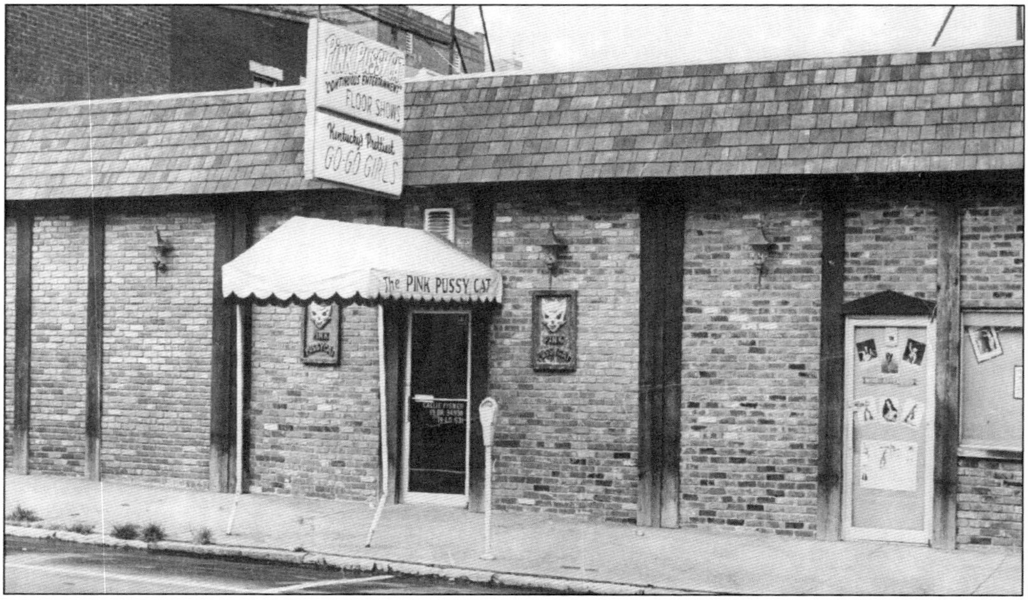

The Pink Pussycat Lounge, located at Sixth and York Streets, was a go-go club that featured exotic dancing. The club was owned by Callie Blaine Eisner. In 1975, a dancer and a frequent patron of the club both testified that prostitution regularly took place at the Pink Pussycat. Eisner was indicted on charges, but insisted she had no prior knowledge of prostitution taking place at her business. (Campbell County Historical Society.)

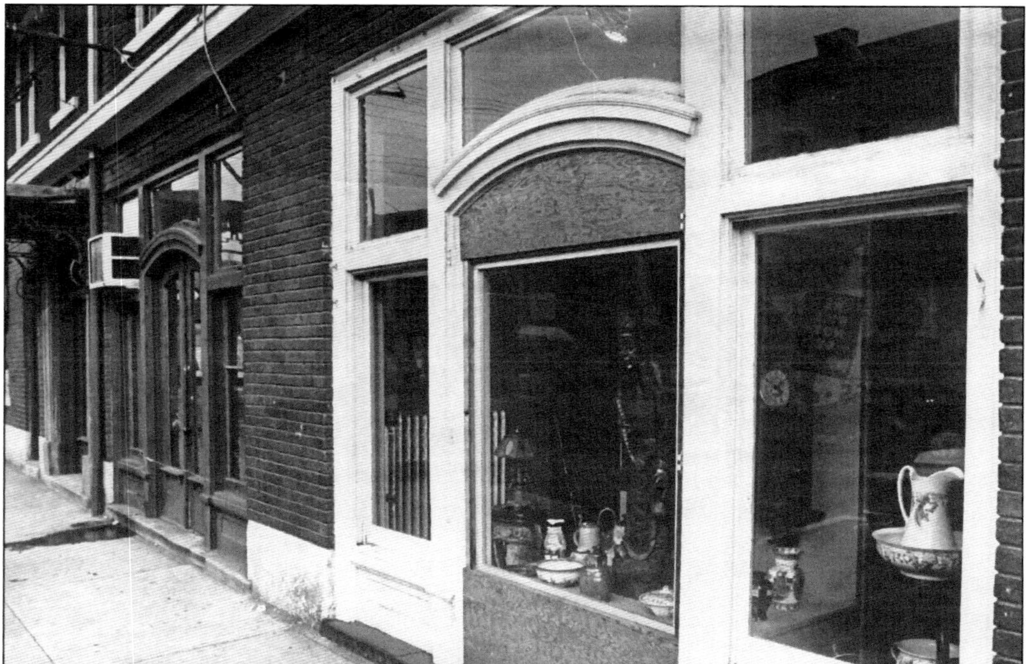

The Antique Shop, located on East Sixth Street, was owned and operated by Sammy Eisner. On July 30, 1972, Eisner was shot three times inside his place of business. His murder investigation was turned over to the Kentucky State Police on August 17, 1972. The murder has never been solved. (Kenton County Public Library.)

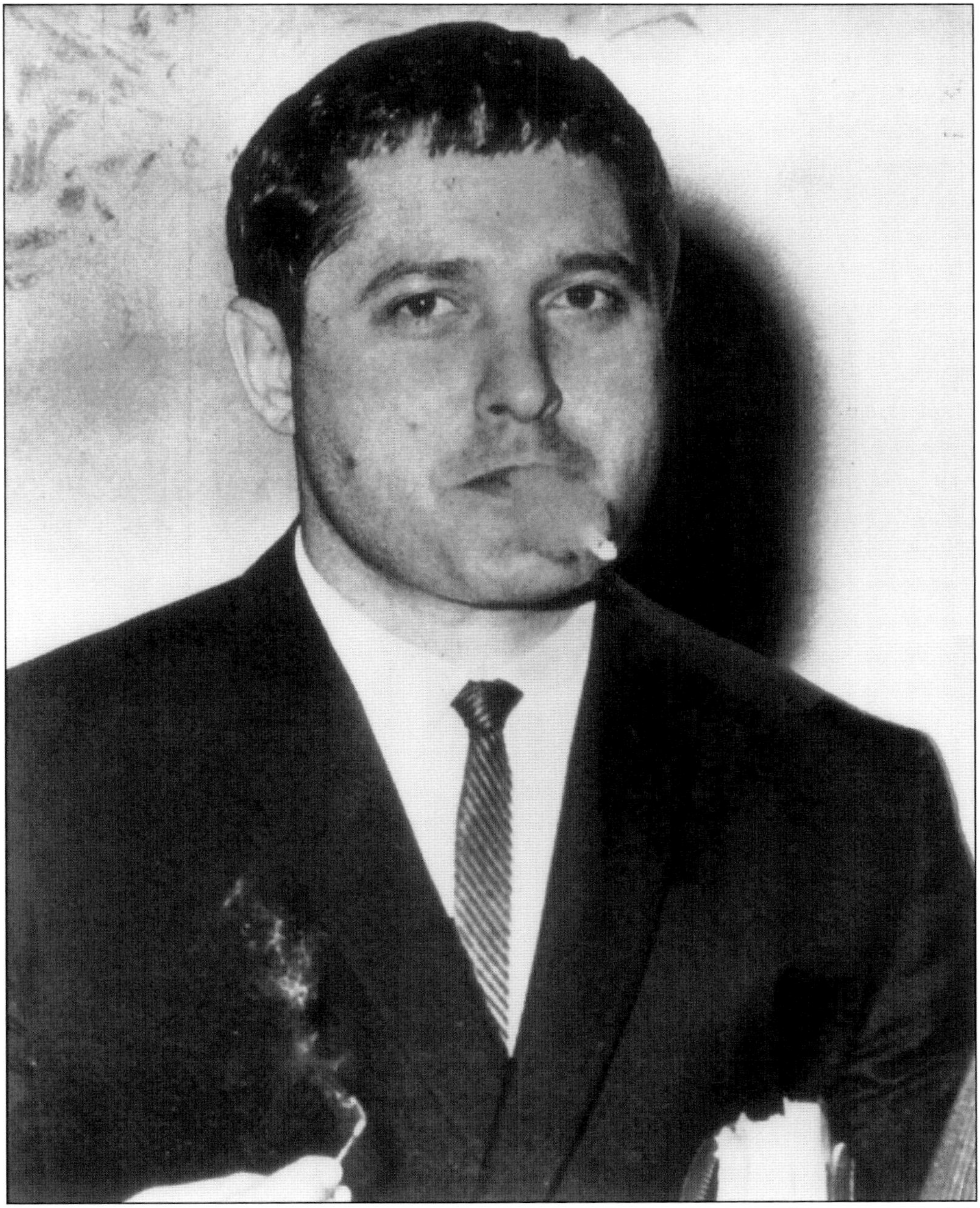

Tito Carinci was a former football star at Xavier University. Carinci was a well known night life figure in Newport who had close ties to the syndicate. A cousin to Dean Martin, Carinci wanted to run his own Vegas style club and was appointed manager of the Glenn Hotel and Tropicana Nightclub. Carinci maintained the club's profitable bookmaking operation and casino and added a strip show and prostitution to the venue. A large Vegas-style, neon sign was installed in front of the club and pictures of nude women were plastered on the windows. Carinci is well known for allegedly taking part in the 1961 conspiracy to frame reform candidate George W. Ratterman. In 1963, Carinci ran unsuccessfully for mayor of Newport. Carinci died in 2006 in California. (Courtesy of the Dave Horn Collection.)

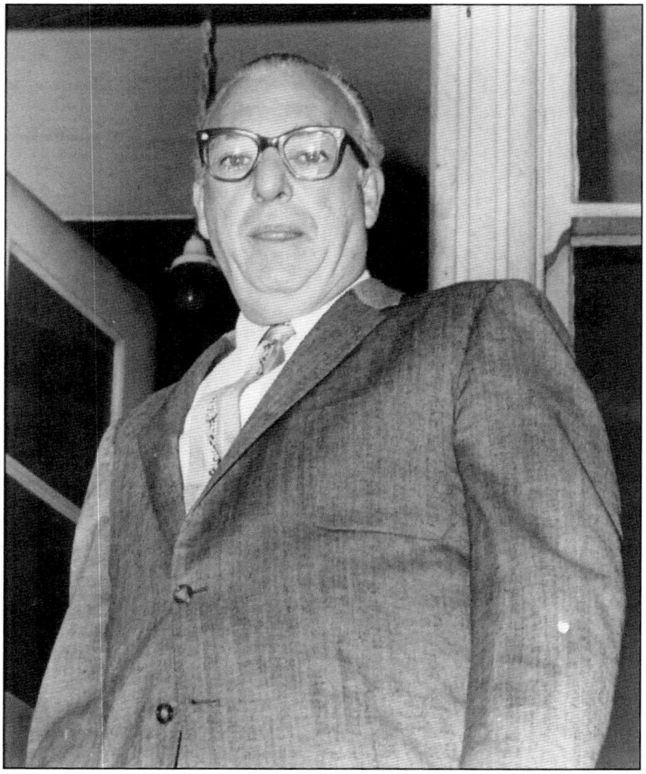

Frank "Screw" Andrews (whose real name is Frank Andriola) operated several casinos and numbers rackets in Newport. He was known as the "Numbers King," and his operations grossed millions of dollars. Andrews operated the Sportsman's Club, the Alibi, the Golden Lounge, and the Latin Quarter. (Kenton County Public Library.)

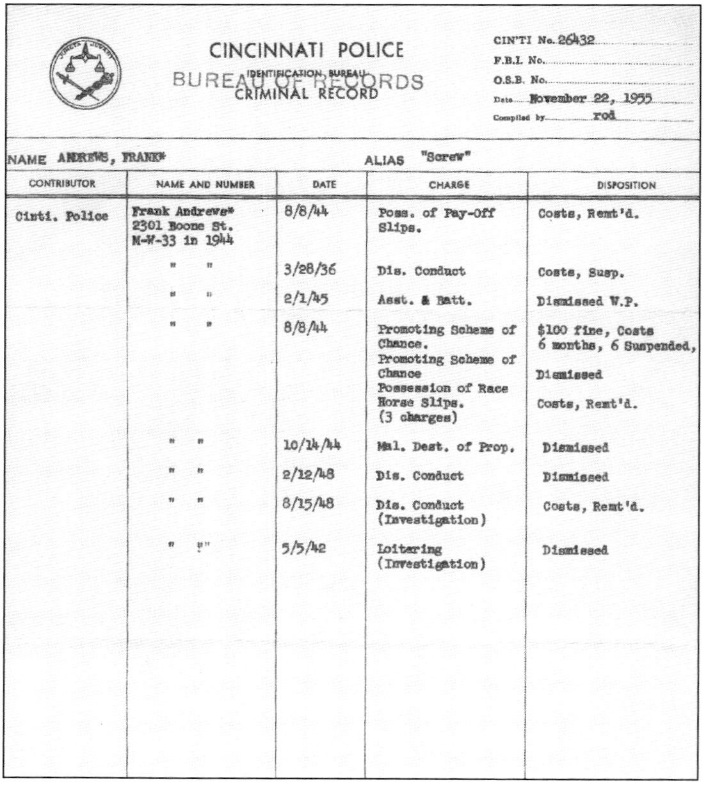

CINCINNATI POLICE
BUREAU OF RECORDS
IDENTIFICATION BUREAU
CRIMINAL RECORD

CIN'TI No. 26432
F.B.I. No.
O.S.B. No.
Date November 22, 1955
Compiled by rod

NAME ANDREWS, FRANK* ALIAS "Screw"

CONTRIBUTOR	NAME AND NUMBER	DATE	CHARGE	DISPOSITION
Cinti. Police	Frank Andrews* 2301 Boone St. M-W-33 in 1944	8/8/44	Poss. of Pay-Off Slips.	Costs, Remt'd.
	" "	3/28/36	Dis. Conduct	Costs, Susp.
	" "	2/1/45	Asst. & Batt.	Dismissed W.P.
	" "	8/8/44	Promoting Scheme of Chance.	$100 fine, Costs 6 months, 6 Suspended,
			Promoting Scheme of Chance	Dismissed
			Possession of Race Horse Slips. (3 charges)	Costs, Remt'd.
	" "	10/14/44	Mal. Dest. of Prop.	Dismissed
	" "	2/12/48	Dis. Conduct	Dismissed
	" "	8/15/48	Dis. Conduct (Investigation)	Costs, Remt'd.
	" "	5/5/42	Loitering (Investigation)	Dismissed

This is an early Cincinnati police record for Frank "Screw" Andrews. He added considerably to his list of convictions over the years. Screw spent time in jail for gambling, murder, assault, theft, and tax evasion. (Dave Horn Collection.)

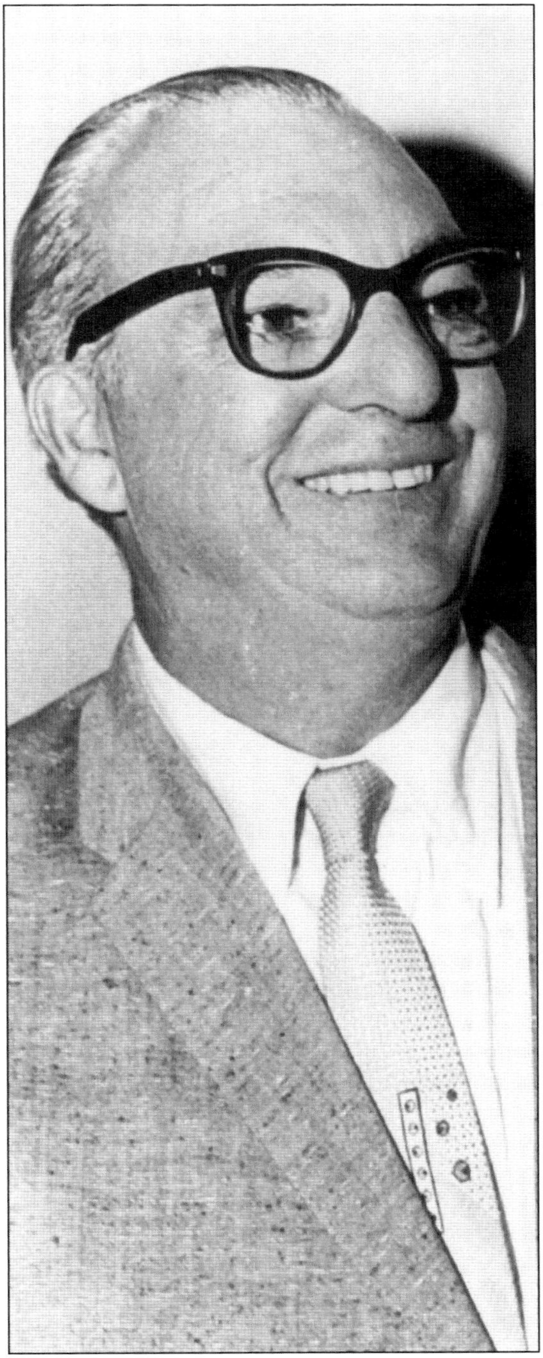

Newport contained several African American gambling clubs, such as the Alibi Club, Coconut Grove, the Congo, the Copa, Golden Lounge, Rocket Club, Varga Club, and the Sportsman's Club. Screw Andrews muscled his way into several of these clubs and took over their numbers rackets. Andrews wanted possession of the Sportsman's Club. The owner of the club, Steve Payne, was murdered in 1948. Andrews was the number one suspect, but was never prosecuted. A month after Payne's murder, the club was sold to Nig Devine, a big shot in the New York Syndicate. Devine gave Andrews control of the club and sold it to him a year later. (Kenton County Public Library.)

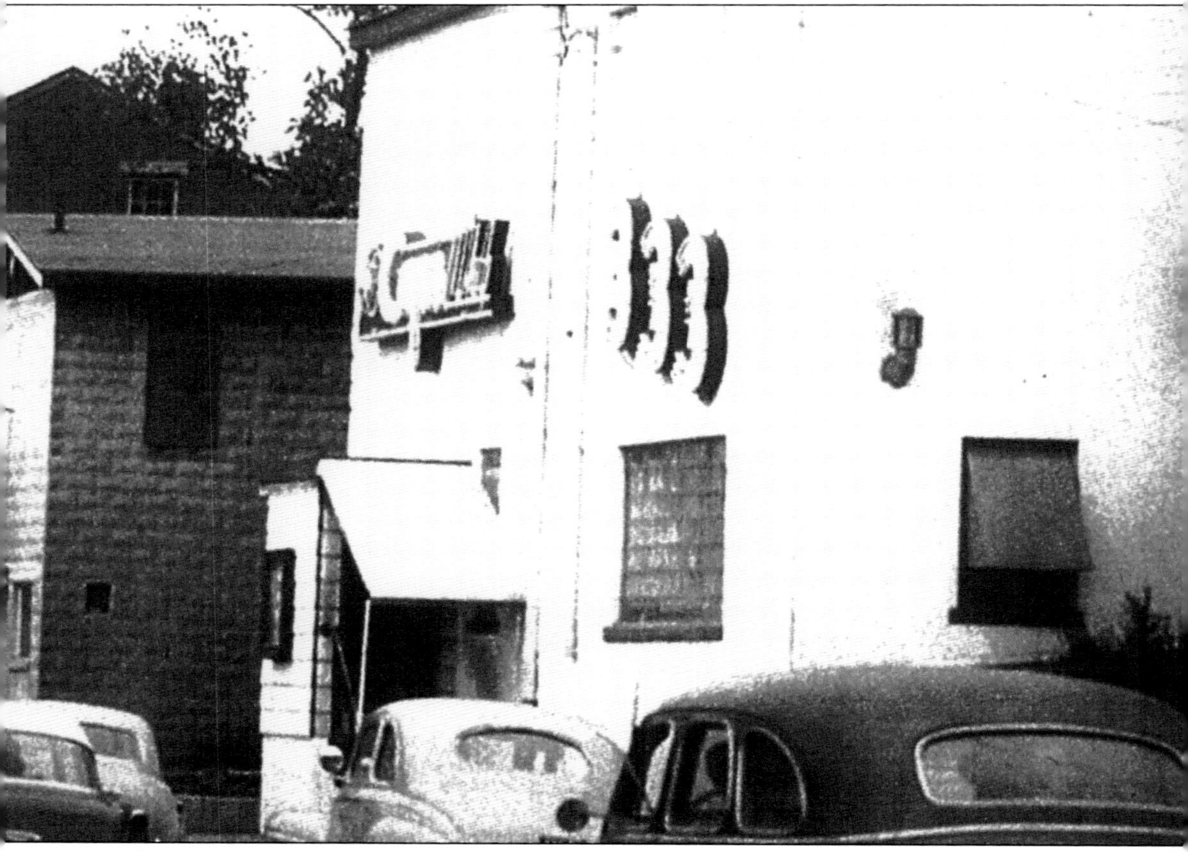

The Copa Club was located at 333 Central Street. It was an African American gambling club that ran a numbers racket. In 1952, Melvin Clark, owner of the Congo, the Copa, and the Coconut Grove, shot and killed Andrew's casino manager at the Alibi Club. Clark was acquitted after pleading self defense. Andrews got revenge several years later by killing Clark and taking over the Coconut Grove. Andrews pleaded self defense and was exonerated. (Author's collection.)

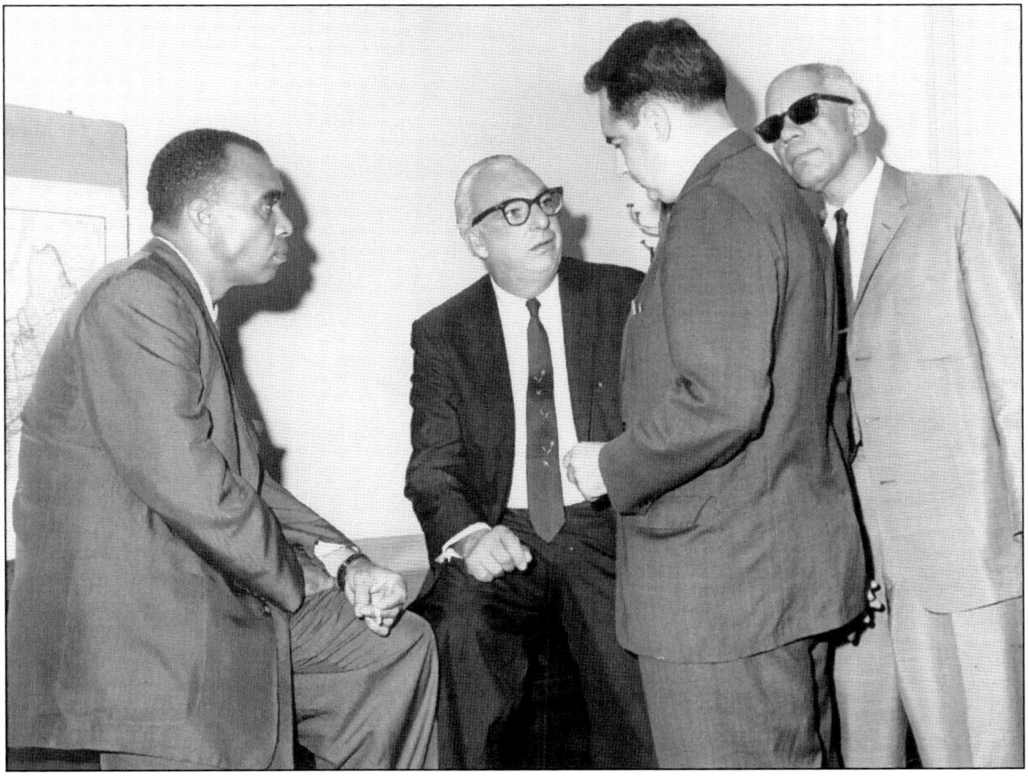

In June 1965, Gus Postell (left), Screw Andrews (center), and Willard Whitley (far right) were convicted of conspiracy to violate Internal Revenue statutes by fraudulently concealing and withholding gambling excise taxes. James L. Cobb (forefront) represented the defendants along with Dan Davies and Morris Weintraub. (Kenton County Public Library.)

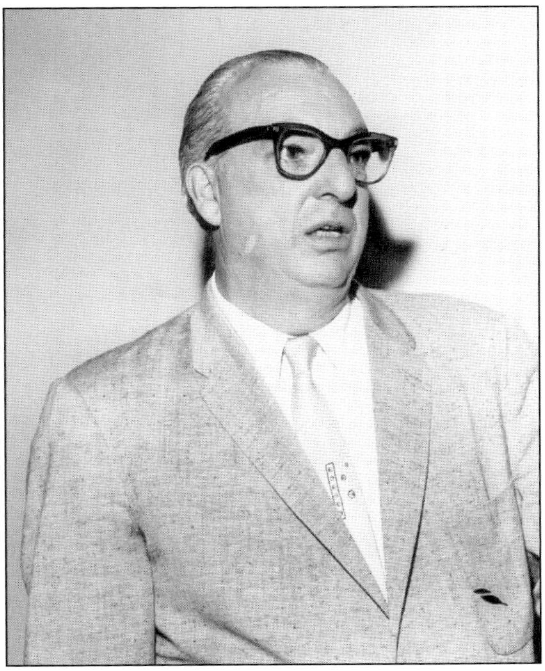

Ann Drahmann Coppola, former wife of notorious syndicate overlord "Trigger" Mike Coppola, wrote a letter to Robert Kennedy claiming Screw Andrews (shown at right) was Mike Coppola's main and most important man in Newport. This picture of Andrews was taken in June 1969. (Kenton County Public Library.)

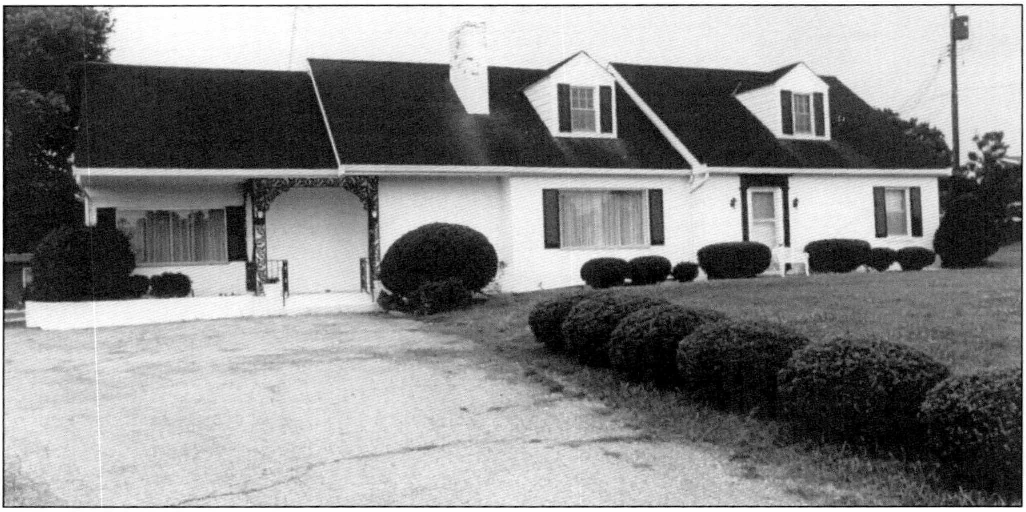

This was the home of Screw Andrews, located in Cold Spring, Kentucky. Rumor has it Screw buried several caches of money somewhere near his property to avoid having the IRS seize all of his assets. Allegedly, the money is still buried somewhere on the property. This legend is repeated in the book *A Guide to Treasure in Kentucky*, by Michael P. Henson. (Kenton County Public Library.)

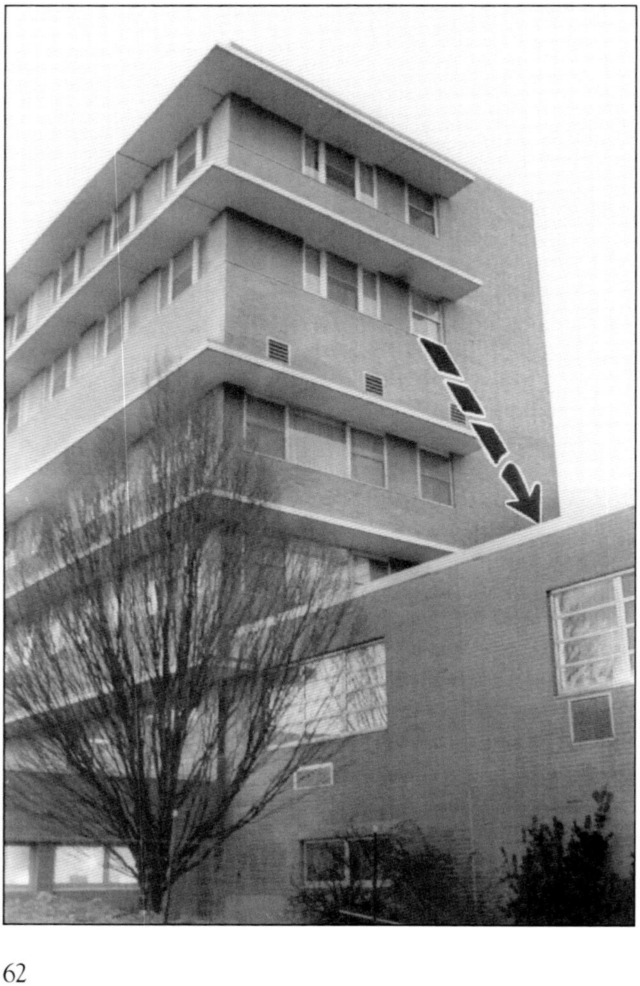

On December 17, 1973, the lifeless body of Screw Andrews was found six stories below his St. Luke hospital room window. Authorities concluded the ailing Andrews committed suicide by jumping to his death. Over the years, stories about the incident have surfaced, and several staff members have admitted that several men in suits approached Andrew's room and ordered the nurses to "take a walk." (Kenton County Public Library.)

Lawrence Riedinger Jr. (left) and Charles Lester (right) started their law careers by fighting vice and requesting court orders to padlock known houses of prostitution. Here the two attorneys stand outside of their law office at 501 York Street. Charles Lester eventually drifted toward the criminal's side and began defending many of Newport's underworld figures. He became involved in shady deals with the Cleveland Syndicate and found himself on trial several times. (Campbell County Historical Society.)

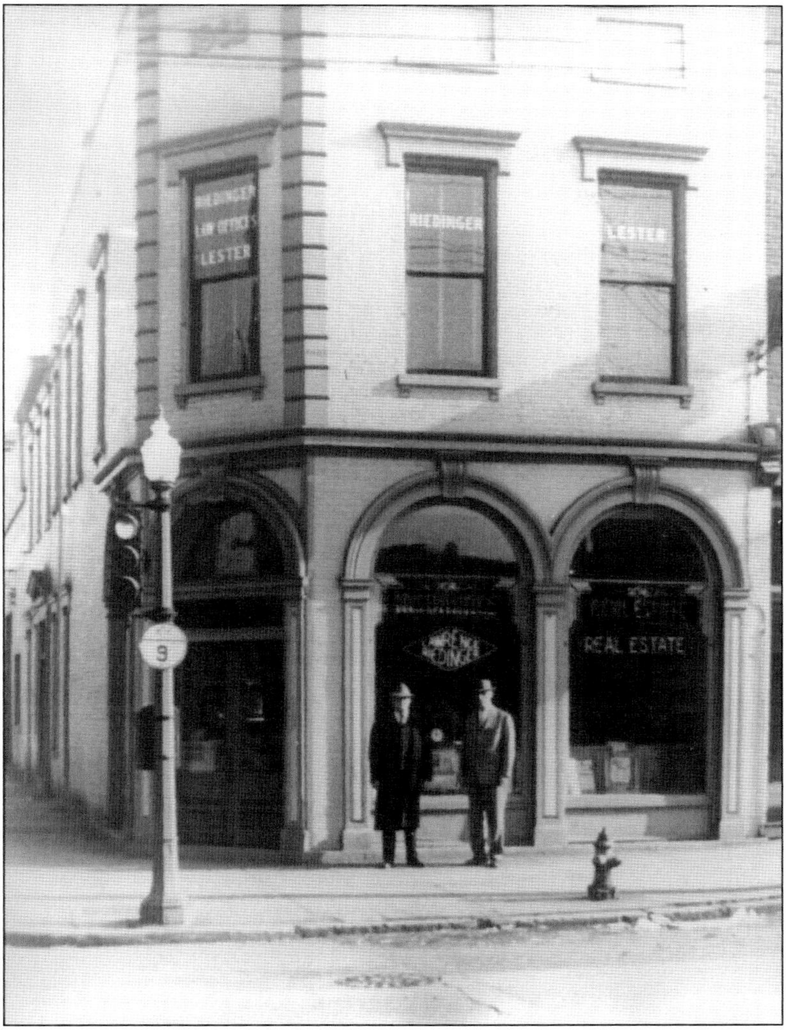

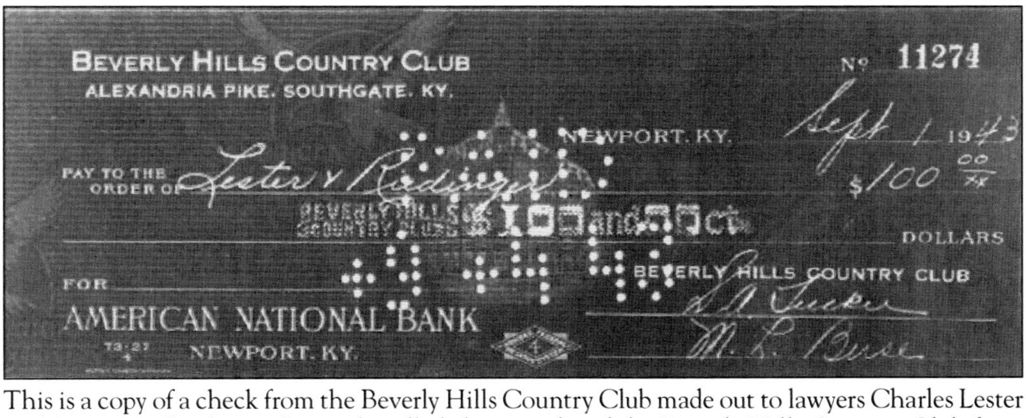

This is a copy of a check from the Beverly Hills Country Club made out to lawyers Charles Lester and Lawrence Riedinger. Lester handled the transfer of the Beverly Hills Country Club from Pete Schmidt to the Cleveland Syndicate in 1940. The date on this check is September 1, 1943, indicating that the syndicate kept Lester under retainer to handle their legal needs in Newport. The check is signed by Sam Tucker, member of the Cleveland Syndicate. (Dave Horn Collection.)

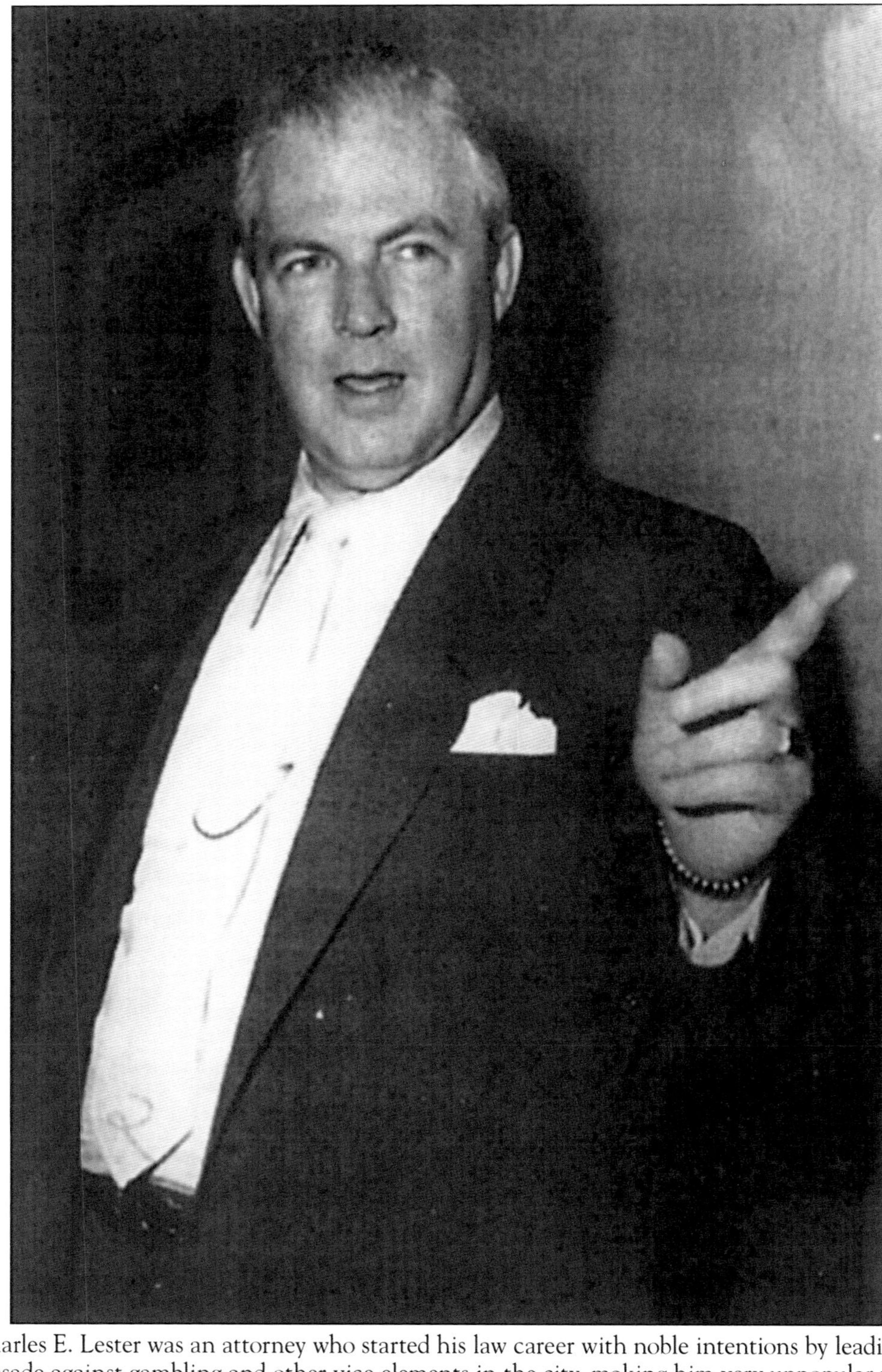

Charles E. Lester was an attorney who started his law career with noble intentions by leading a crusade against gambling and other vice elements in the city, making him very unpopular with Newport's underworld. After receiving death threats, Lester must have figured, "if you can't beat them, join them," because he began representing many of Newport's notorious underworld figures. (Dave Horn Collection.)

Three

Gambling, Girls, and Graft

The Cleveland Syndicate became powerful and wealthy during Prohibition. After its repeal, the syndicate transferred its activities to the even more lucrative field of gambling. They operated several casinos in Cleveland and the outlying areas before officials closed the clubs and successfully brought a halt to their gambling enterprise in Ohio. They were forced to move their operations across the Ohio River into Kentucky, where wide-open gambling was tolerated. The syndicate's casinos were often plush and luxurious venues that offered all forms of gambling such as numbers games, roulette, craps, chuck-a-luck, razzle dazzle, blackjack, slot machines, and bookie services. Illegal lotteries known as "numbers games" or "policy betting" were popular because the odds were much higher than those offered by state lotteries. The smaller club operators ran crooked games that gained them a reputation as a "bust out joint." The term was used because patrons were usually busted by the time they left. Bookmaking was an important source of income for organized crime. The Bobben Realty Company at Fourth and York Streets housed a large bookmaking operation, which evolved into the largest layoff bank in the country. It is thought to have been created by Meyer Lansky and his associates in New York and run by local criminals. Bookmakers offered off-track betting to the people who were not able to attend the races at the track. The wire service obtained instantaneous results from racetracks throughout the country, enabling on-the-spot collections and payoffs. The Ace Research Service supplied wire service to more than 100 bookmakers in nearby Covington and more than 60 in Newport.

Local independent casino operators also participated in running illegal games, and many became involved in the operation of brothels. Prostitution was rampant in the city and consisted of "day" houses and "night" houses. During World War II, the military condemned prostitution during their Fit to Fight campaign. West Newport was deemed off limits to servicemen stationed at the Fort Thomas Military Reservation to prevent them from contracting venereal diseases from the city's brothels. Competing local establishments were eventually absorbed by the syndicate, but sometimes they operated in conjunction with local partners. Whatever the syndicate wanted, the syndicate took.

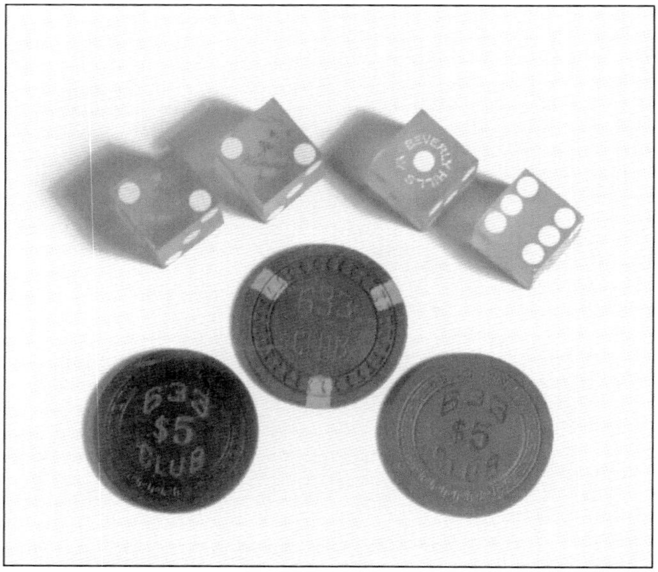

Most clubs had personalized gambling pieces such as dice and money chips that bore the name or insignia of the club on them. The dice and chips shown here are from the Beverly Hills Country Club. Gambling memorabilia is much sought after by collectors. (Kenton County Public Library.)

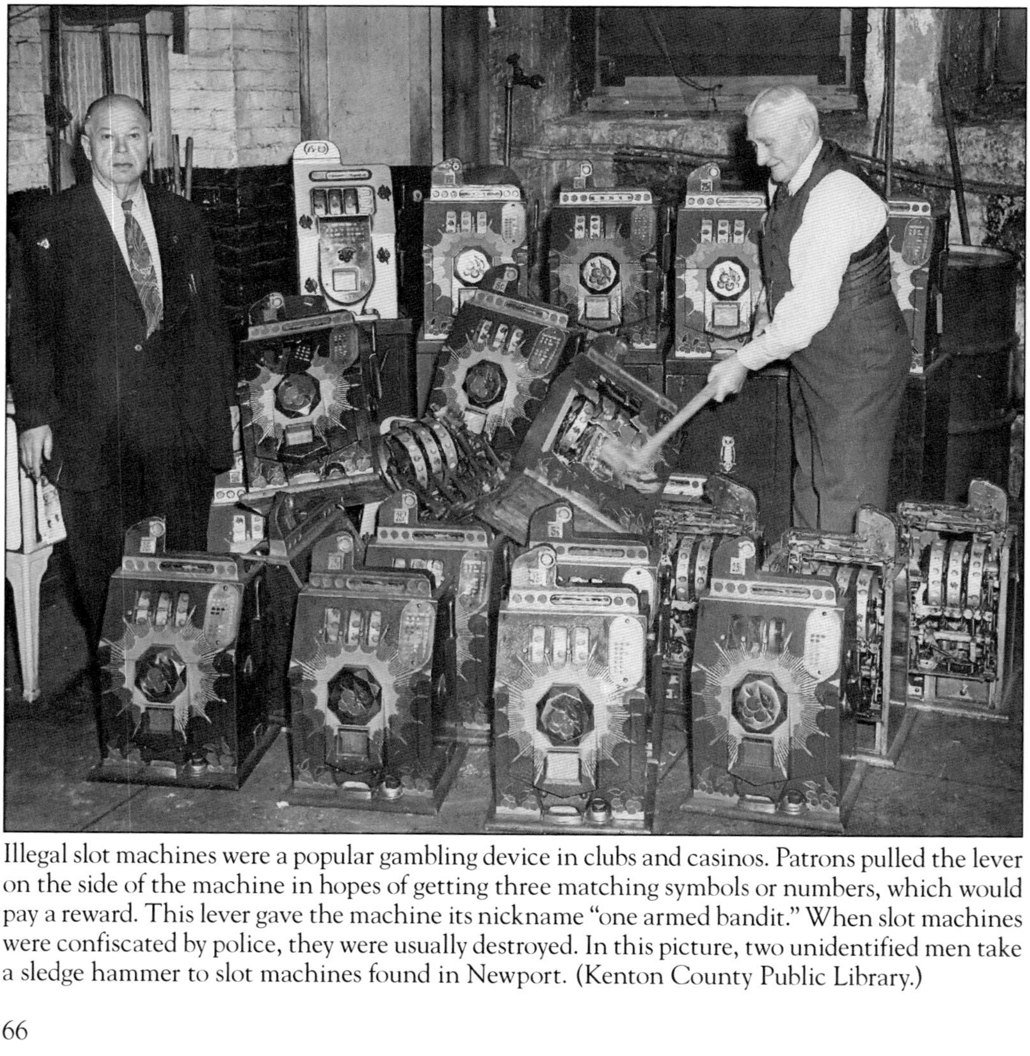

Illegal slot machines were a popular gambling device in clubs and casinos. Patrons pulled the lever on the side of the machine in hopes of getting three matching symbols or numbers, which would pay a reward. This lever gave the machine its nickname "one armed bandit." When slot machines were confiscated by police, they were usually destroyed. In this picture, two unidentified men take a sledge hammer to slot machines found in Newport. (Kenton County Public Library.)

Betting boards, like this one photographed in a Newport bookie joint, showed immediate results from racetracks throughout the country. Most Newport bookmakers offered their clients off-track betting and were able to "lay off" large bets. (Dave Horn Collection.)

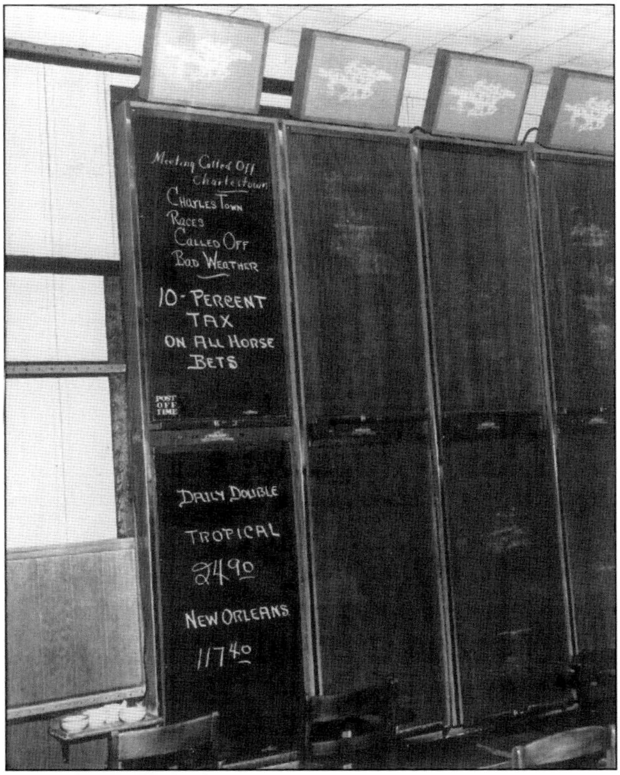

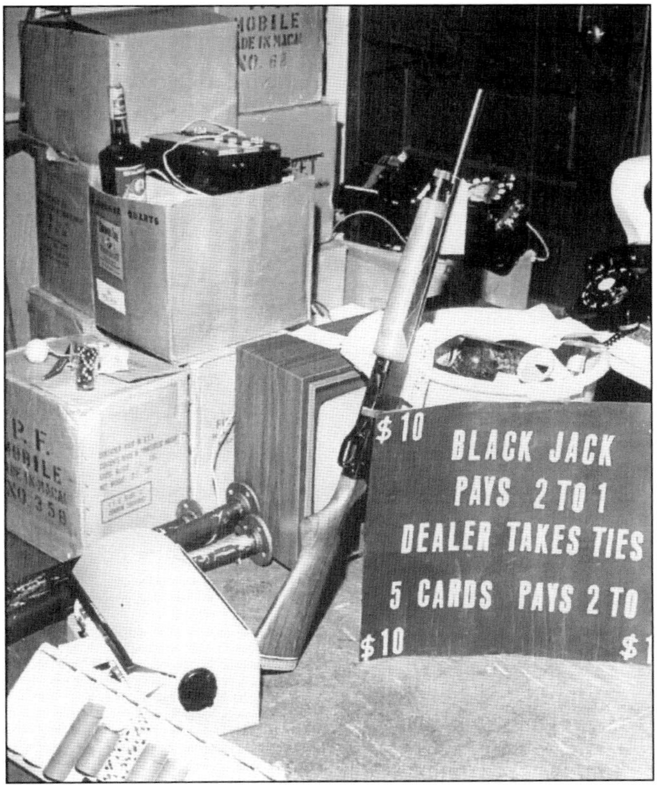

Gambling merchandise seized by Newport officials often included telephones, as seen in this picture. Numerous phone lines were used by bookies to take bets and obtain results. Incriminating evidence was often attained through court-approved wire taps. In 1961, the state public service commission issued a regulation that allowed telephone companies to disconnect phones being used in gambling establishments. (Kenton County Public Library.)

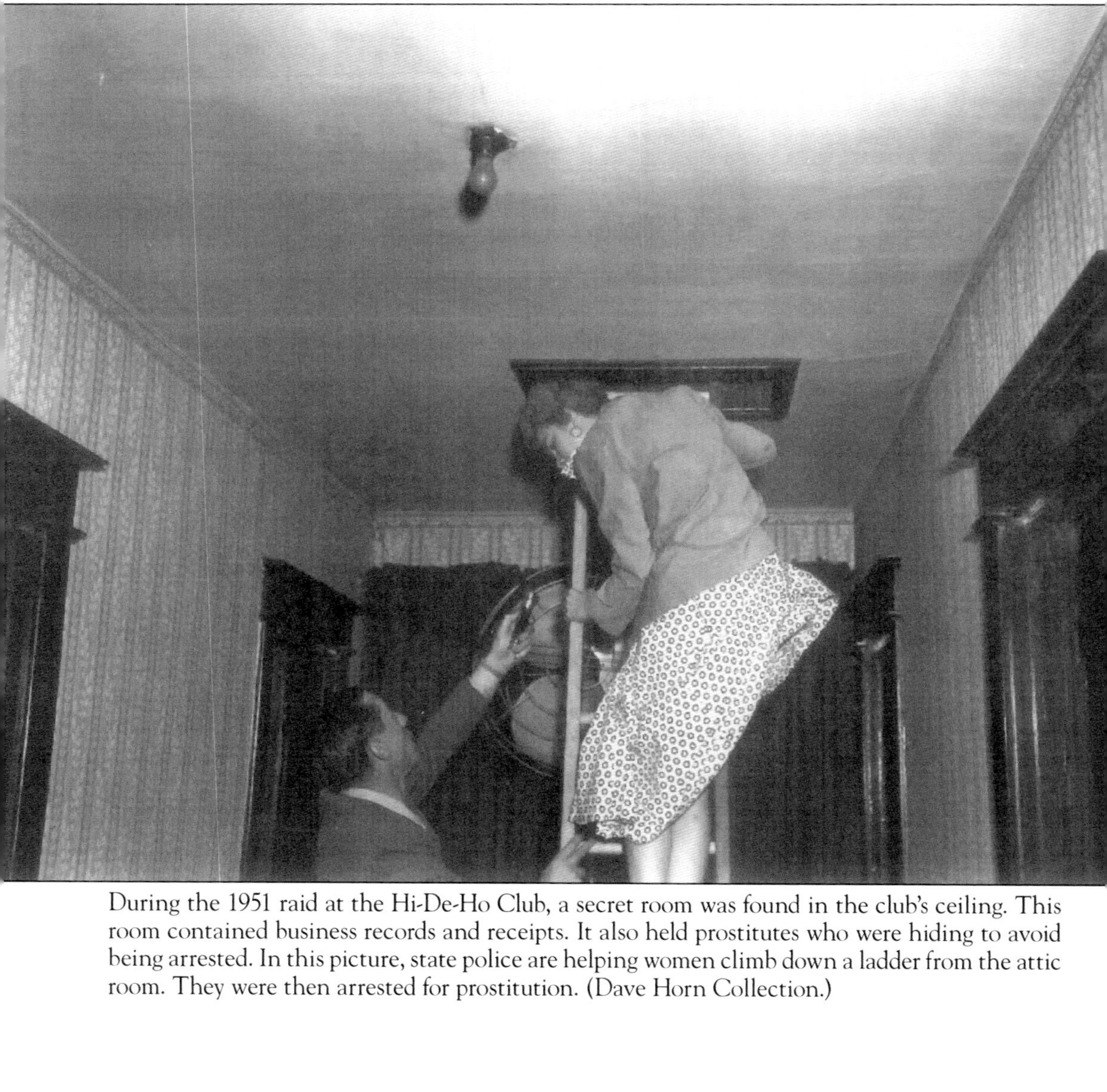

During the 1951 raid at the Hi-De-Ho Club, a secret room was found in the club's ceiling. This room contained business records and receipts. It also held prostitutes who were hiding to avoid being arrested. In this picture, state police are helping women climb down a ladder from the attic room. They were then arrested for prostitution. (Dave Horn Collection.)

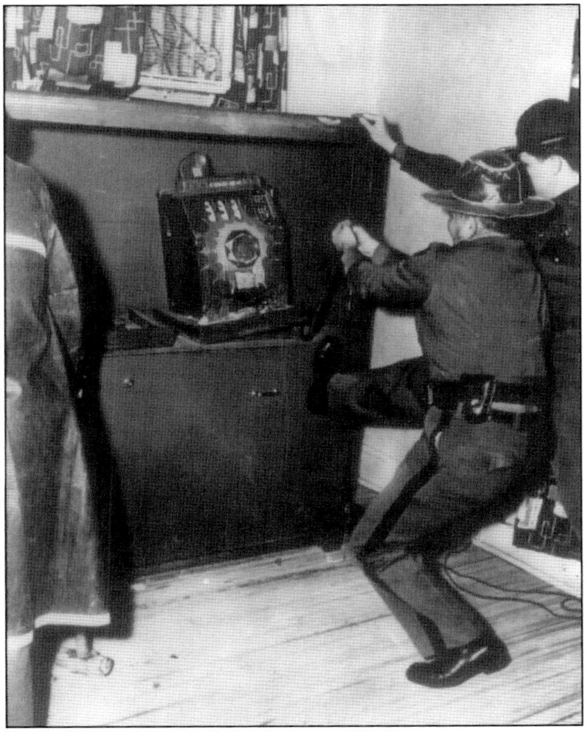

During the Hi-De-Ho raid, state police took sledge hammers to the slot machines. Allegedly, casinos first introduced slot machines to entertain the wives and girlfriends of gamblers. The casinos hoped this tactic would occupy the women so the men would feel free to spend more time gambling. Mechanical slot machines in casinos were commonplace until the 1960s, when the first electromechanical slot machine was introduced. Police in this picture are pulling the machines off of the shelves. (Both images, Dave Horn Collection.)

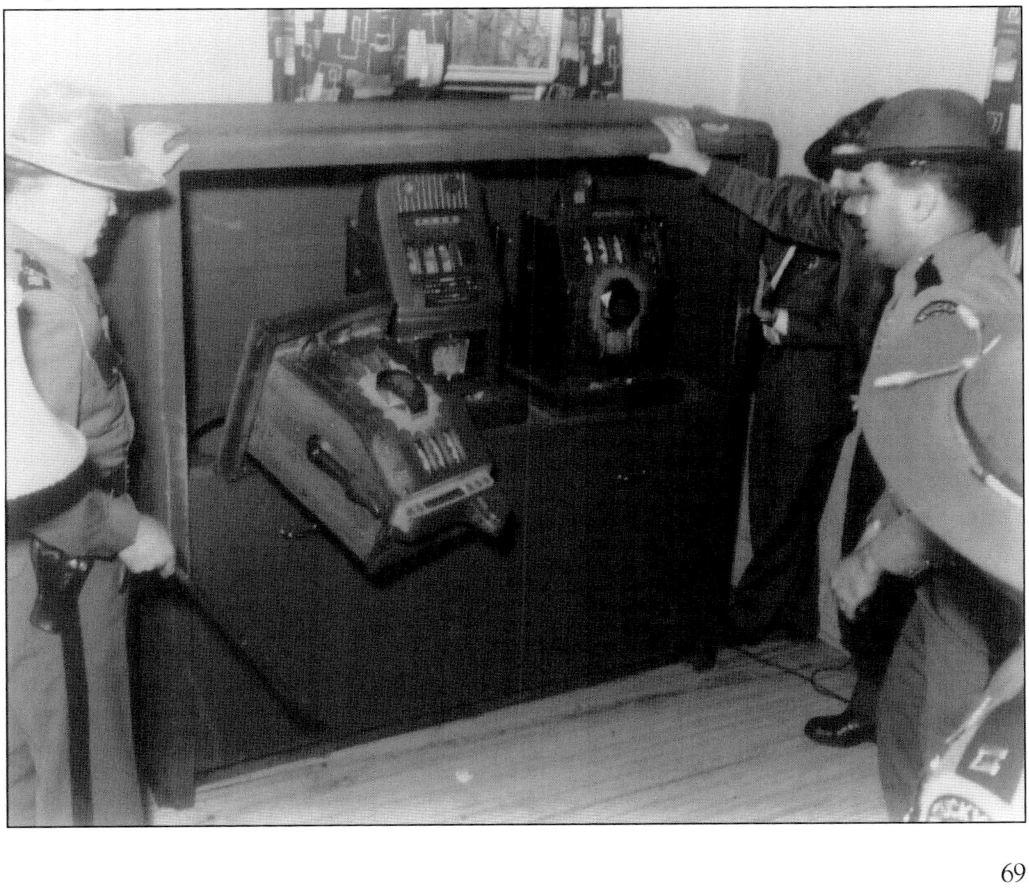

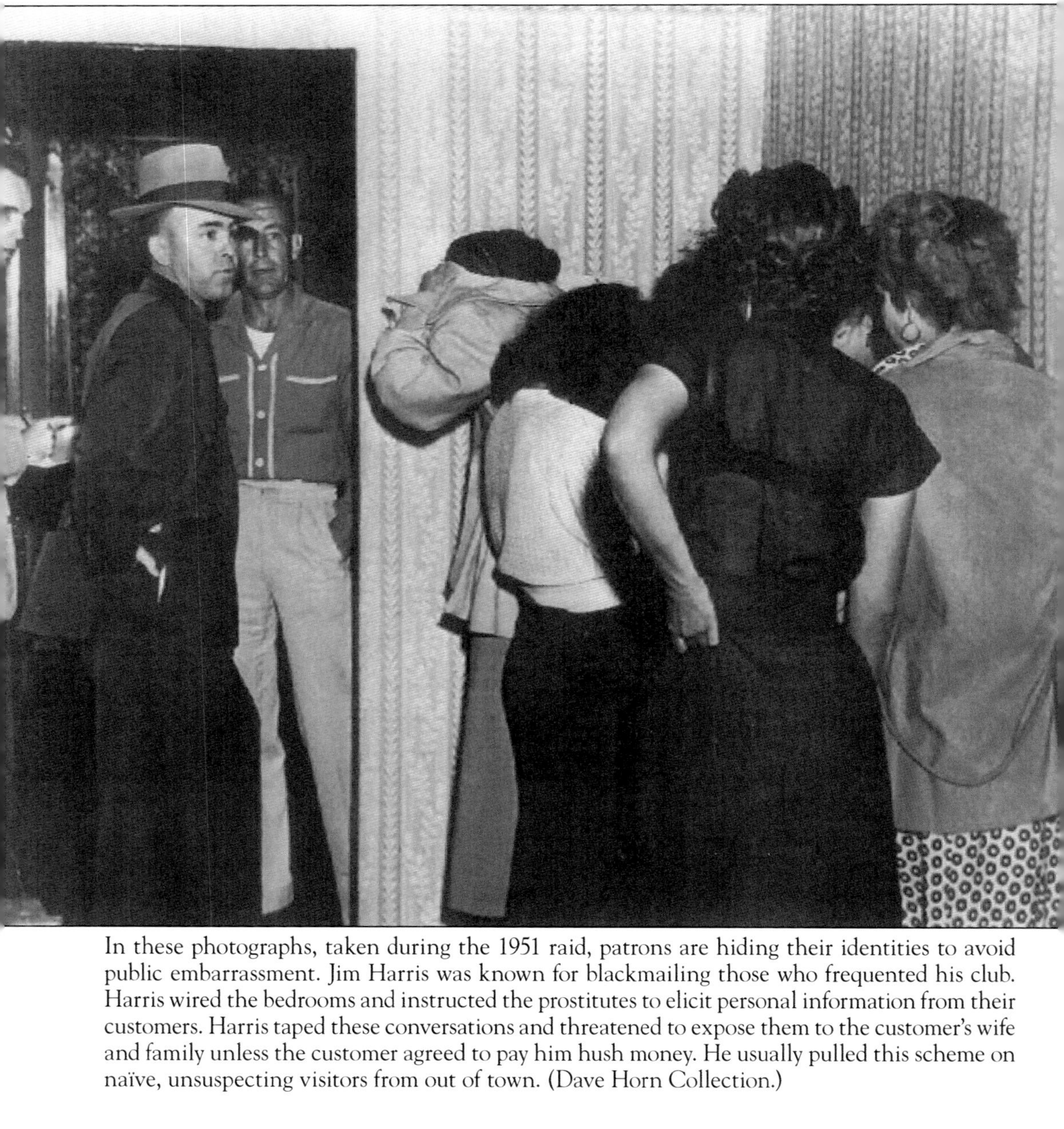

In these photographs, taken during the 1951 raid, patrons are hiding their identities to avoid public embarrassment. Jim Harris was known for blackmailing those who frequented his club. Harris wired the bedrooms and instructed the prostitutes to elicit personal information from their customers. Harris taped these conversations and threatened to expose them to the customer's wife and family unless the customer agreed to pay him hush money. He usually pulled this scheme on naïve, unsuspecting visitors from out of town. (Dave Horn Collection.)

In 1951, Pete Schmidt opened the Glenn Schmidt Playtorium on East Fifth Street. The syndicate-controlled citizens group known as the Newport Civic Association (NCA) ordered a raid on the casino. Red Masterson, operator of the Merchants Club, was behind the pre-arranged raid. Schmidt had become a nuisance to the syndicate, and Masterson hoped to put him out of business. In this picture, the police and detective are confiscating money chips and cash boxes. (Dave Horn Collection.)

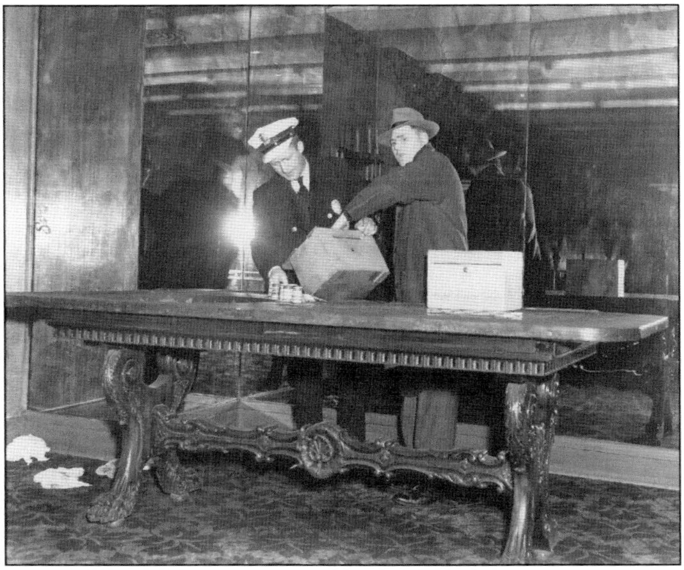

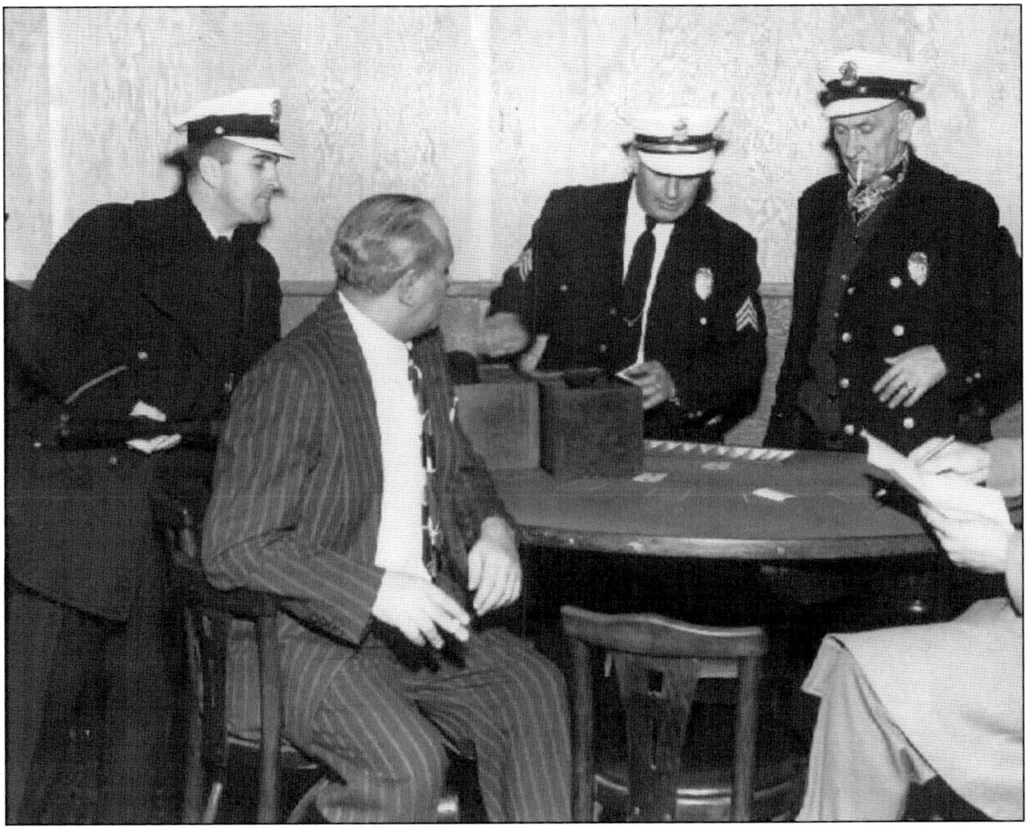

After the raid at the Glenn Schmidt Playtorium, Pete Schmidt and attorney Charles Lester arranged for their contacts on the police force to launch a retaliatory raid on the syndicate's Merchants Club. Pictured here are, from left to right, Officer Ed Gugel, gambler Davey Polinsky, Sgt. Jack Thiem, and Officer Jack Schnelle. (Dave Horn Collection.)

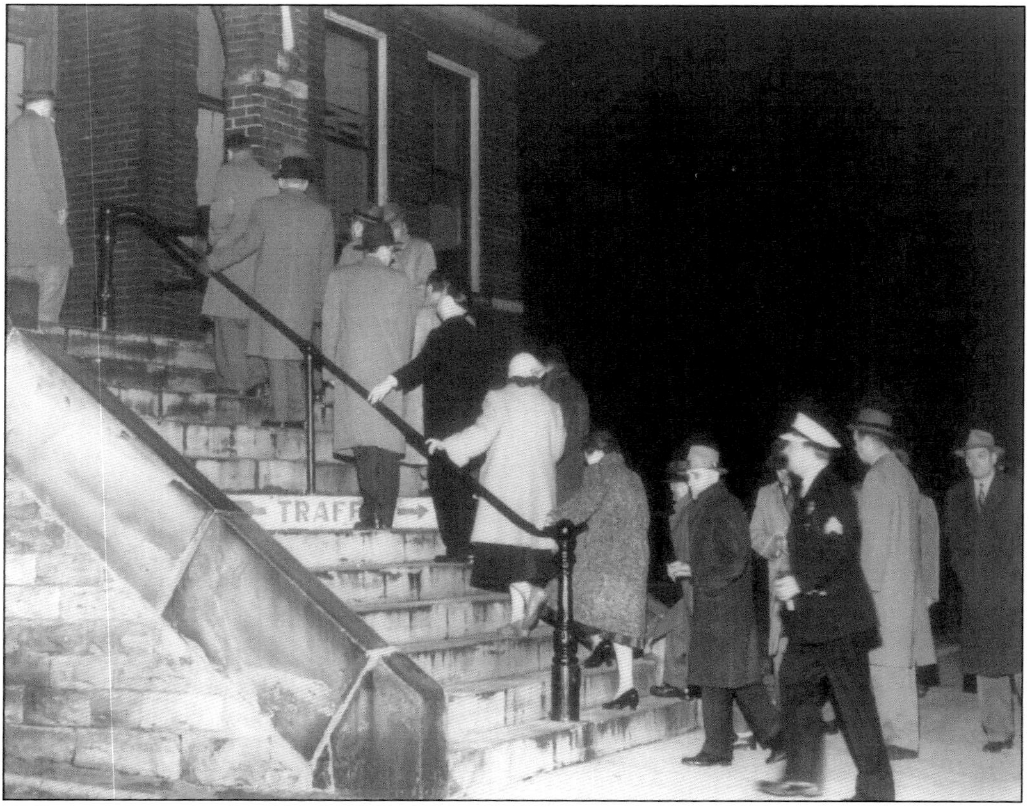

After the raid at the Merchants Club, the customers were placed under arrest and read their rights. Sgt. Jack Thiem marched the group down Fourth Street to the Newport Police Station. (Dave Horn Collection.)

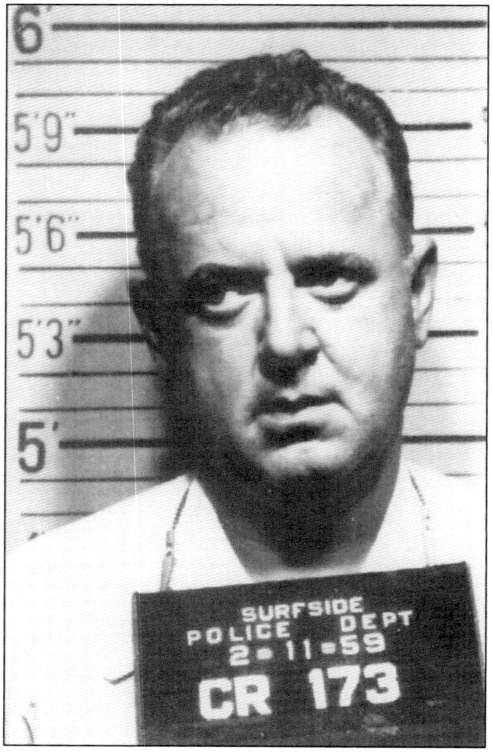

Newport was once the largest center of layoff betting east of Las Vegas. The Bobben Realty Company, located at Fourth and York Streets, was managed by Nig Devine and Bob and Ben Lasoff. Meyer Lansky's New York Syndicate ran the operation. In the 1940s, Gil "the Brain" Beckley (pictured here) partnered with Ed Levinson and took control of the layoff bank, turning it into the largest in the country. (Dave Horn Collection.)

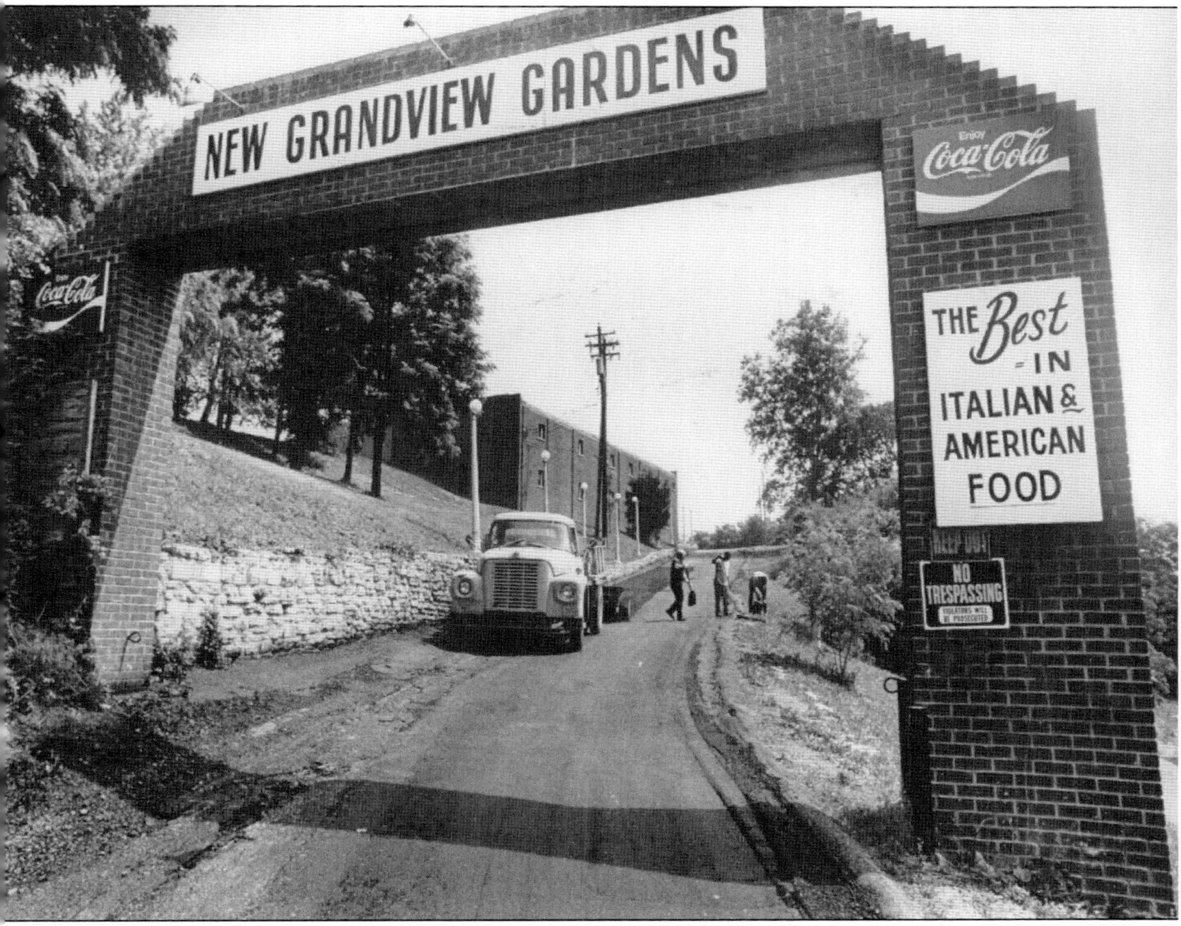

From 1933 through the early 1970s, the Santini and Peluso families owned and operated Grandview Gardens at the top of Widrig Street in South Newport, off of Grandview Avenue. This Italian restaurant was home to fireworks in the summer, boxing events, political party gatherings, fish fries, gambling, and other questionable events. Pasquale Santini ran it until 1967, when he sold the place to Johnny "TV" Peluso, who renamed it the New Grandview Gardens. Peluso once proposed building a cable car ride from the site (across the Ohio River) to Mount Adams, an entertainment district on the east side of downtown Cincinnati. In 1988, developers gained zoning approval for a 56-unit housing project, which is known as the Grandview Condominiums today. (Campbell County Historical Society.)

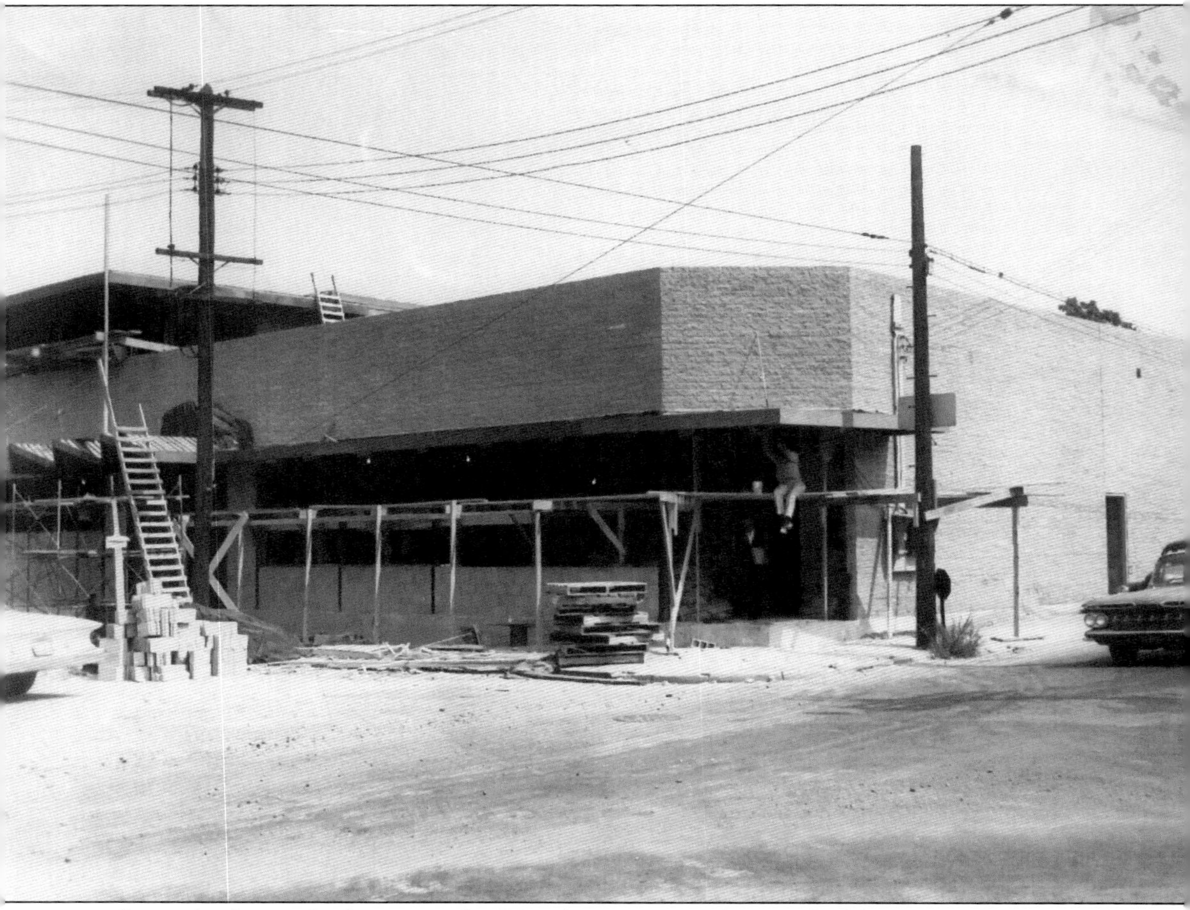

Screw Andrews, also known as the "Numbers King," took control of the Sportsman's Club after the murder of its owner, Steve Payne. The original club was located at 330 Central Avenue. This became the headquarters for Screw Andrew's numbers racket. On August 22, 1961, a squad of special federal agents launched a raid on the club. It was shut down, and Andrews went to prison for conspiracy to promote gambling, excise tax evasion, and violation of the Federal Communications Act. In 1965, Andrews was released from prison and opened a newly built Sportsman's Club (seen here). He continued to operate an illegal gambling casino until the club was closed down in 1968. (Kenton County Public Library.)

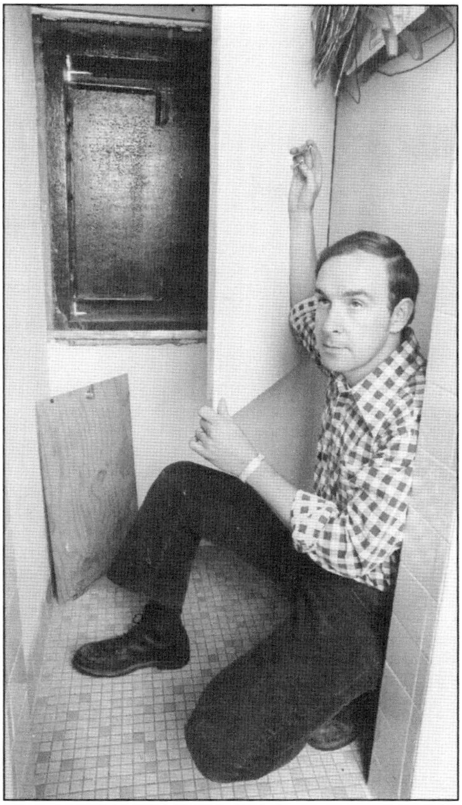

During the 1961 raid of the Sportsman's Club, agents found secret rooms and hidden panels concealed throughout the club. In these two pictures, an unidentified man demonstrates how to gain access to a secret room. In the back of a closet, agents discovered a copper wire lying on the floor and two nails about eight inches apart sticking out of the wall. By touching the nails with the wire, the agents discovered a panel in wall that opened to reveal a door leading to another room, where Andrews kept money, records, and receipts. (Both images, Dave Horn Collection.)

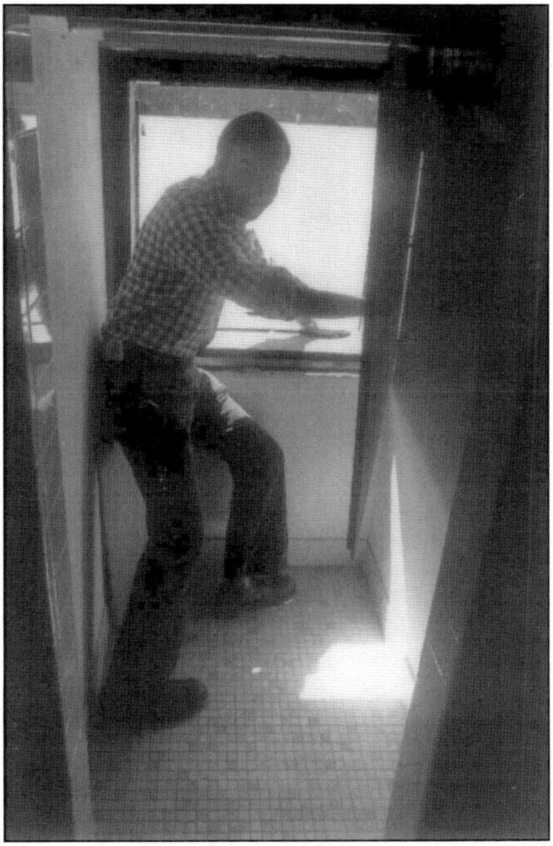

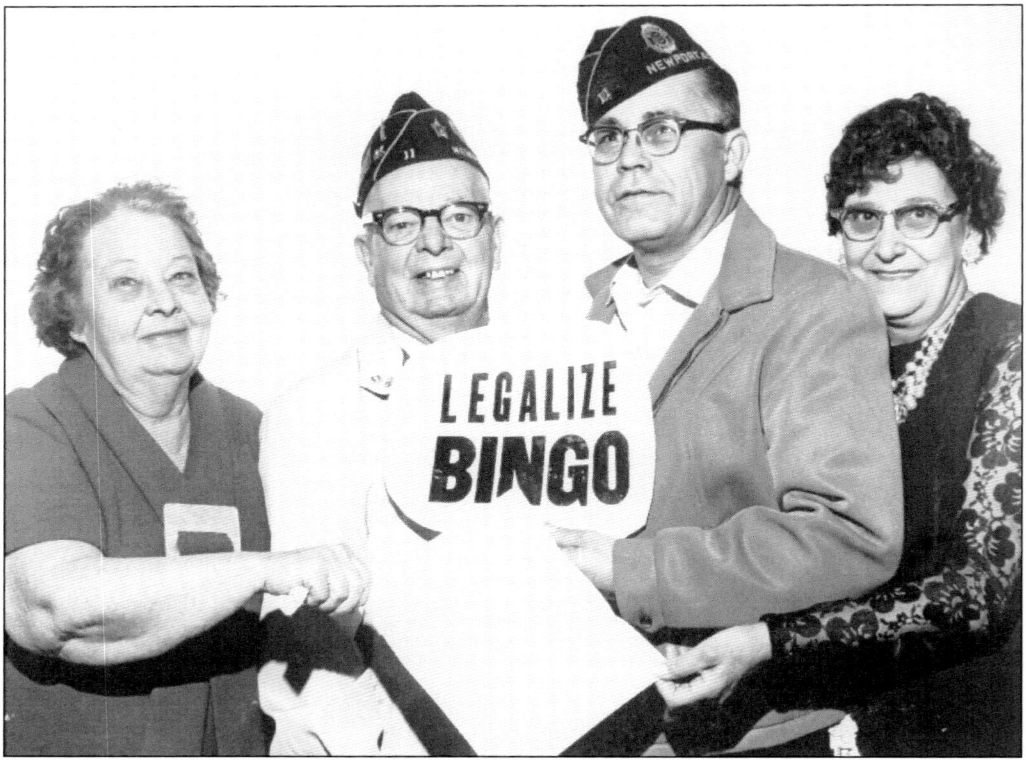

In 1940, the state attorney general's office declared bingo is gambling, not amusement, and therefore illegal. Many clubs and halls were raided and cited for operating bingo games. In the 1980s, a bill was introduced to legalize charitable bingo games. Pictured above, from left to right, Alberta Gutapful, Frank Schwed, Robert Bowds, and Louise Hunt lobby to legalize bingo. (Kenton County Public Library.)

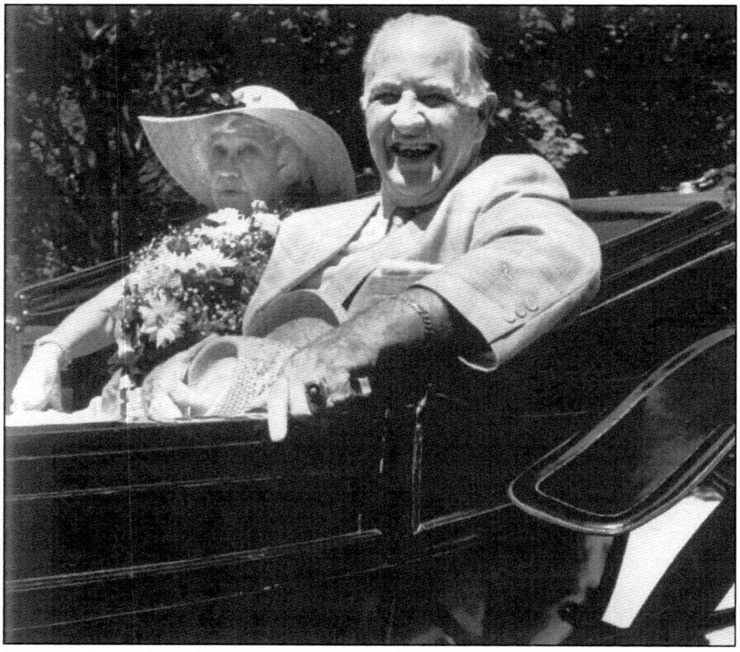

Albert "Happy" Chandler was governor of Kentucky from 1936 to 1939 and again from 1955 to 1959. Chandler sent state police detectives to Newport to collect evidence from the various casinos, brothels, and bookie joints. He supposedly used this data to secure campaign contributions by promising not to interfere in local affairs. Chandler once declared, "The people of Newport have a right to have it dirty." (Kenton County Public Library.)

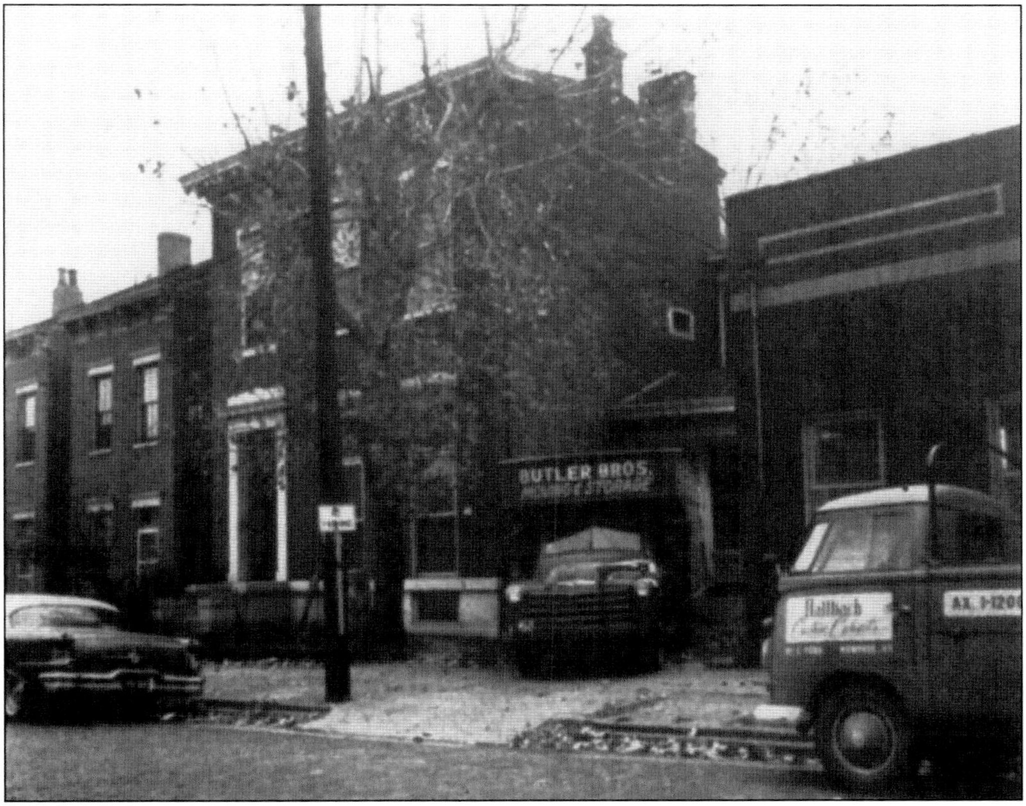

Vivian Schultz ran one of Newport's popular bordellos (seen above), located at 21 West Third Street. The city offered many day and night houses of prostitution to accommodate visitors. Schultz operated the Fourth Street Grill, a well-known brothel, which was located across the street from the police station. Many clubs had special, private rooms set aside for carnal pleasures. (www.nkyviews.com.)

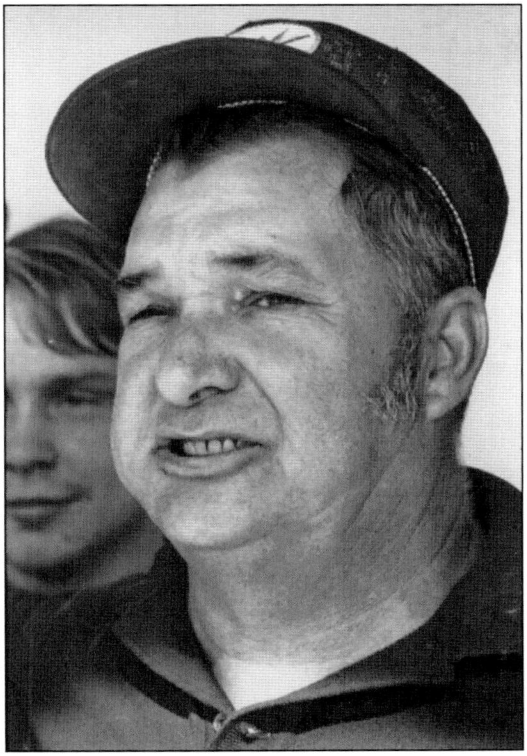

The Bridewell brothers, Ray (right), James, Ralph, and Emil, ran several gambling joints such as the 345 Club, the Kid Able, and the Mecca Club. It is rumored that the Bridewells operated many of Newport's renowned houses of ill repute. The Bridewells persistently denied conducting prostitution on their premises. In 1961, a former madam testified to the Campbell County Grand Jury that she and the Bridewells operated a brothel together. The Bridewells were sent to prison for perjury. (Kenton County Public Library.)

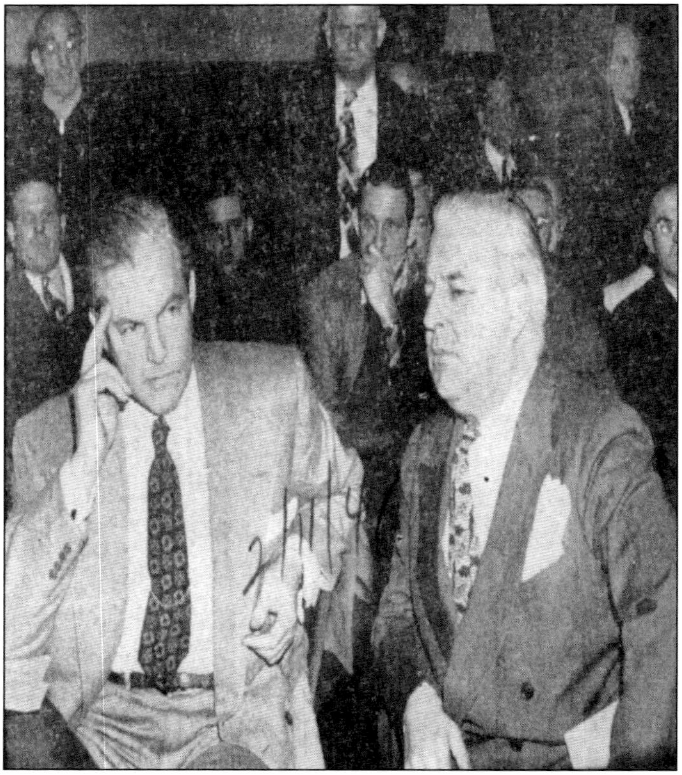

Attorney Charles Lester (left) and Newport police chief George Gugel (right) sit during Gugel's trial for wrongful imprisonment of *Louisville Courier Journal* photographer George Bailey. The newspaper photographer attempted to take a picture of Chief Gugel during a raid at Glenn Schmidt's Playtorium. Gugel was trying to thwart the raid led by Det. Jack Thiem. Gugel seized Bailey's camera, destroyed his film, and had the cameraman thrown in jail. A grand jury indicted Gugel for nonfeasance of duty and for violating Bailey's civil rights. Gugel was fined $1,000 and forced to take a temporary leave of absence from the force. (Campbell County Historical Society.)

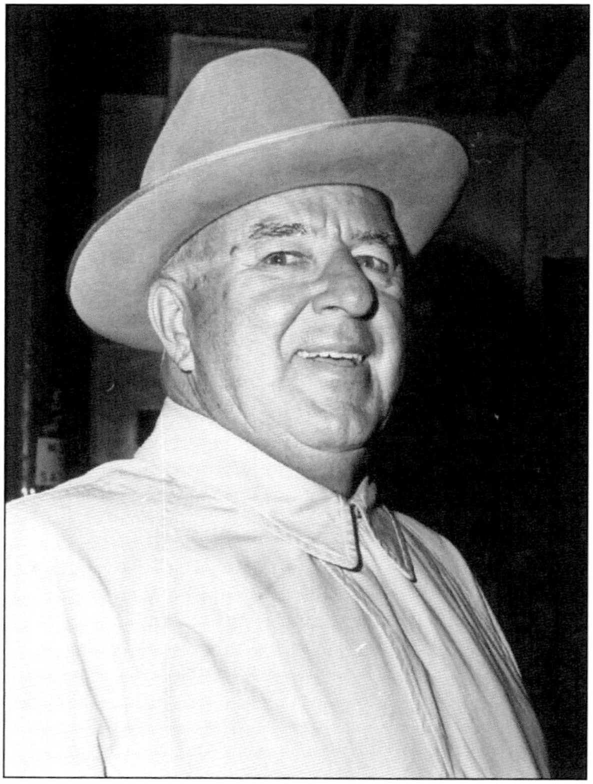

George Gugel was Newport's Chief of Police from 1946 to 1961. The Kefauver Committee subpoenaed Gugel in 1951 to question him about the wide open gambling occurring in his jurisdiction. Gugel's response was, "What gambling?" In 1961, a Campbell County special grand jury began investigating corruption in city hall. Gugel was indicted, but acquitted, on charges of conspiracy to pervert, corrupt, and obstruct justice. Gov. Bert T. Combs signed an order ousting Chief Gugel, preventing him from holding public office for four years. Gugel died in January 1972. (Kenton County Public Library.)

Ralph Mussman was Newport's city manager from 1957 to 1958. He served as mayor of Newport from 1960 to 1964. He was one of the many public officials indicted by the 1961 Campbell County special grand jury that ousted Newport's corrupt officials. Mussman was accused of neglecting his duties as mayor by allowing vice conditions to exist in the city. He was acquitted of these charges and allowed to finish his term as mayor. He was elected city manager from 1977 to 1980 and again from 1980 to 1984. (Kenton County Public Library.)

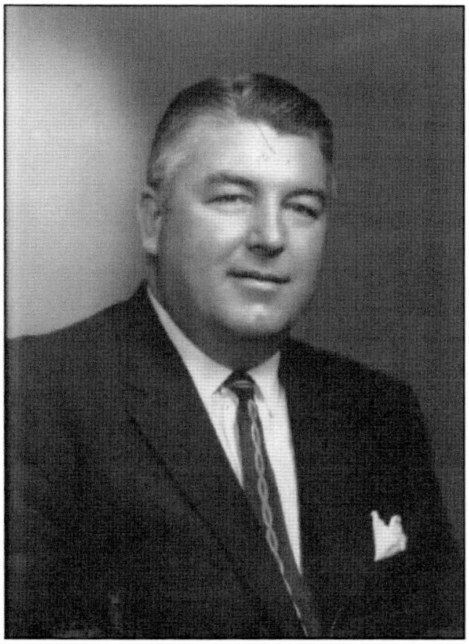

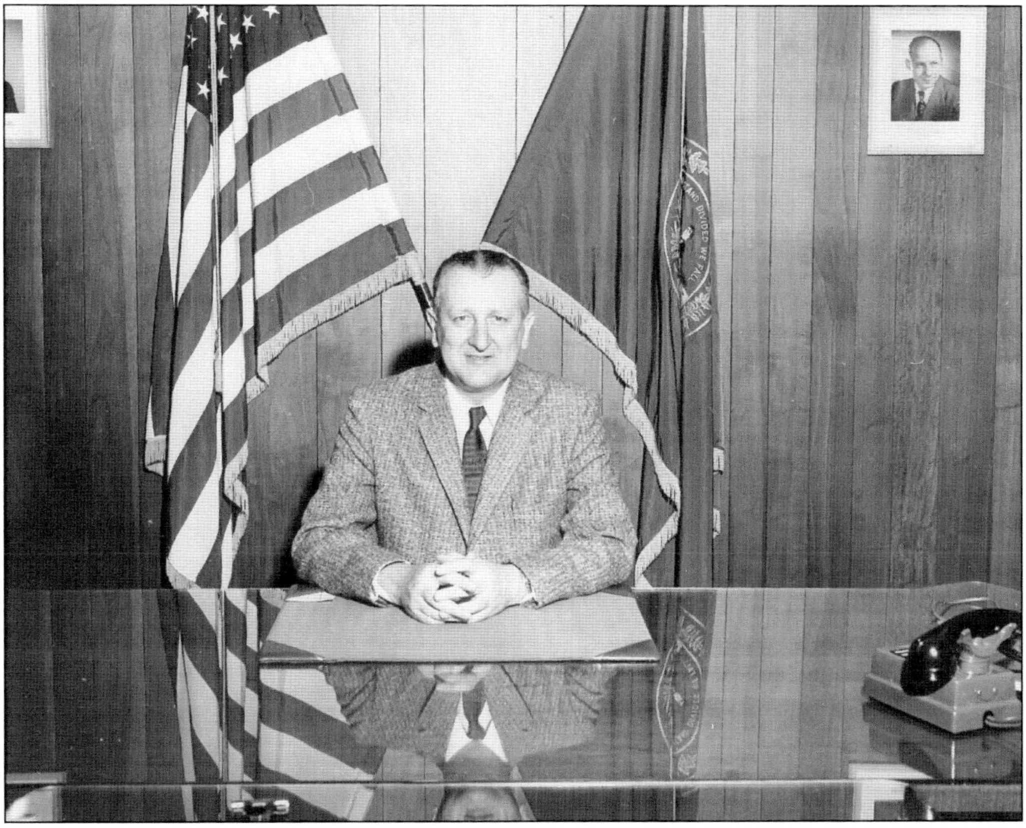

Norbert W. Roll was Campbell County sheriff from 1958 to 1962. In 1961, a Campbell County special grand jury indicted Roll after he stated under oath that illegal gambling did not exist in the county. The sheriff was charged with failing to enforce the law by neglecting to uphold the state anti-gaming statutes. Roll was ousted from his position as sheriff but later acquitted on the charges of nonfeasance. He was later found guilty of failing to file federal income taxes. Roll died in May 1973. (Kenton County Public Library.)

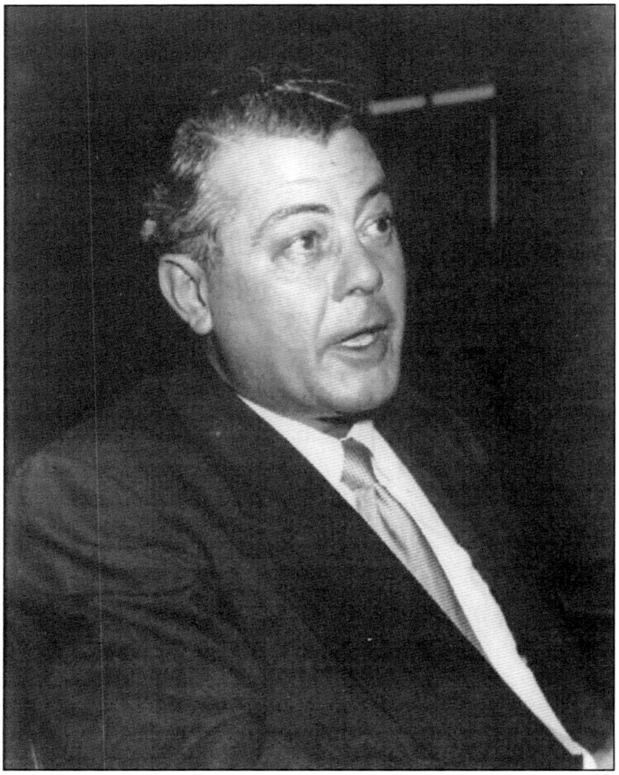

William Wise was the Commonwealth's attorney and accused of turning a blind eye towards vice conditions in Newport. He claimed, "Newport was no worse than any other city." Wise appeared before the Kefauver Committee in 1951 to answer questions about organized crime in Newport. In 1961, he was investigated by a Campbell County special grand jury for allegedly accepting payoffs and allowing the gambling casinos to operate without interference. He was not indicted, but the jury reprimanded him for not making full use of his abilities and powers to stop gambling and vice. (Dave Horn Collection.)

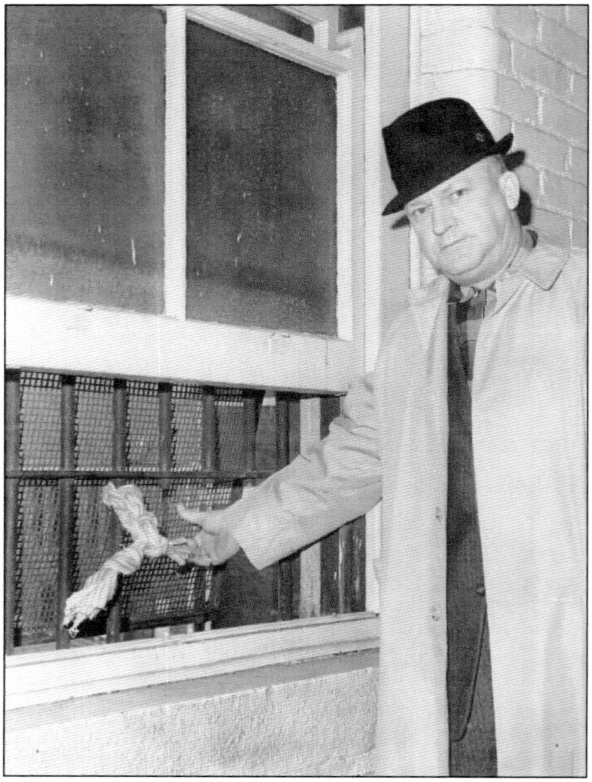

Upshere White started out as an officer on the Newport police force. He was promoted to detective, became chief of police in 1961, and held this position until 1967 . In 1961, a former madam testified before a Campbell County grand jury that she made graft payments to White and several other officers. The grand jury did not return any indictments for bribery, but White and 12 others were indicted, but acquitted, on charges of conspiracy to corrupt and pervert justice. (Kenton County Public Library.)

Patrick Ciafardini was a well known Newport detective who served 25 years on the force. Ciafardini was accused by a former madam of accepting bribes and was investigated during a Campbell County grand jury. No indictments were returned against him for bribery. Another grand jury indicted Ciafardini and twelve others for corrupting and perverting justice. All were later acquitted. He was also indicted but acquitted of violating the civil rights of George Ratterman. (Kenton County Public Library.)

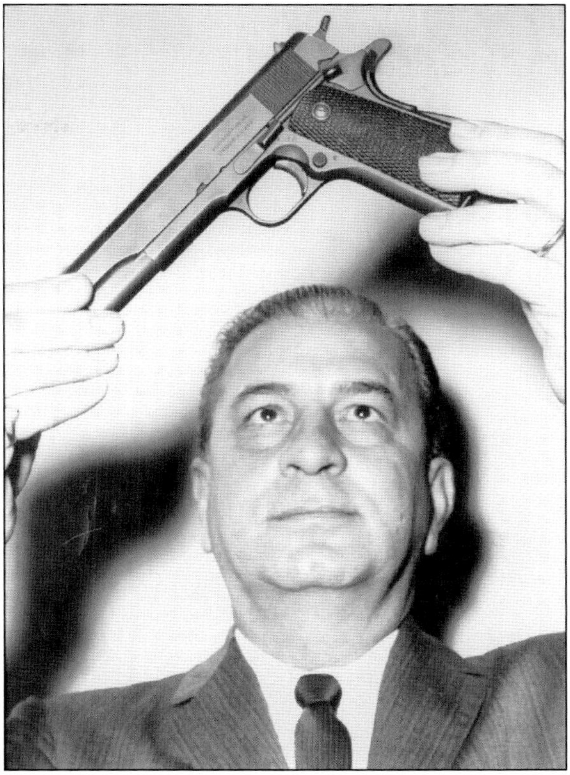

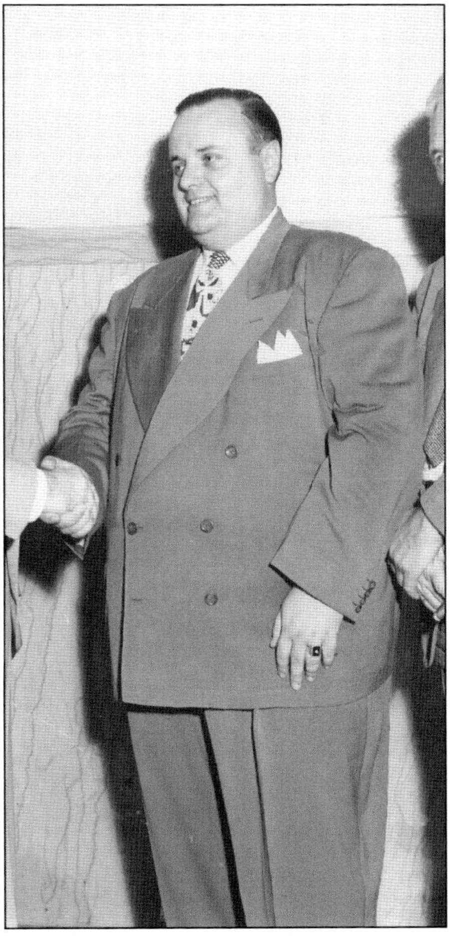

Robert Sidell was part of the local musical group known as the Bob Sidell Trio. He conducted the intermission orchestra at the Beverly Hills Country Club from 1937 to 1940. He became close friends with Pete Schmidt during this time, and Schmidt urged Sidell to run for public office. He was elected to the Newport city commission in 1944. He was elected mayor in 1952. In 1961, Sidell was charged with complicity in illegal gambling for leasing the Belmont Snax Bar to bookies for gambling purposes. Sidell was sentenced and fined $1,250. He was Newport's city manager from 1966 to 1968 and again from 1972 to 1976. Sidell died in December 1991. (Kenton County Public Library.)

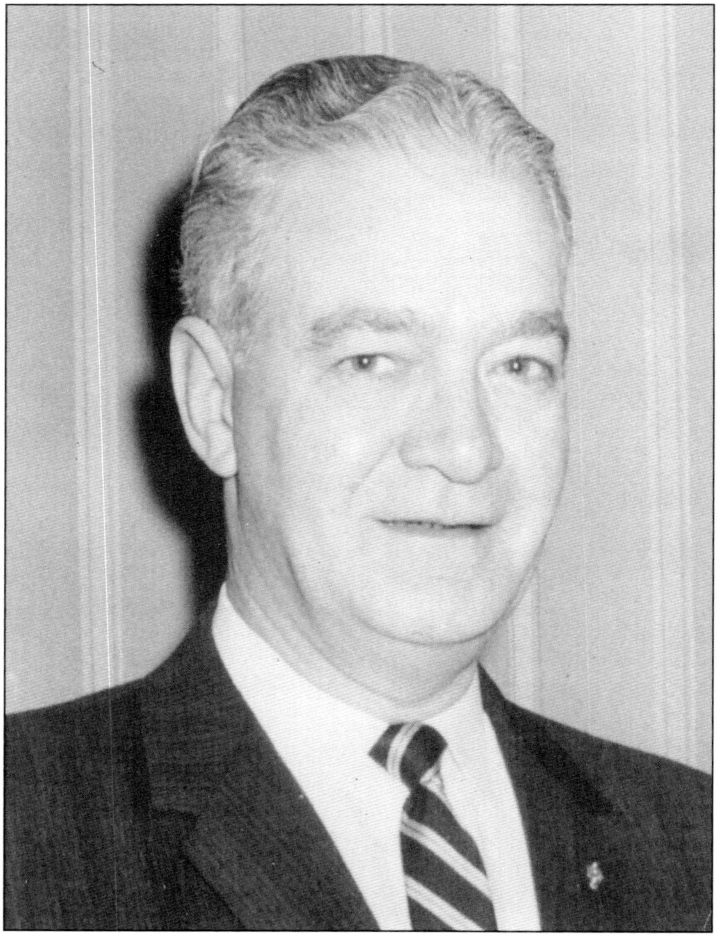

A. J. "Tony" Warndorf (left) was a Newport city commissioner indicted in 1981 on charges of bribery of a public servant. Nightclub owner "Big Jim" Harris paid Warndorf bribe money in exchange for Warndorf's promise to secure a promotion for a police officer. Harris told a Campbell County grand jury he had made payoffs to past and present city commissioners. Videotape evidence of Warndorf accepting payoff money from Harris was shown in court. Warndorf pleaded not guilty. A political campaign sign urging people to vote for Warndorf hangs above a strip club (below). (Both images, Kenton County Public Library.)

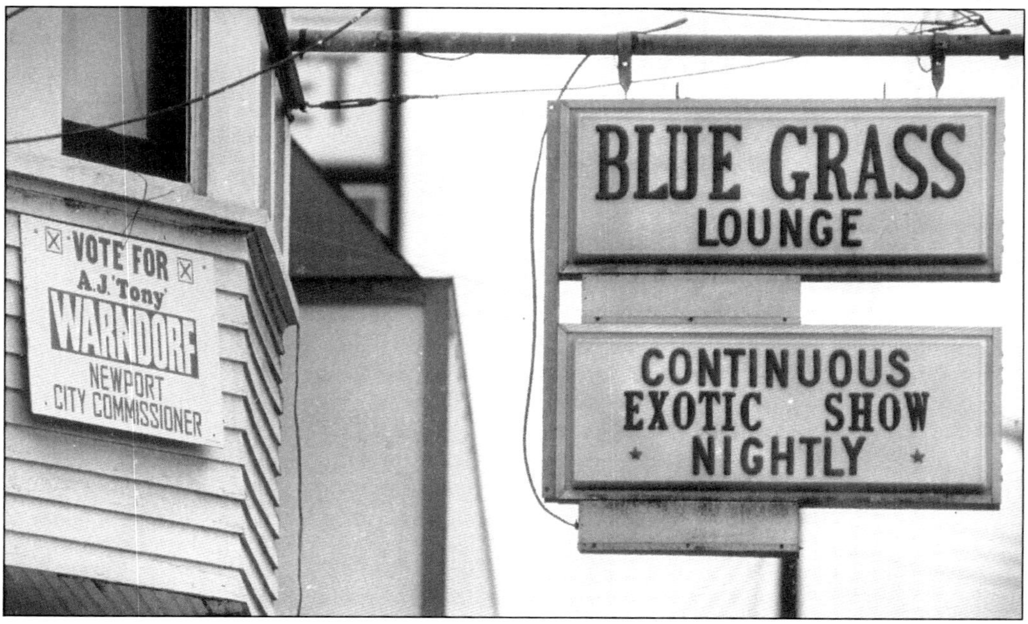

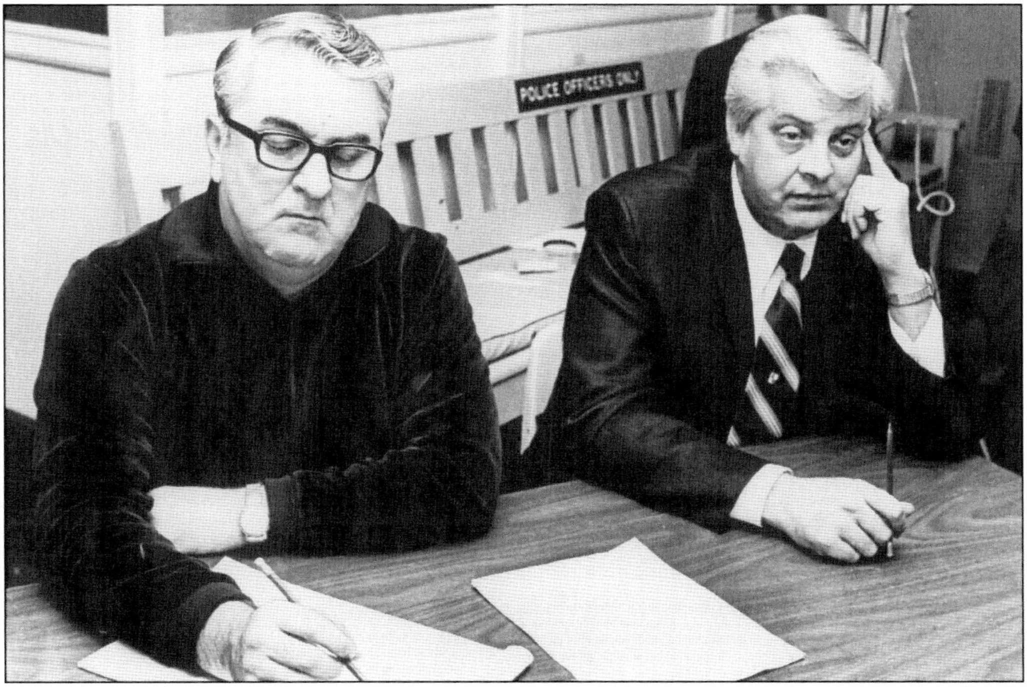

In 1972, a Campbell County grand jury investigating vice and crime in Newport returned nine indictments against city officials, including several police officers. Newport police chief Edward Gugel (left) was indicted on bribery charges. Night chief Donald Faulkner (right) was indicted on charges of robbery and receiving stolen property. They were both suspended by the city and later acquitted. (Kenton County Public Library.)

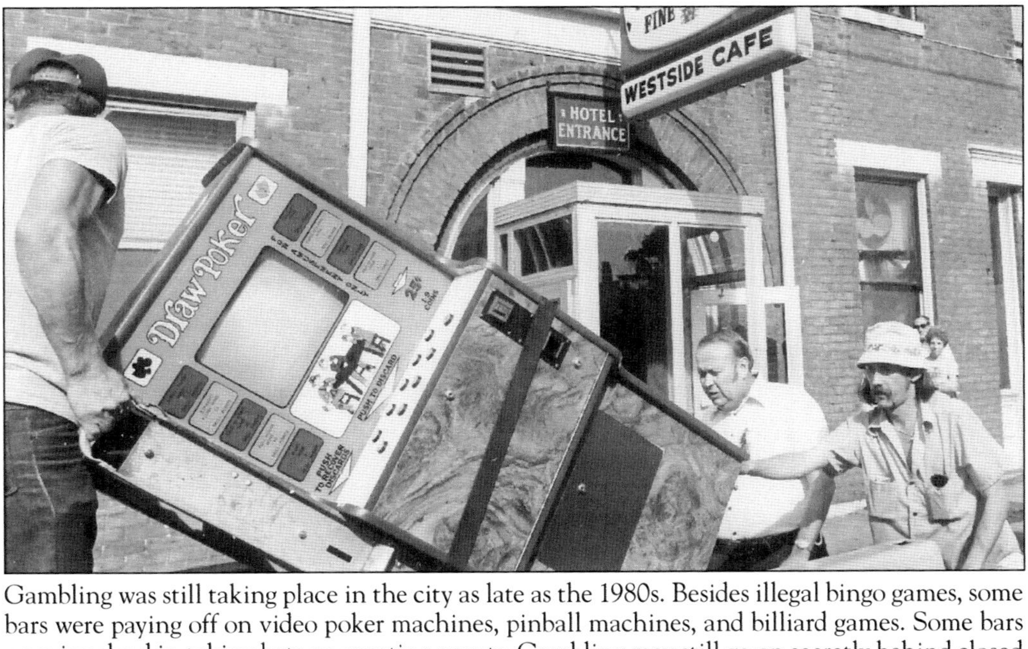

Gambling was still taking place in the city as late as the 1980s. Besides illegal bingo games, some bars were paying off on video poker machines, pinball machines, and billiard games. Some bars were involved in taking bets on sporting events. Gambling may still go on secretly behind closed doors, but it is no longer wide open in Newport. In this picture, a poker machine is confiscated from the West Side Café at 438 West Eleventh Street. (Kenton County Public Library.)

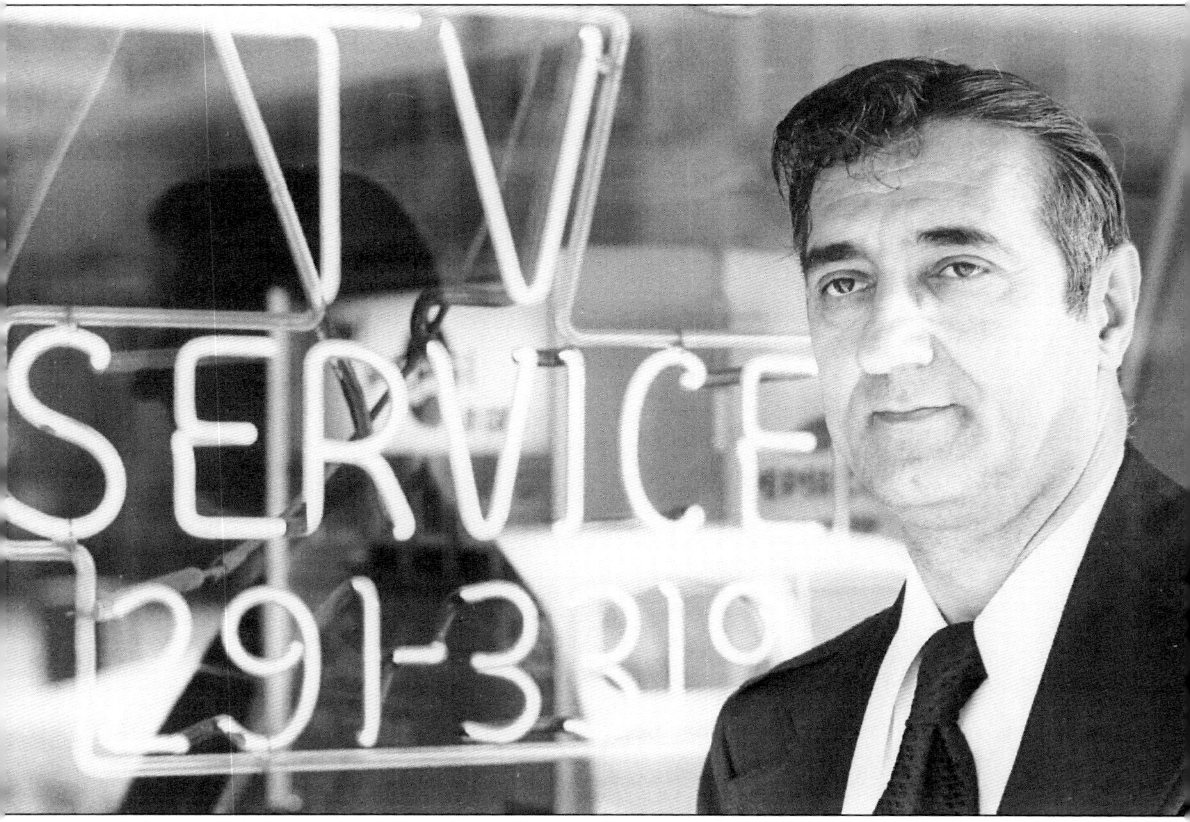

Johnny "TV" Peluso (right) got his nickname from the television repair shop he once operated in Newport. He served as mayor and city commissioner in Newport for 16 years. He was first elected mayor in 1964 and served his last term as commissioner in 1982. Convicted of running an illegal bingo game and lying to a federal grand jury, he was sentenced to four years in prison. Peluso was also known for his compassion and generosity towards the city's downtrodden. He was known to buy groceries and shoes for needy families. In 1999, Kentucky governor Paul Patton restored his rights to vote and hold office. Peluso unsuccessfully ran for Campbell County sheriff in 2006 at the age of 82. (Kenton County Public Library.)

Four

NEWPORT CLEANS UP

Several unsuccessful attempts at reform were made throughout the years. On May 3, 1950, the Senate established a special committee known as the Kefauver Committee to expose the growth of powerful crime syndicates and their impact on the nation's larger cities. Hearings were televised as the committee questioned notorious underworld figures about their involvement in certain business ventures. Combined with the efforts of Atty. Gen. Robert Kennedy, this put an enormous amount of heat on the syndicate operating in Newport. One reform group, the Newport Ministerial Association, was comprised of Newport clergymen who gathered evidence of gambling's existence throughout the city. This group was ignored and considered only a nuisance. In 1956, the Newport Ministerial Association sponsored another group, the Social Action Committee (SAC). Its membership consisted of a minister and two parishioners from each of the city's Protestant churches.

The SAC wrote to FBI director J. Edgar Hoover for advice on how to rid the city of vice and political corruption. Hoover suggested that the group bring public attention to the city's shocking conditions. The SAC contacted *Louisville Courier* reporter Hank Messick, who visited Newport and wrote a series of articles on the deplorable conditions in the city. The SAC gathered and presented evidence and testimony to a Campbell County Grand Jury, proving gambling and prostitution were widespread throughout the city. The grand jury turned a blind eye toward the evidence and refused to hand out indictments.

The following year, the SAC once again presented proof gathered from their investigations. The grand jury admitted a laxity in law enforcement, but once again refused to return indictments. The SAC and the Newport Ministerial Association declared February 12, 1961, "United Sunday." The clergy in area churches preached about the evils of vice and corruption. This united effort enabled them to raise enough in contributions to pay legal fees and continue their investigation. In March 1961, a new reform organization joined the cause. The Committee of 500 described itself as "religiously non-sectarian and politically non-partisan." The committee's objective was to persuade the governor to remove officials who refused to enforce the law and to support reform candidates possessing honesty and integrity. The committee nominated hometown football hero George Ratterman for Campbell County sheriff. For city commissioners, they endorsed Jack Cowens, Carl Giancola, Milton Pandorf, and Ralph Stevens. Their campaign motto was "Switch to Honesty." The Committee of 500 grew to include several thousand members.

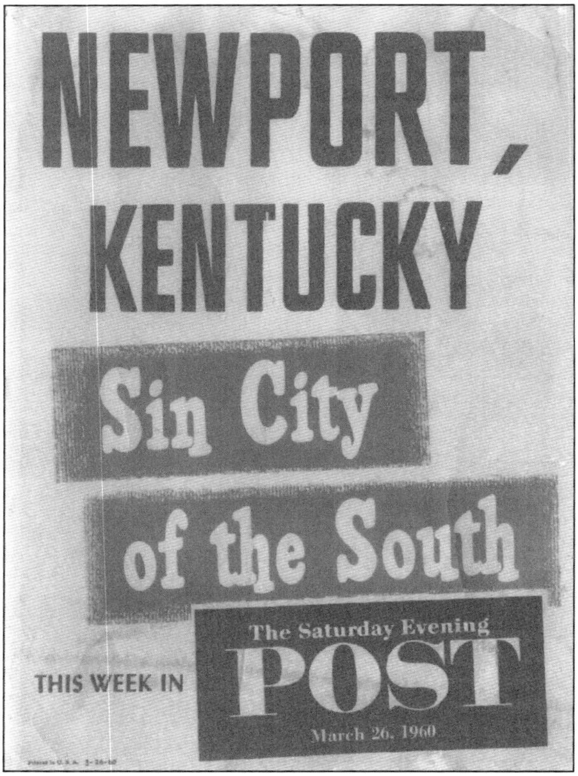

The *Saturday Evening Post* ran an expose on Newport on March 26, 1960. The article brought national attention to the vice conditions in the city. It also highlighted the reform efforts of the Social Action Committee. Pictured at left is the front page of the magazine featuring its lead story about Newport. (Author's collection.)

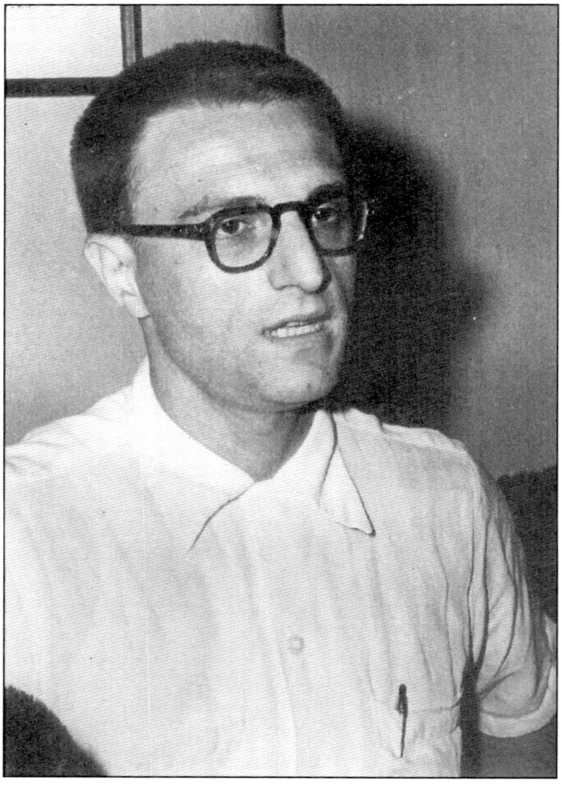

Rev. George Bennett of the First Presbyterian Church in Newport was a founding member of the Social Action Committee. Bennett helped arrange a "United Effort Day" on Sunday, September 13, 1959. On that date, all Newport pastors preached on the evils of vice and corruption. They also distributed pledge cards asking their congregations to sign them and uphold the promise to support honest political candidates who vow to enforce the laws. (Dave Horn Collection.)

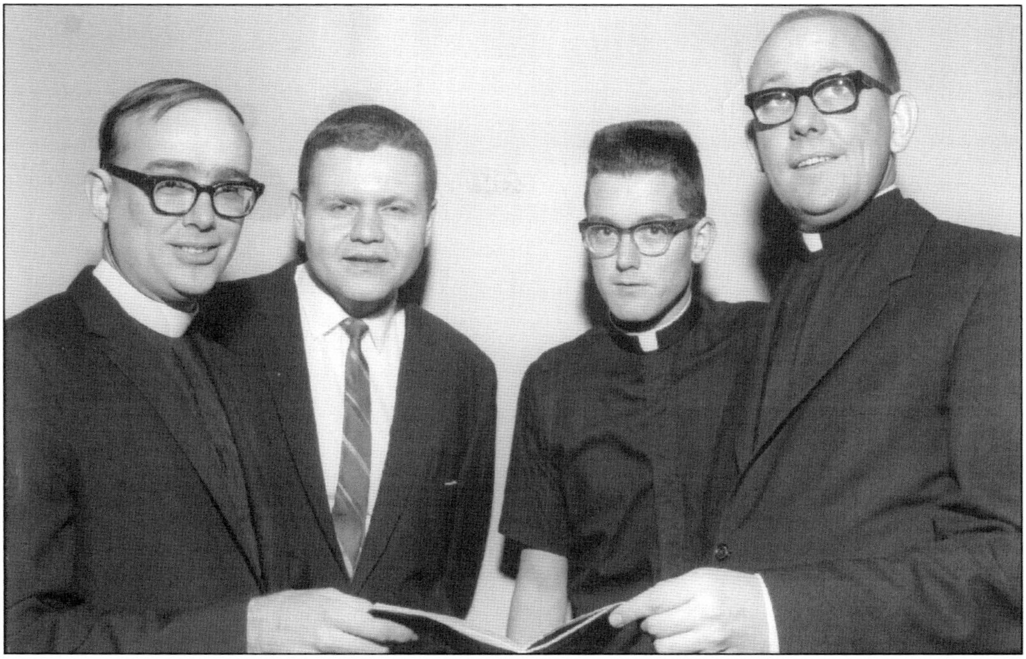

The Social Action Committee began raising funds through their churches to finance their legal proceedings in their quest to oust corrupt local officials who were neglecting their duties. On United Sunday, pastors throughout Northern Kentucky preached about the evils of the gambling industry and its effect on the communities' moral fiber. The SAC was initially made up of Protestants, but after nominating a Catholic as its first reform candidate for office, many Catholics joined the SAC's cause. Pictured here is Newport's Planning Committee for the week of prayer for Christian unity. From left to right are Rev. Thomas Hunter, pastor, St. Mark's Lutheran Church; Rev. Ron Hill, pastor, Ninth Street Evangelical United Brethren Church; Rev. Ron Brock, assistant pastor, Corpus Christi Church; and Rev. Paul Tenhundfeld, assistant pastor, Immaculate Conception Church. (Campbell County Historical Society.)

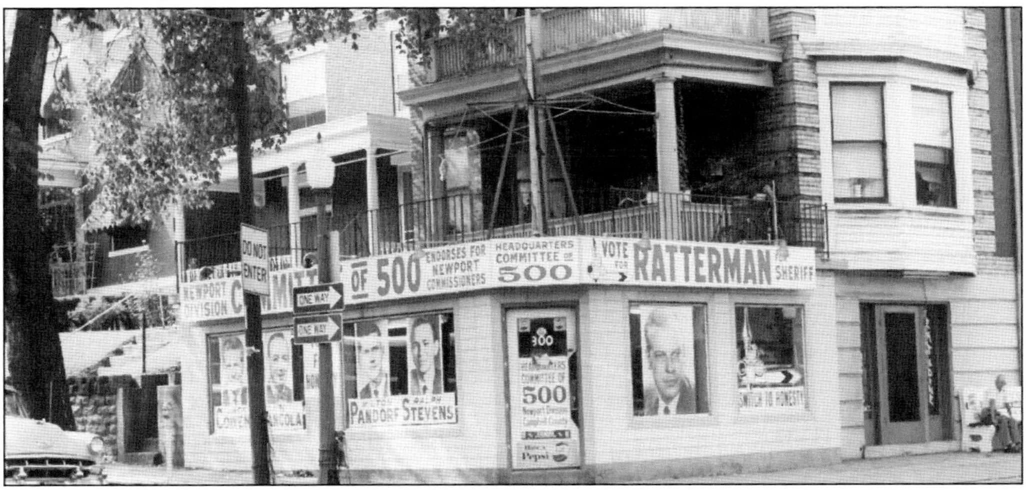

The Committee of 500 was a reform group started by local businessmen looking to change Newport's leadership and values. The committee backed honest candidates willing to enforce the law and drive out vice. The group set up headquarters (shown here) at the corner of Second and York Streets. (Dave Horn Collection.)

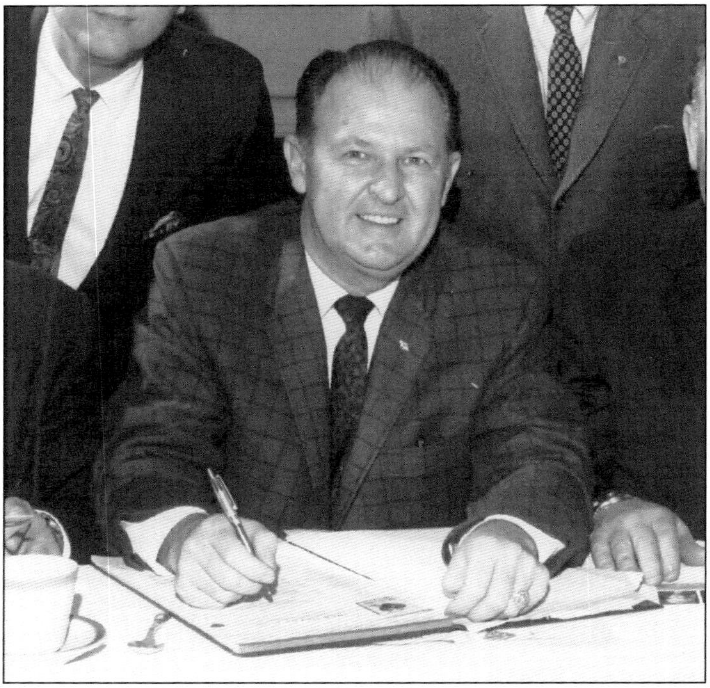

The goals of the Committee of 500 were to rally public support against gambling, pressure the city government to remove corrupt officials, and nominate honest reform candidates in local elections. Fort Thomas businessman Henry Hosea was the first president of the Committee of 500. (Kenton County Public Library.)

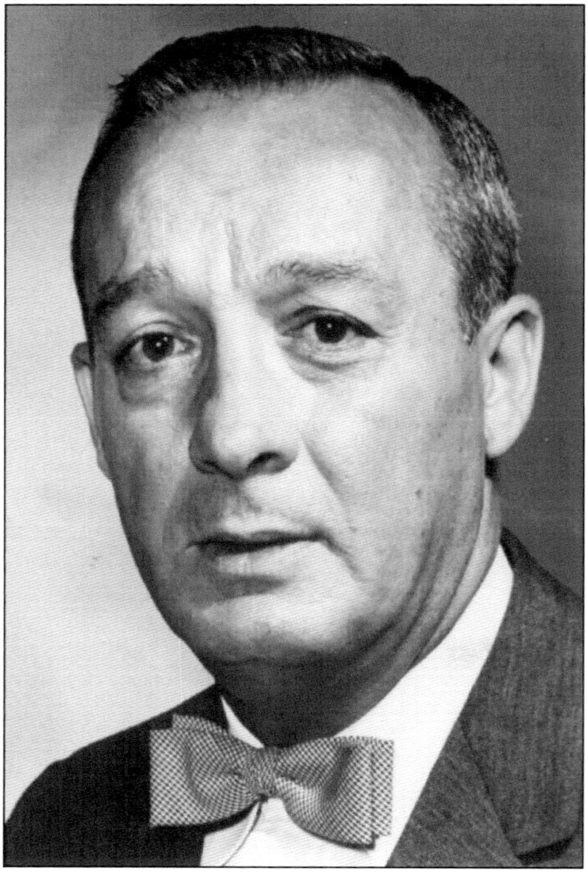

In 1960, Carl Giancola presided as foreman in the special grand jury that indicted Sheriff Norbert Roll. Giancola was considered an honest candidate, and the Committee of 500 endorsed his nomination when he ran for Newport city commission in 1961. (Kenton County Public Library.)

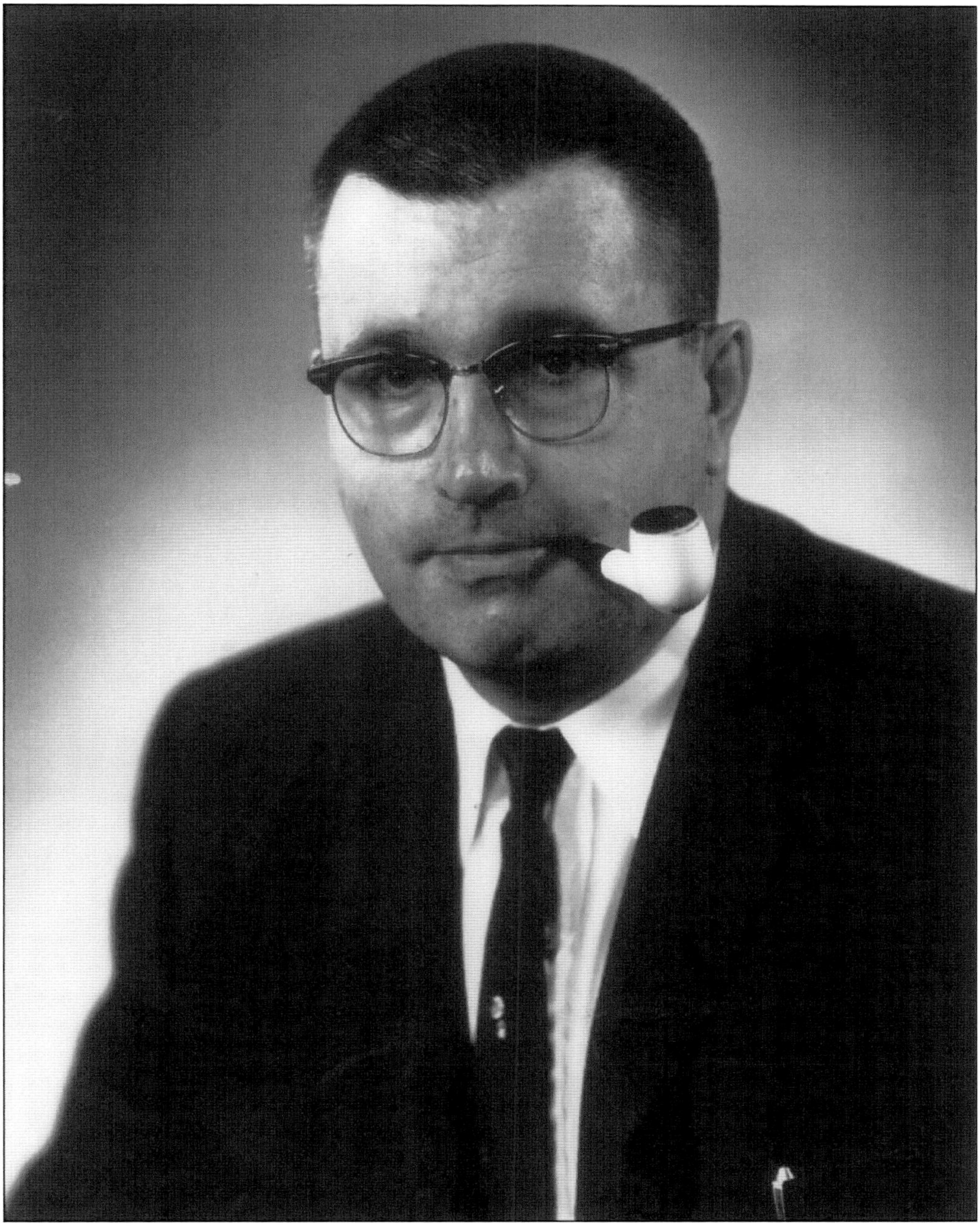

Hank Messick, a reporter for the *Louisville Courier Journal*, visited Newport on numerous occasions and wrote many articles chronicling the vice and corruption occurring in the city. Messick helped bring statewide attention to the conditions in Newport. He wrote several books about organized crime. *Razzle Dazzle* and *Syndicate Wife* both feature stories about Newport's days as a gambling mecca. (Dave Horn Collection.)

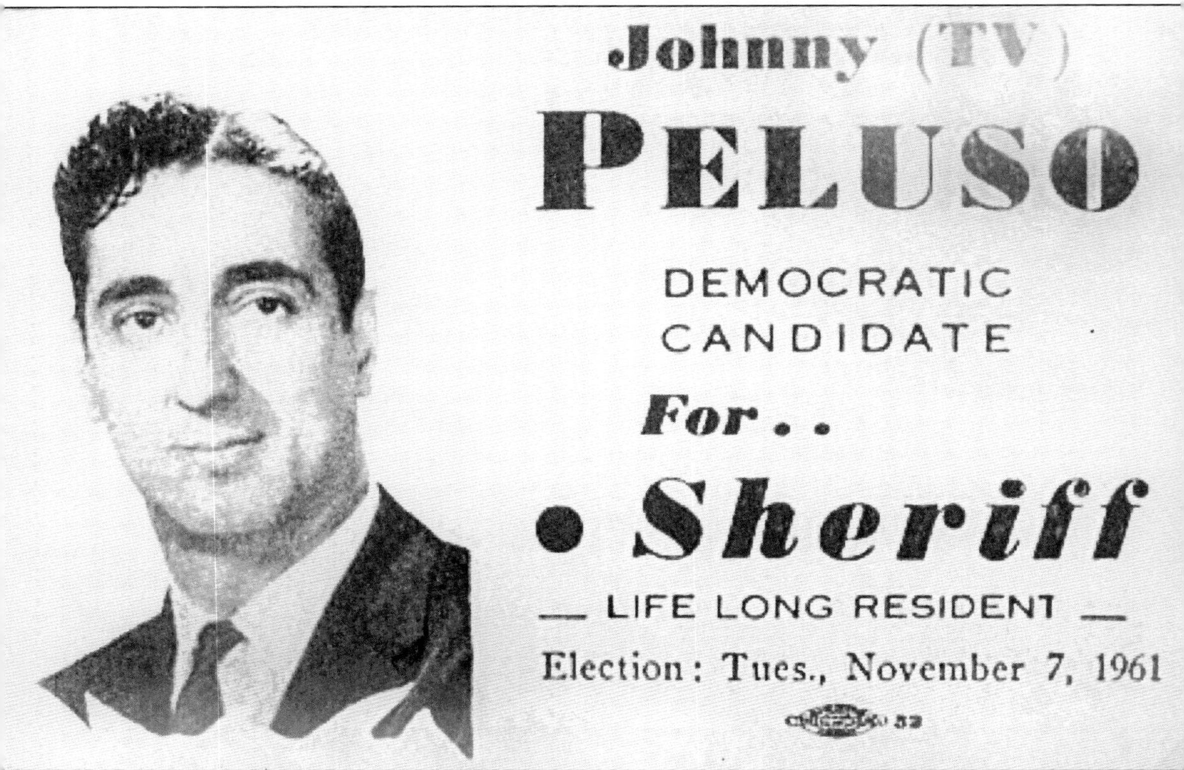

Johnny "TV" Peluso was a longtime resident who operated a television repair shop in Newport. He entered the race for Campbell County sheriff in 1961. The Committee of 500 nominated a reform candidate to run against Peluso. Pictured here is a card handed out by Peluso's campaign volunteers. He would later become mayor of the city. (Author's collection.)

Five

The Quarterback Gets Sacked

The Committee of 500 endorsed candidate George Ratterman for county sheriff. A former football star, Ratterman was a family man with an honest reputation. Ratterman accepted the nomination and promised to enforce the laws. The leading club owners devised a plan to ruin Ratterman and cause him to lose the election. On May 8, 1961, Tito Carinci, operator of the Tropicana nightclub, arranged a meeting with Thomas Paisley and George Ratterman at a hotel in Cincinnati. Acting as if he wanted to leave organized crime and aid the reform movement, it was alleged in Newport Police Court that Carinci slipped 'knock out drops' into Ratterman's drink. After leaving the restaurant , Carinci and Paisley accompanied Ratterman back to the Glenn Hotel. The Newport Police received an anonymous call reporting that prostitution was taking place in room 314 at the Hotel. When Newport police arrived at room 314, they found a partially clothed Ratterman with a stripper named April Flowers. Newport Police arrested Carinci for breach of peace, Ratterman for resisting arrest, and April Flowers on suspicion of soliciting prostitution. The event made national headlines. Ratterman proclaimed his innocence and a blood test revealed the presence of a massive dose of chloral hydrate. During the trial there was a general outpouring of sympathy and support for Ratterman and his family. Sufficient evidence suggested that Ratterman was drugged and the case was thrown out.

The national press coverage during this trial prompted Ky. Governor Bert T. Combs to order an investigation of Campbell County's elected officials. During these investigations, a Newport madam named Hattie Jackson testified that she made weekly payoffs to various officials. She claimed that she paid the county judge, the police chief, and officers on the police force. A special grand jury was assembled to investigate graft, as well as gambling and vice in Newport. No indictments were returned for bribery. However, the jury did return indictments against police and city officials for perverting and obstructing justice. The Governor issued a state of emergency and state police were brought in to arbitrate and enforce laws.

On October 27, 1961, a federal grand jury held its own inquest into the Ratterman case. During these proceedings, six people were named in a federal indictment for conspiring to violate Ratterman's civil rights. Tito Carinci's lawyer, Charles Lester, was found to be one of the masterminds of the set-up and was convicted of conspiracy charges in August 1963. Tito Carinci and three detectives involved in the arrest were acquitted. George Ratterman was elected county sheriff in November 1961 and the new anti corruption campaign began.

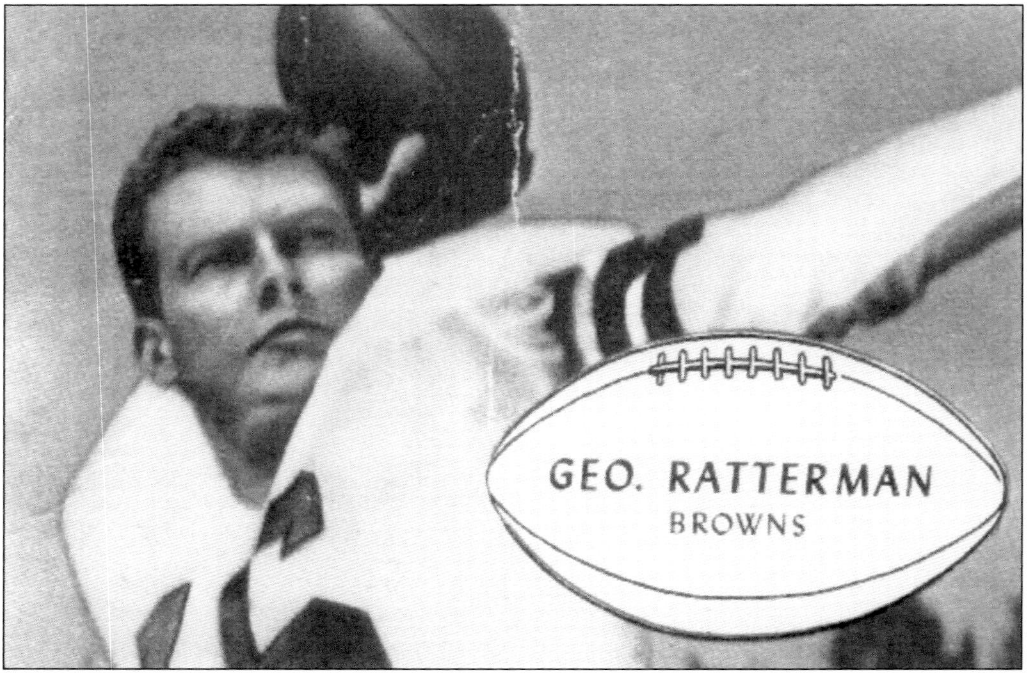

The Committee of 500 nominated hometown sports hero George Ratterman for sheriff. Ratterman had a successful college and pro football career until a knee injury forced him to retire. He worked as a sports commentator and eventually moved to his wife's hometown of Fort Thomas, Kentucky. He announced his candidacy for Campbell County sheriff in April 1961. (www.nkyviews.com.)

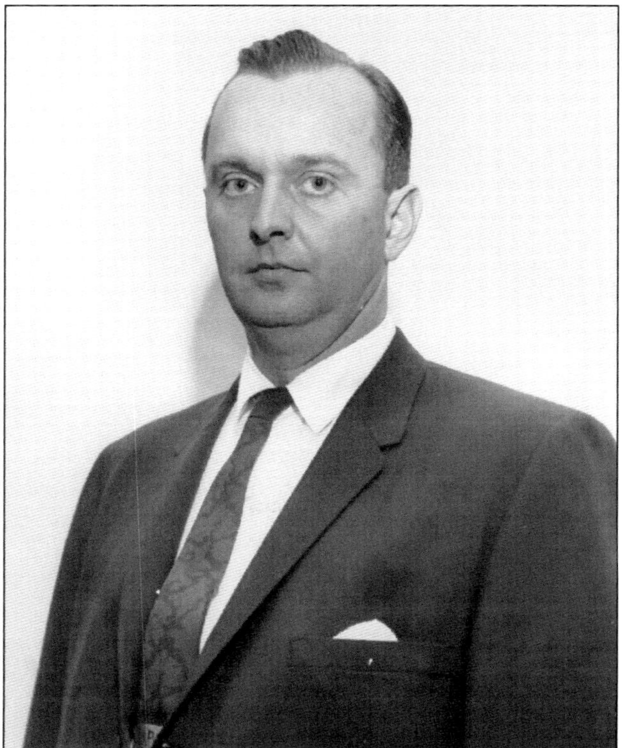

Thomas J. Paisley of Medina, Ohio, was a mutual friend of both George Ratterman and Tito Carinci. In April 1961, Carinci asked Paisley to arrange a meeting with Ratterman. After meeting the following month in Cincinnati, Paisley brought a drugged Ratterman to the Glenn Hotel. (Kenton County Public Library.)

On May 8, 1961, Tito Carinci spiked Ratterman's drink with chloral hydrate drops and took him back to the Glenn Hotel. Carinci arranged for a stripper to join Ratterman and planned to photograph the two together in bed, but the photographer never showed up. Carinci called the Newport Police Department and had Ratterman arrested. (Kenton County Public Library.)

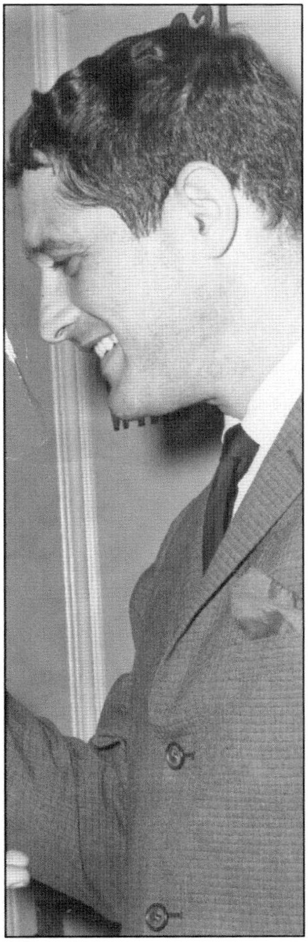

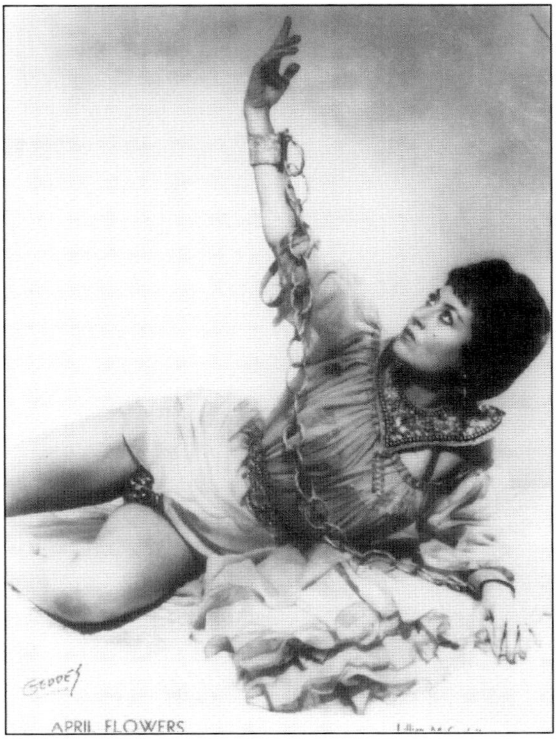

Juanita Hodges, "April Flowers," worked at the Tropicana and was the exotic dancer found in room 314 with George Ratterman. After testifying during the Newport Police Court Trial held May 16, 1961 she perjured her testimony. She approached the FBI and after taking a lie detector test testified for the prosecution. After three days of deliberation in the second trial held in federal court the jury convicted Charles E. Lester and Marty Buccieri of the conspiracy. (Dave Horn Collection.)

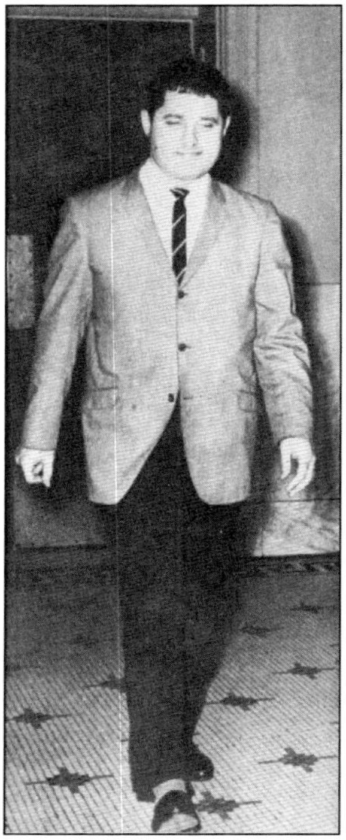

Tito Carinci is seen here entering a Newport courtroom on May 16, 1961. Carinci was charged with breach of the peace for allegedly trying to prevent the police officers from entering his apartment to arrest Ratterman and Flowers. During the trial, more than 300 people packed into the 75-seat courtroom. National media, including the *New York Times* and *Time* magazine, were in attendance. The local newspaper reported, "A city is on trial in a stuffy little courtroom rocking with sin and shame." (Dave Horn Collection.)

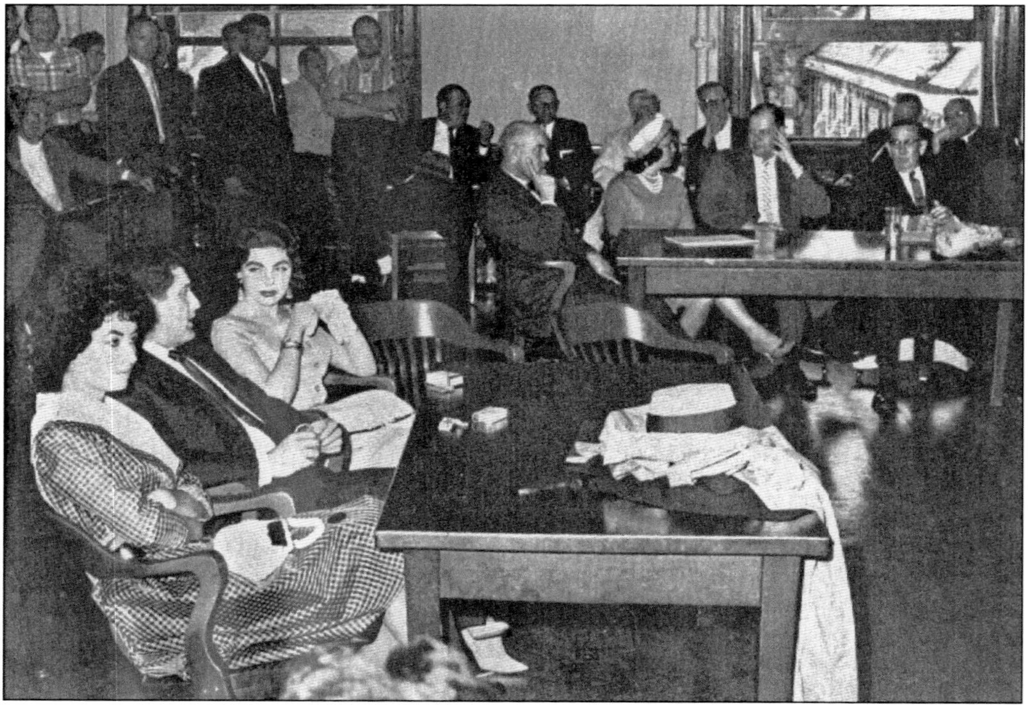

Sitting in the Newport courtroom at the table on the left are, from left to right, April Flowers, Tito Carinci, and Rita Desmond. Seated at the table toward the right of the picture are, from left to right, unidentified, Ann Ratterman, George Ratterman, and Henry Cook. Flowers was on trial for engaging in prostitution, Carinci was charged with breach of peace, and Ratterman was accused of breach of peace, disorderly conduct, and resisting arrest. (Dave Horn Collection.)

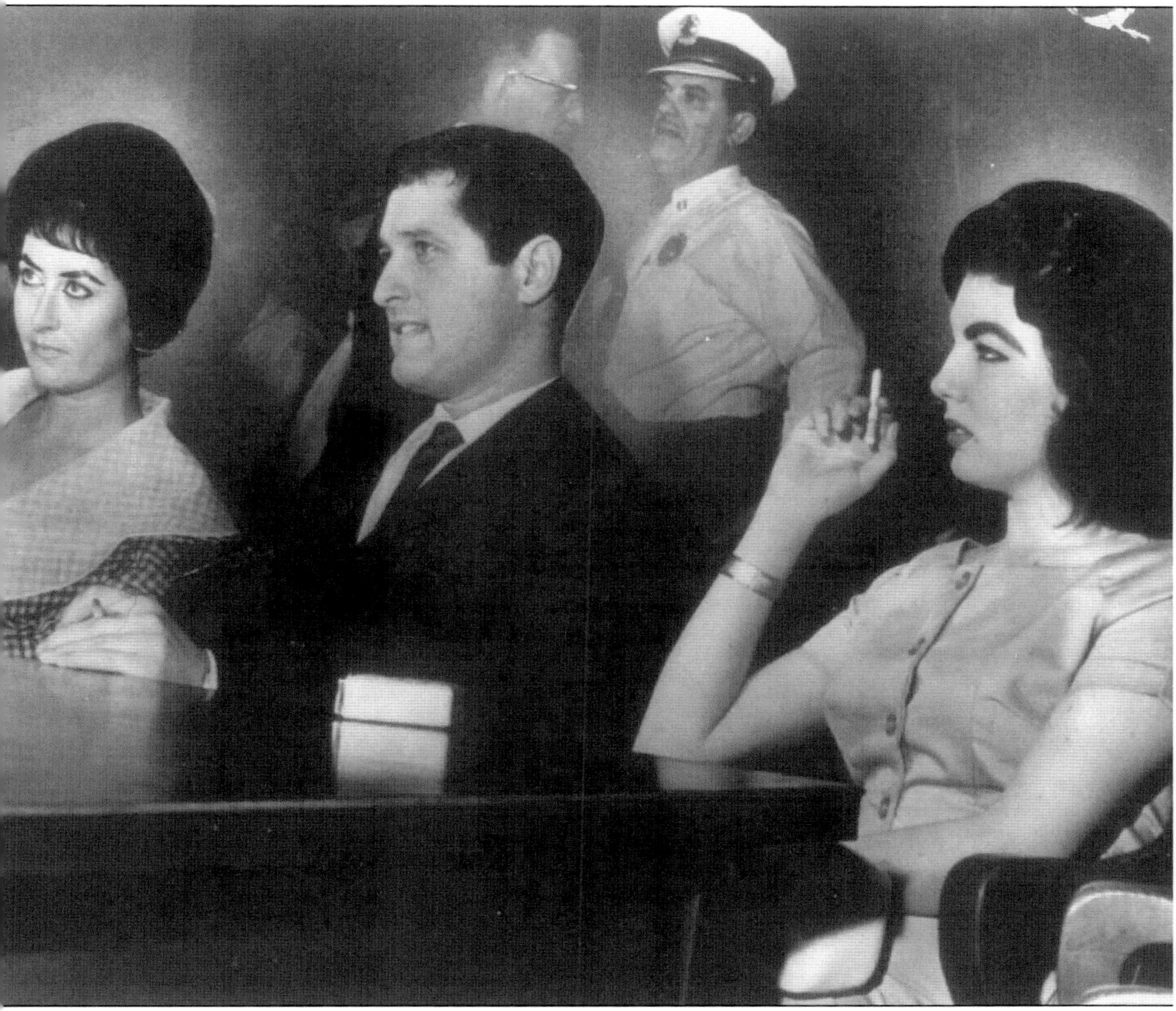

April Flowers (left), Tito Carinci (center), and Rita Desmond (right), sit in the courtroom waiting to testify. Desmond testified that she and Thomas Paisley avoided arrest because they left the Glenn Hotel to spend the evening at Paisley's hotel in Cincinnati. Flowers testified that she and Ratterman were getting intimate in Carinci's apartment before the Newport police interrupted them. Carinci testified that Ratterman willingly went to the Glenn Hotel on his own accord in search of women. All three defendants changed their stories several times. (Courtesy of the Dave Horn Collection)

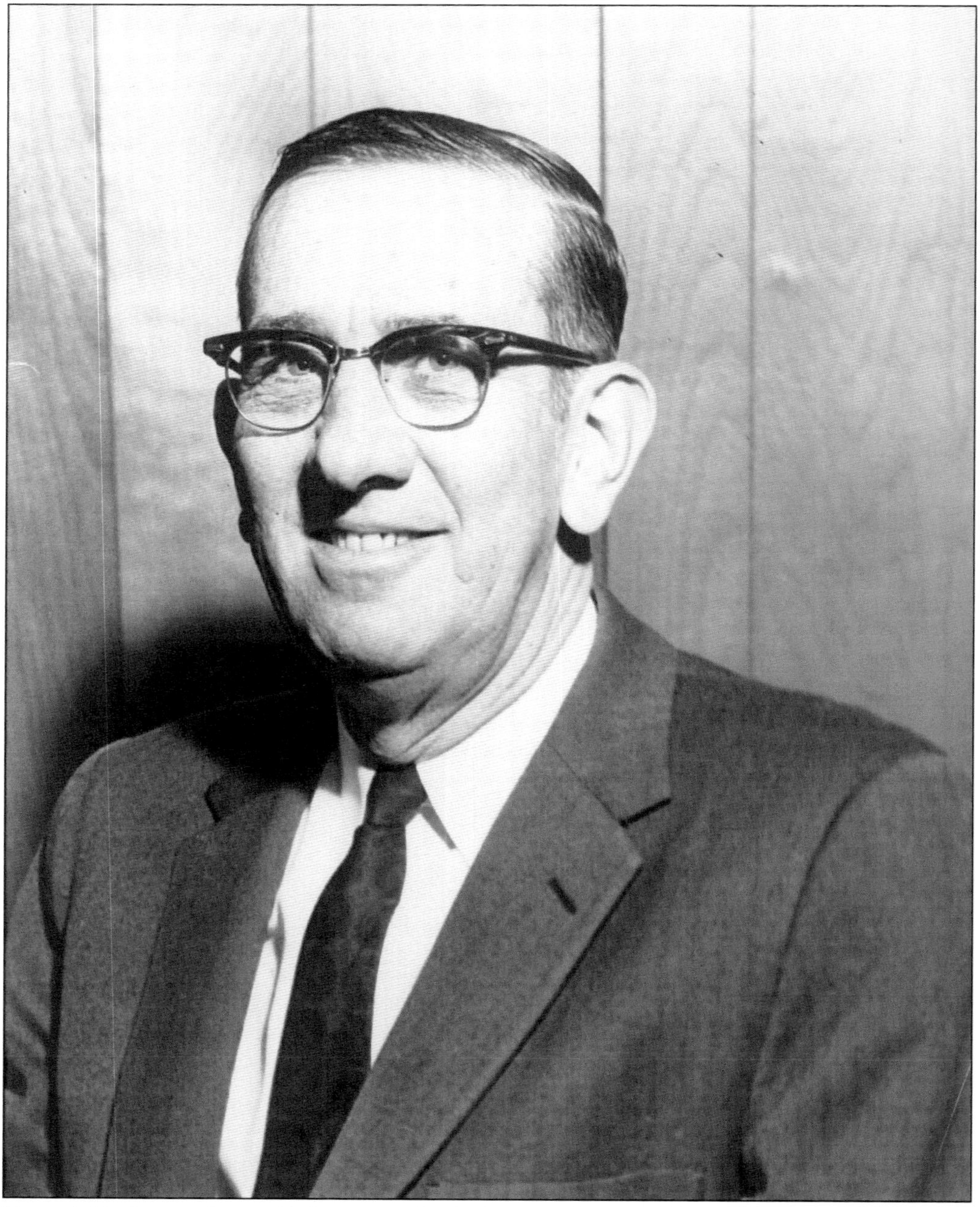

Henry J. Cook was a former U.S. attorney for the Eastern District of Kentucky. Cook provided legal council for the Committee of 500 and was George Ratterman's attorney during the famous trial. Cook called local photographer Thomas Withrow, who testified that Charles Lester approached him about taking pictures at the Glenn Hotel. Withrow stated that he met with Marty Buccieri, owner of the hotel, who told Withrow he needed him to take incriminating pictures of a man and a woman in bed together. Withrow was told he would be well paid for the job and given protection. He decided he did not want any part of the suspicious job and ignored Buccieri's late-night phone calls. His testimony, along with that of his wife and grandmother, helped Henry Cook prove Ratterman had been framed. (Kenton County Public Library.)

In May 1961, the Newport Ministerial Association asked Gov. Bert T. Combs (pictured at right) for aid in ousting Newport's corrupt officials. The governor sent Alcohol Beverage Control investigators to Newport to raid casinos for liquor license violations, and he sent the state fire marshal to close casinos violating fire laws. Governor Combs also instituted ouster proceedings against top Campbell County law enforcement officials. Four officials were prosecuted: the sheriff and police chief of Campbell County, the police chief of Newport, and an attorney. Governor Combs declared a state of emergency in Campbell County and sent state police to Newport to enforce the law. (Kenton County Public Library.)

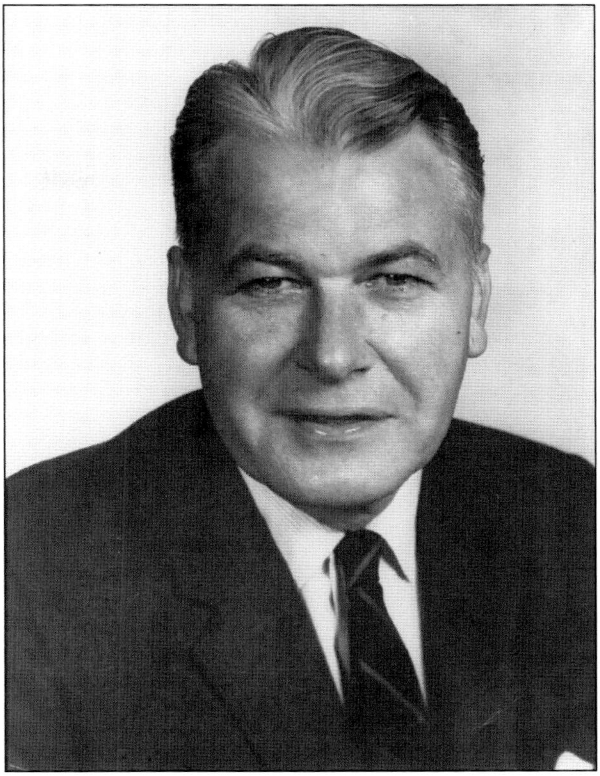

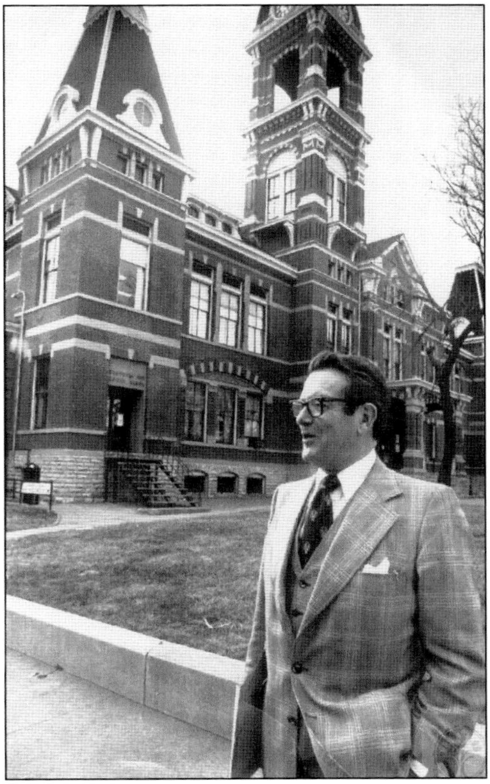

Pictured here is John Breckinridge (1913–1979) standing in front of the Campbell County courthouse. He was Kentucky's attorney general from 1960 to 1964 and again from 1968 to 1972. As the attorney general, John Breckinridge represented the Commonwealth during the ouster hearings in Campbell County. Breckinridge helped put an end to corruption and commercialized vice in Newport. Breckinridge served as a member of the U.S. House of Representatives from 1973 to 1979. (Kenton County Public Library.)

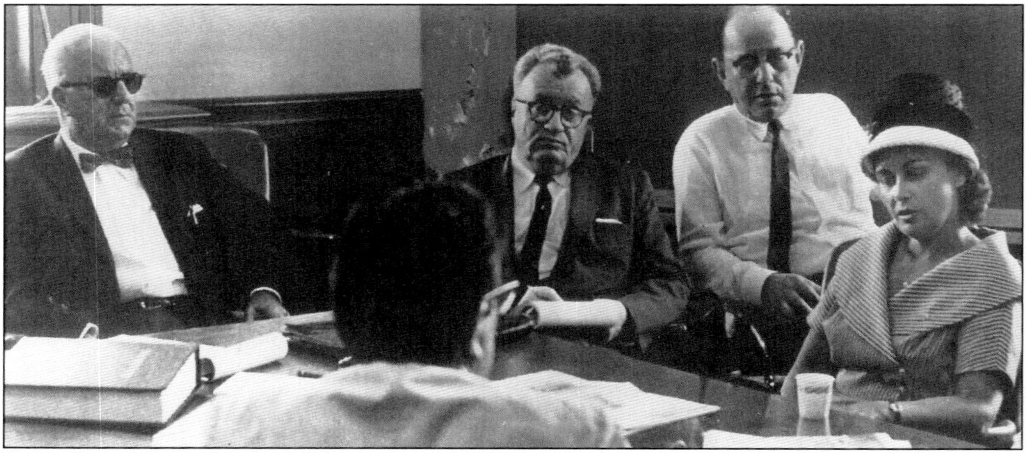

During the ouster hearings, Hattie Jackson, a former Newport brothel madam, testified that she made regular weekly payments to city officials and policemen to continue operating without interference. She began working at the 316 Club for notorious madam Vivian Schultz in 1947. Part of her job was to handle the "payroll" and put money into individual envelopes for officials and police officers. In 1954, Jackson went into business with the Bridewell brothers and became madam of her own house, where she continued the tradition of doling out hush money. She supplied the court with a list of names of those she paid off. A special grand jury was called to investigate the allegations, resulting in the indictment of 13 city officials for conspiracy to pervert and corrupt justice. All were acquitted. (Dave Horn Collection.)

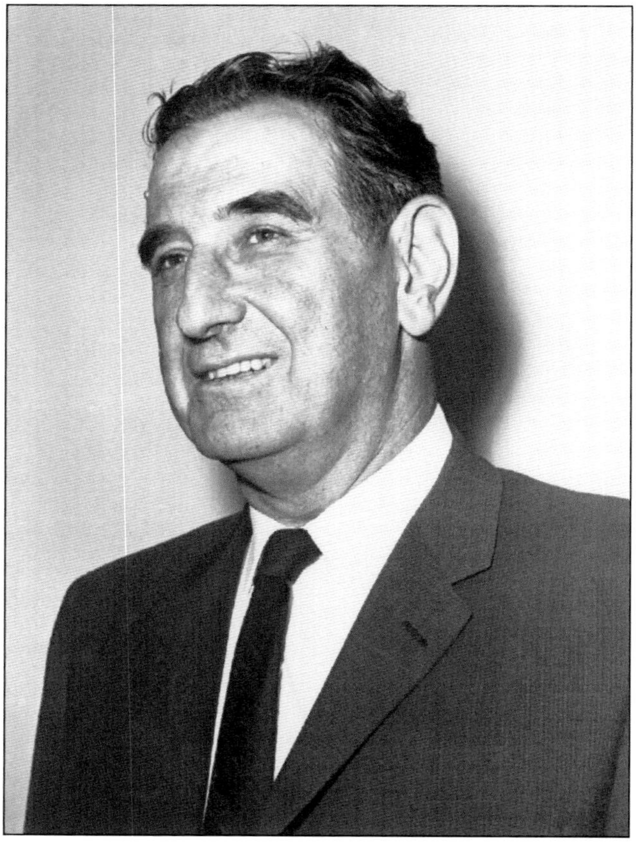

U.S. attorney general Robert F. Kennedy, who took a special interest in the Ratterman case, sent FBI agents to Newport to launch a broad-scale grand jury investigation into payoffs to public officials and to determine if Ratterman may have been kidnapped and taken across the state line. They were also probing into the case to determine if Ratterman's civil rights had been violated. Frank Staab (shown at left) was the local FBI agent assigned to the case. (Kenton County Public Library.)

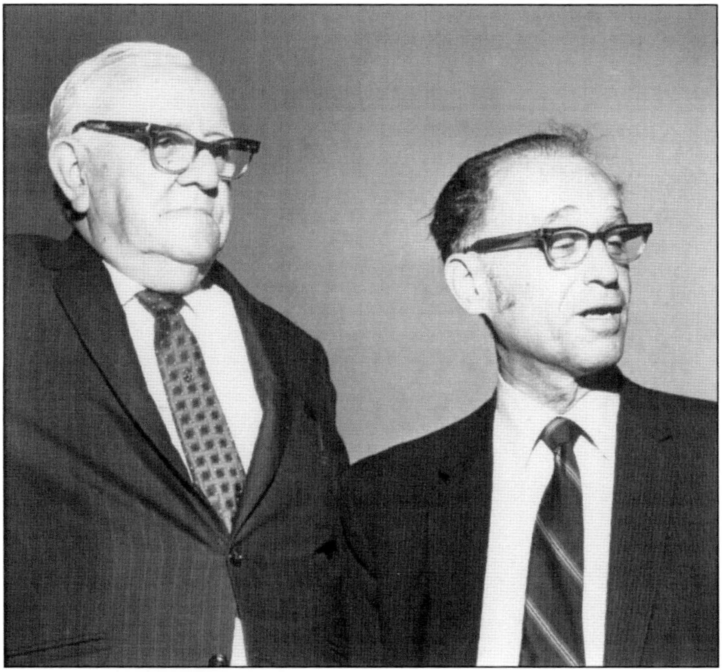

Dan Davies (left) and Morris Weintraub (right) were two local attorneys who were well known for representing many of Newport's club owners and nightlife figures. The two attorneys represented the three Newport police detectives accused of conspiring to violate Ratterman's constitutional rights. Davies and Weintraub argued that the detectives were merely performing their duties by investigating the prostitution tip and arresting the participants at the hotel. (Kenton County Public Library.)

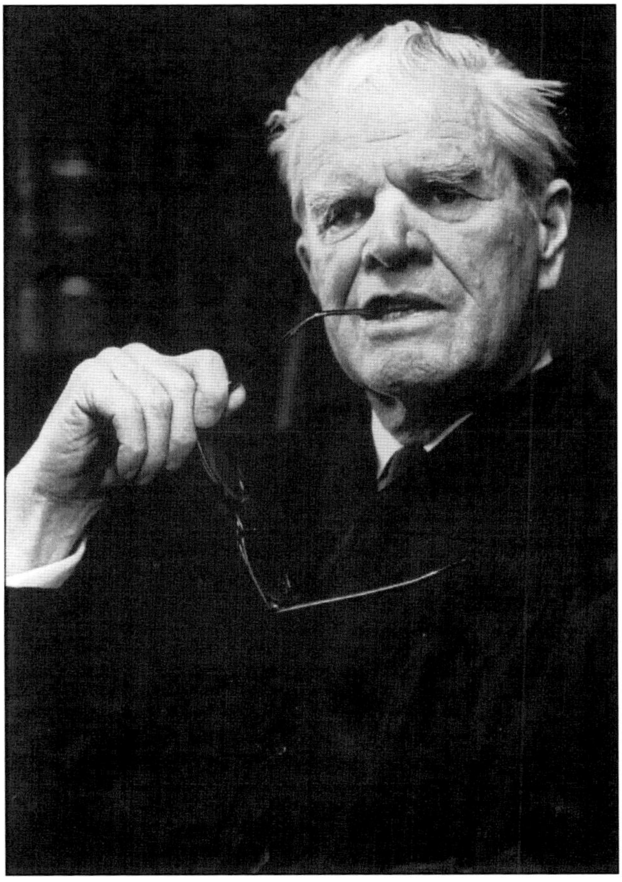

Federal judge Mac Swinford officiated over the federal grand jury case titled *U.S. v. Lester, et al.*, otherwise widely referred to as "the Ratterman case." The FBI was convinced attorney Charles Lester was the mastermind behind the scheme. The case was tried at the federal courthouse in Covington, Kentucky, on June 5, 1962. It resulted in a hung jury. A second trial began on July 15, 1963. This time, a jury found Charles Lester and Marty Buccieri guilty of the conspiracy charge. Tito Carinci and Newport police detectives Ciafardini, Quitter, and White were acquitted. (Kenton County Public Library.)

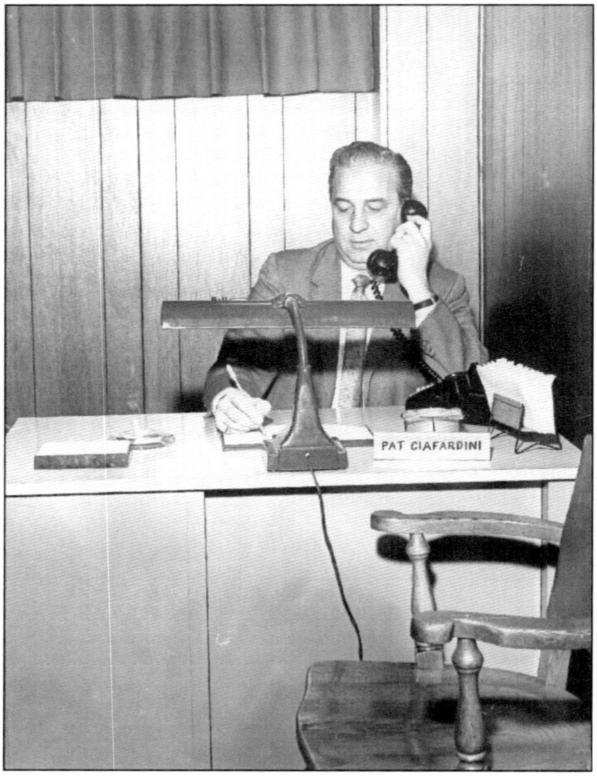

Newport police detective Pat Ciafardini, along with fellow detectives Upshere White and Joseph Quitter, went to the Glenn Hotel to investigate a tip that prostitution was occurring on the premises. The detectives stated that when they entered room 314, they found a scantily clad stripper in bed with reform candidate George Ratterman. (Kenton County Public Library.)

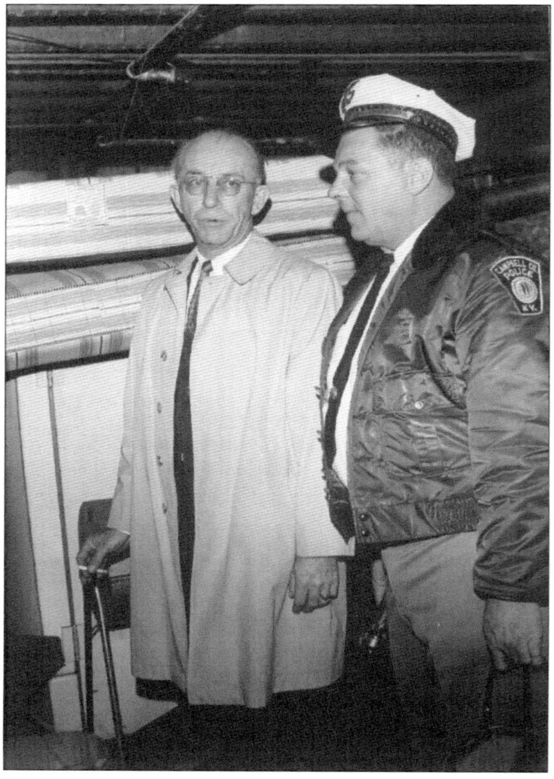

Campbell County Police Detective Joseph Quitter (left) is pictured here with Campbell County Police Lieutenant Al Seifried (right) after a Newport raid in 1968. Quitter was one of the Newport police detectives who arrested George Ratterman. He and the other arresting officers stood trial for violating Ratterman's civil rights and all were found "not guilty". (Courtesy of the Campbell County Historical Society.)

Upshere White was one of the Newport Police Detectives who arrested Ratterman at the Glenn Hotel. White, along with the other detectives, was acquitted of the charge of violating Ratterman's civil rights. The detectives were accused of taking Ratterman's pants off while he was unconscious and lying about the entire incident. Upshere White testified that Ratterman was trying to console a sobbing Carinci on the way to the police station by saying, "Don't cry, Tito. It's just one of these things that happen. We just got nailed, that's all." (Kenton County Public Library.)

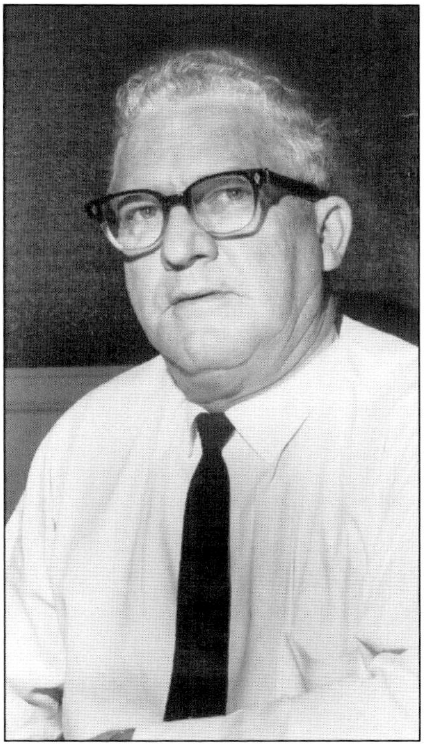

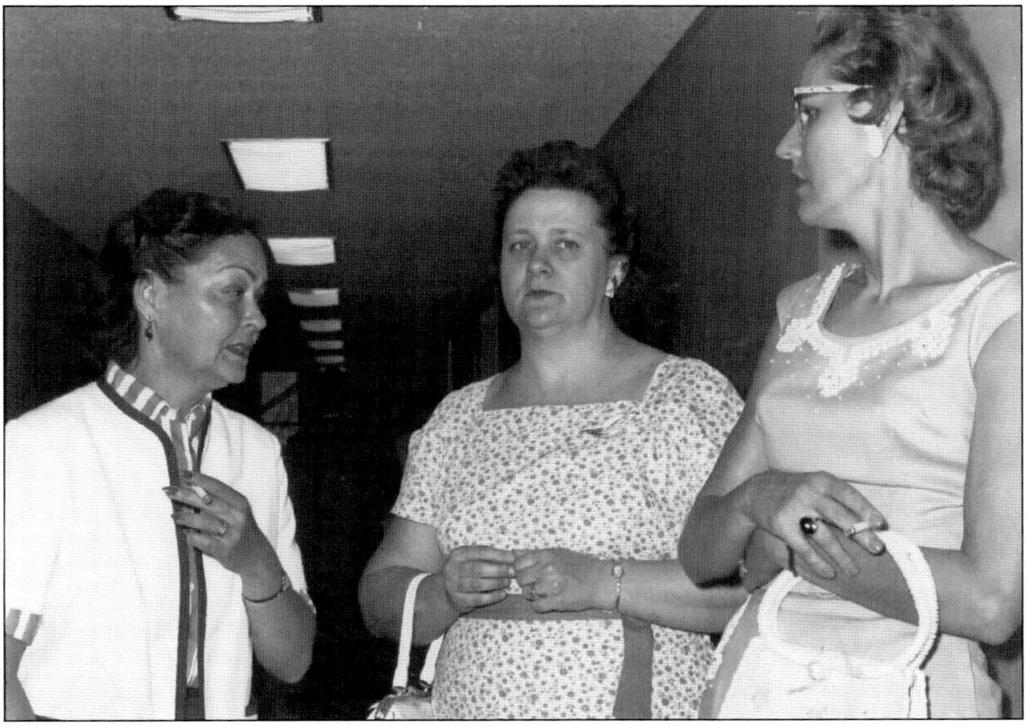

Dorothy White (left), Annora Quitter (center), and Alma Ciafardini (right) take a break during their husbands' trial. The three Newport police detectives were acquitted of the charge of conspiracy to violate George Ratterman's civil rights. (Kenton County Public Library.)

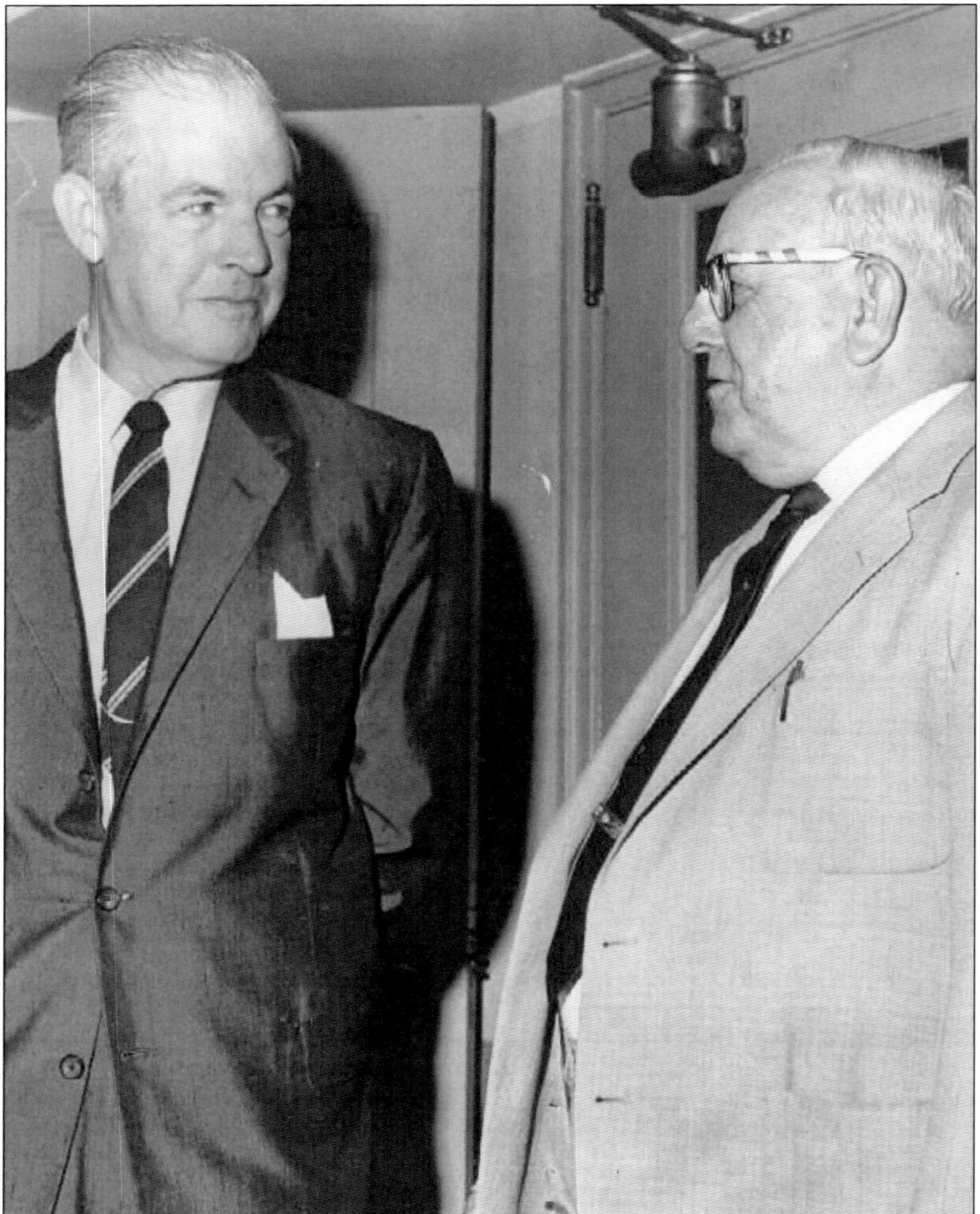

Attorney Charles Lester (left) is seen here with attorney Dan Davies (right). The two lawyers were notorious for representing club owners being prosecuted on illegal gambling charges. During the Ratterman case, Lester was deemed to be the instigator and leader behind the plot to frame the reform candidate. While the other defendants accused of taking part in the conspiracy were acquitted, Lester and Glenn Hotel owner Marty Buccierei were convicted in 1963 of violating George Ratterman's civil rights. Both were sentenced to one year in federal prison. Lester was disbarred from the state in 1968. (Dave Horn Collection.)

George Ratterman (right) was elected sheriff of Campbell County in November 1961. Once he took office, Ratterman and his deputies, with the assistance of federal agents, raided all of the bookie joints and clubs in Newport. By the end of Ratterman's term, nearly all of the illegal gambling dens in Newport were shut down. Many of the club owners left town and headed for Miami or Las Vegas. After unsuccessful bids for county judge-executive and Congress, Ratterman moved his family to Colorado, where he died in 2007. (www.nkyviews.com.)

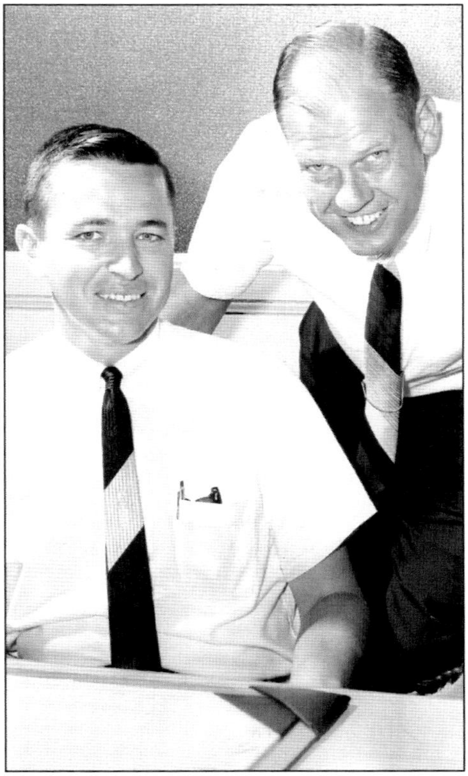

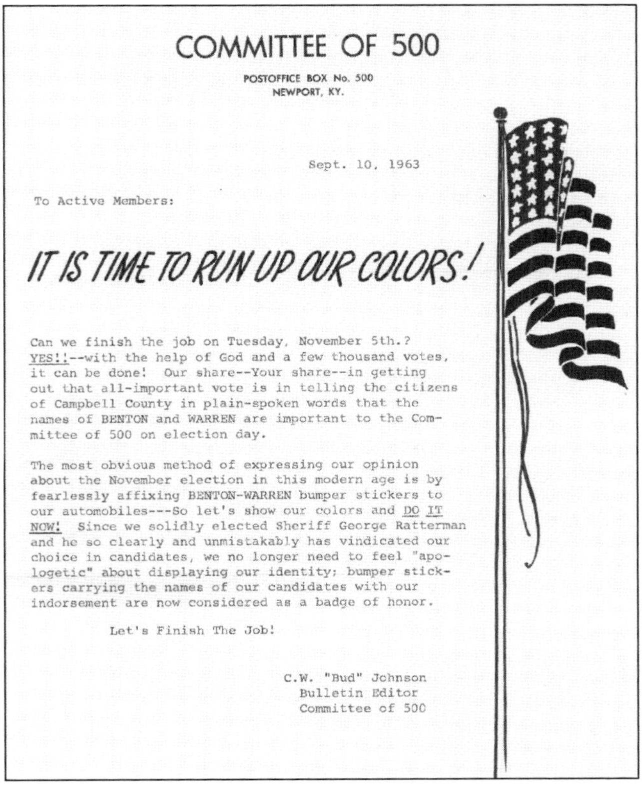

COMMITTEE OF 500

POSTOFFICE BOX No. 500
NEWPORT, KY.

Sept. 10, 1963

To Active Members:

IT IS TIME TO RUN UP OUR COLORS!

Can we finish the job on Tuesday, November 5th.? YES!!--with the help of God and a few thousand votes, it can be done! Our share--Your share--in getting out that all-important vote is in telling the citizens of Campbell County in plain-spoken words that the names of BENTON and WARREN are important to the Committee of 500 on election day.

The most obvious method of expressing our opinion about the November election in this modern age is by fearlessly affixing BENTON-WARREN bumper stickers to our automobiles---So let's show our colors and DO IT NOW! Since we solidly elected Sheriff George Ratterman and he so clearly and unmistakably has vindicated our choice in candidates, we no longer need to feel "apologetic" about displaying our identity; bumper stickers carrying the names of our candidates with our indorsement are now considered as a badge of honor.

Let's Finish The Job!

C.W. "Bud" Johnson
Bulletin Editor
Committee of 500

The Committee of 500 continued to support reform-minded candidates. In 1963, this letter was sent to the citizens of Campbell County encouraging them to vote for committee-endorsed candidates Frank Benton and Fred Warren. This letter urges citizens to display fearlessly their Benton-Warren bumper stickers as a badge of honor. (Dave Horn Collection.)

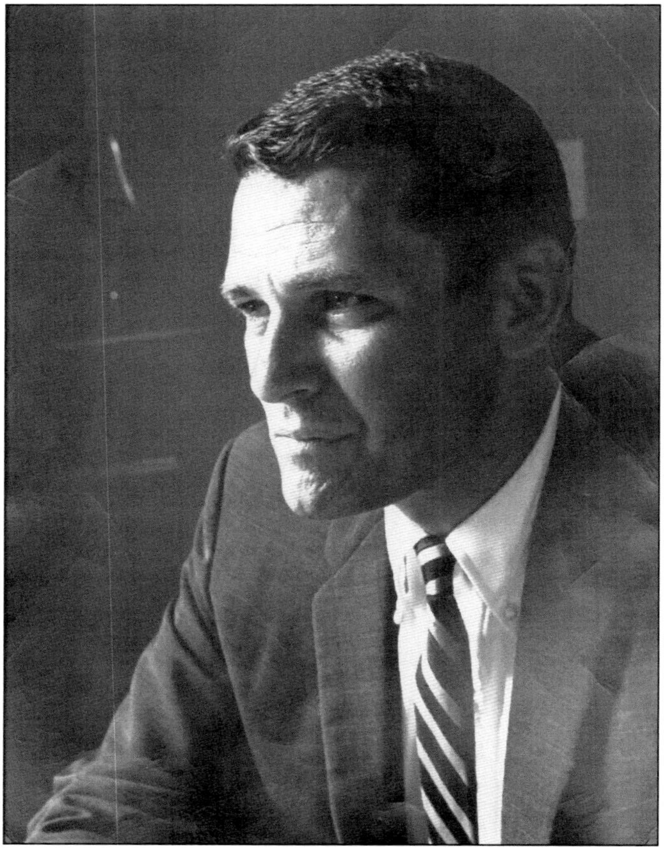

Frank Benton III was elected as Campbell County's commonwealth attorney in 1963, replacing William Wise. Benton made valiant efforts to enforce vice statutes and vigilantly prosecute criminals. (Kenton County Public Library.)

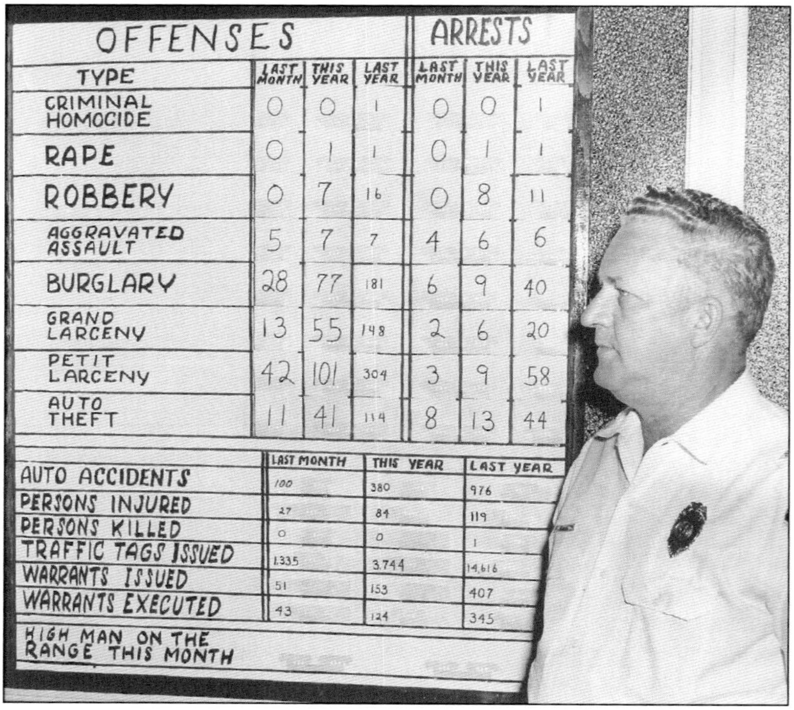

Police chief Upshere White displays a crime scoreboard in June 1964. The chart lists major crimes and their number of offenses and arrests. The chart made comparisons with the previous year so the police department could determine if any particular crime was on the rise. (Kenton County Public Library.)

Six

NEWPORT GETS DIRTY AGAIN

In 1962, the Campbell County sheriff's office teamed with federal agencies and launched a war on vice in Newport. The syndicate networks left town and headed to Vegas. Sheriff Ratterman succeeded in closing most of Newport's gambling emporiums, but could not prevent the economic slump that soon occurred. Over $100,000 in payroll taxes and licensing fees were lost from the city treasury after the casinos closed. By the 1970s, most of the old clubs turned into exotic strip tease outlets that provided a front for prostitution. Porn shops, peep shows, and adult bookstores took the place of the once thriving clubs. In the 1980s, Newport experienced a decline in population and many businesses moved out of the area, including the city's biggest employer, the Wiedemann Brewery. Reform-minded citizens banded together to create organizations and committees aimed at improving Newport's economic future. The Newport Citizens Advisory Council (NCAC) encouraged residents to get involved in city government as well as their neighborhoods to promote civic pride.

Adult entertainment venues became a nuisance, but the city was not sure how to fix the problem. A political action group known as the Newport Political Action Committee (NEWPAC) rallied citizens to elect a slate of commission candidates focused on closing strip bars and improving the city's image. Steve Goetz, Laura Bradley, Tom Ferrara, and Fred Osburg, along with Mayor Irene Deaton, took the initiative and started the city on its path to redemption. Much improvement was made concerning city administration, the police department, and public housing. In 1982, the city enacted an ordinance prohibiting nudity in establishments that sold alcoholic beverages. The city stated the ordinance was necessary to prevent blight and deterioration of the city's neighborhoods and to decrease the incidence of crime, disorderly conduct, and juvenile delinquency. They also enacted strict zoning regulations that blocked additional adult entertainment businesses from opening in the city. In the 1990s, the city enacted an ordinance creating an adult entertainment fee of $5,000 for bars with liquor licenses, mandated that the dancers cover up by wearing "pasties and G-strings," banned private dances away from the main stage, and required dancers to be at least three feet away from patrons. The ordinance also prohibited bar workers known as "B-girls" from soliciting high-priced drinks from customers. These tough restrictions caused the steady demise of the adult entertainment business and opened the door for rehabilitation and revitalization throughout the city.

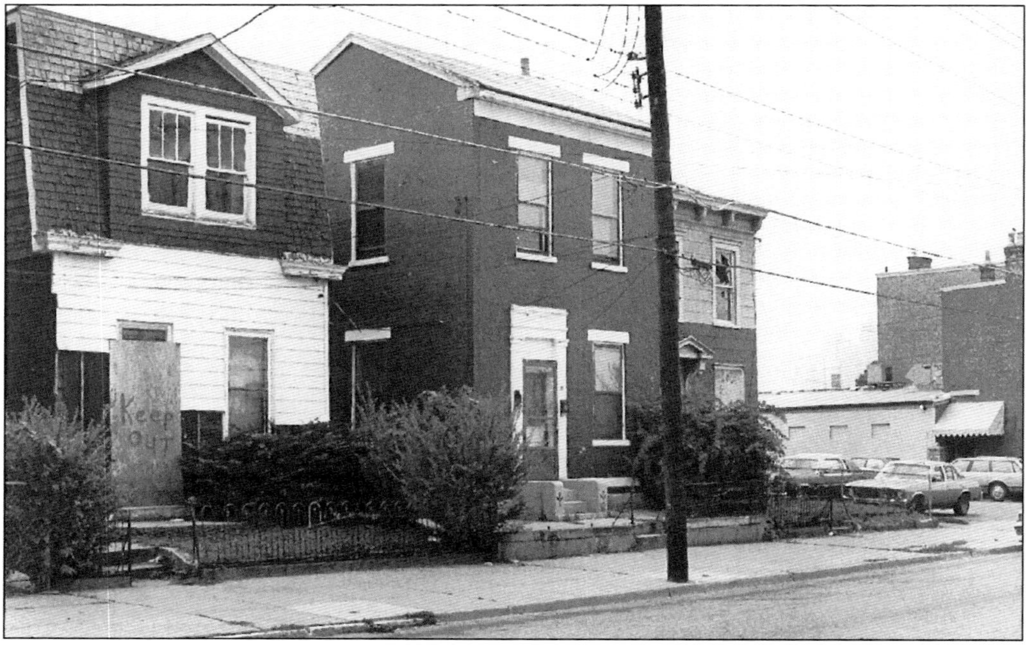

After Newport's clubs and casinos closed, the city experienced an economic slump. The city treasury lost revenue from the payroll taxes and licensing fees. Newport's population declined as many structures, such as these boarded-up houses on Washington Avenue, fell into a dilapidated state. Adult entertainment in the form of strip clubs, adult bookstores, peep shows, and a pornographic theater replaced the old gambling clubs on Monmouth Street. (Kenton County Public Library.)

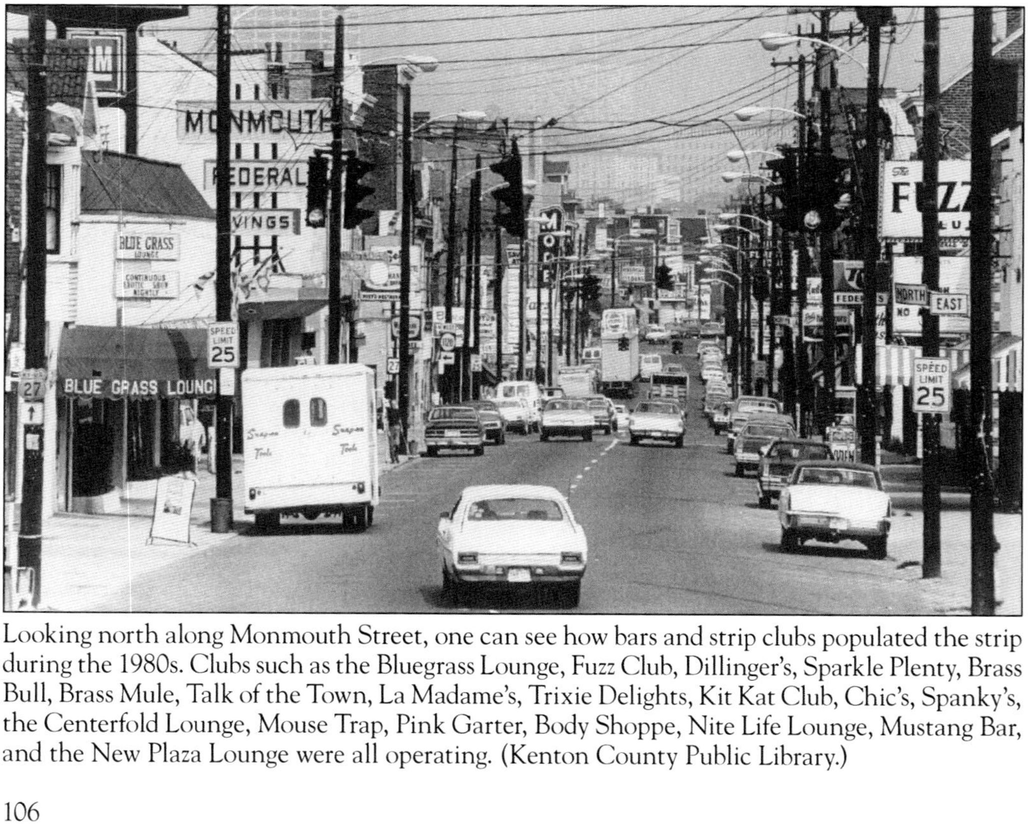

Looking north along Monmouth Street, one can see how bars and strip clubs populated the strip during the 1980s. Clubs such as the Bluegrass Lounge, Fuzz Club, Dillinger's, Sparkle Plenty, Brass Bull, Brass Mule, Talk of the Town, La Madame's, Trixie Delights, Kit Kat Club, Chic's, Spanky's, the Centerfold Lounge, Mouse Trap, Pink Garter, Body Shoppe, Nite Life Lounge, Mustang Bar, and the New Plaza Lounge were all operating. (Kenton County Public Library.)

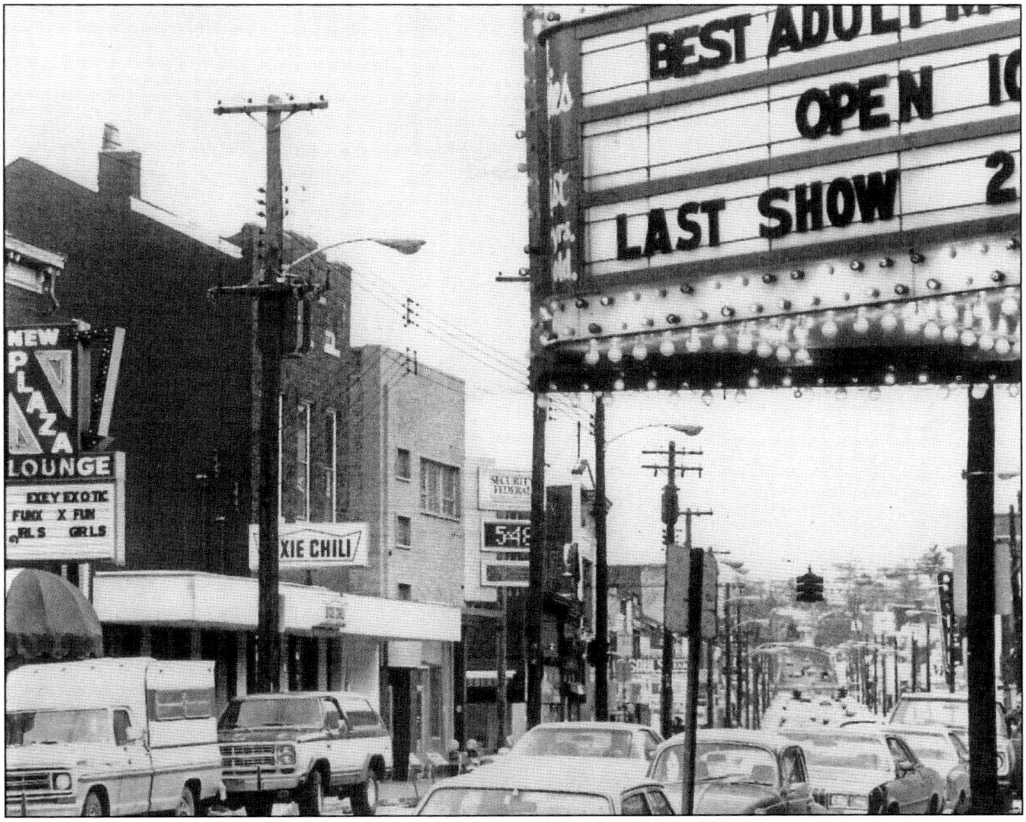

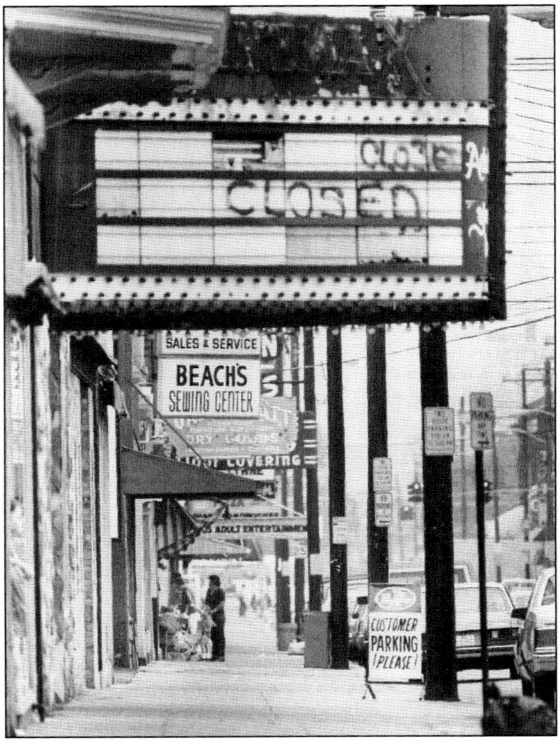

The Cinema X Theater was located at 716 Monmouth Street. It featured adult entertainment in the form of X-rated, pornographic movies. In 1971, city and county officials launched an anti-pornography campaign against the theater. In 1973, police seized the film *Deep Throat* from the theater, which led to a grand jury investigation. The film's star, Linda Lovelace, was subpoenaed to testify in a Newport courtroom. While a jury found the film obscene, the Supreme Court decided that communities have the right to set their own obscenity standards. In April 1980, state and county police raided the theater and confiscated two X-rated films. Several more raids took place before the theater was permanently closed on February 3, 1982. The city acquired the property, demolished the building on March 1, 1983, and later turned it into a parking lot. (Both images, Kenton County Public Library.)

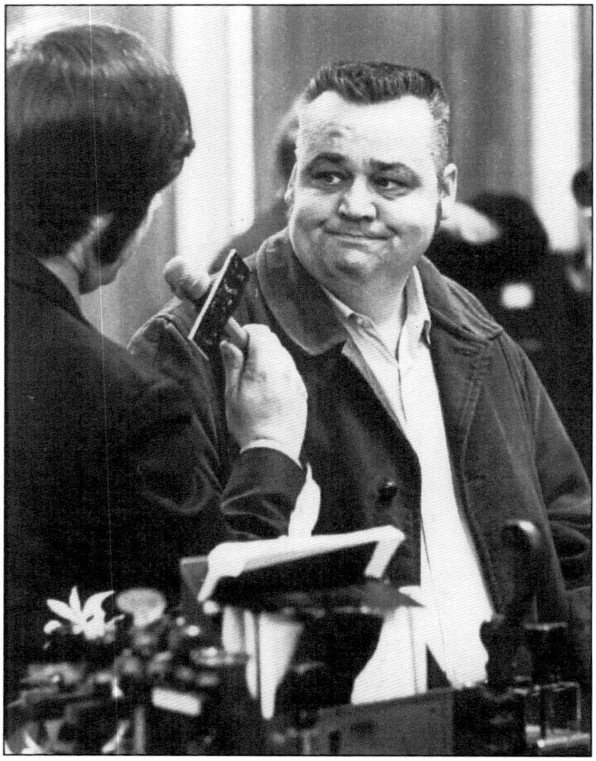

Bill Schweinefuss and Sammy Eisner were partners who operated several clubs together, including the 202 Bar, Midwestern Bar, and the Pink Pussycat. Schweinefuss, a bail bondsman, operated the United Bonding Company on West Fourth Street. After Eisner was found murdered, Schweinefuss became a suspect, but was never charged. Here Schweinefuss is being asked questions by a WCKY news reporter. (Kenton County Public Library.)

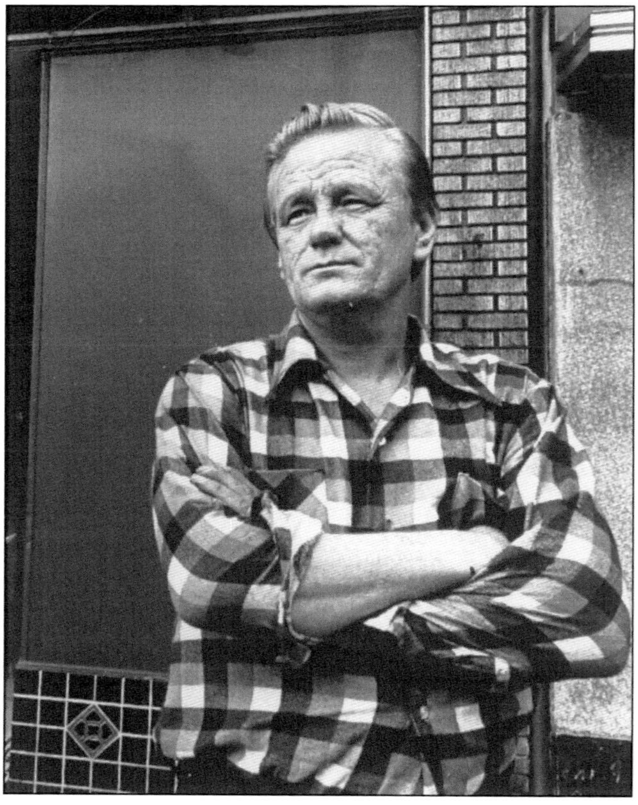

James "Bucky" Lewallen (seen at right) and Sammy Wright operated the Monmouth Street Theater and Variety Store at 721 Monmouth Street. It was also known as Wright's Bookstore. Selling X-rated movies and pornographic books and magazines, it was cited for obscenity in 1980. Wright also owned the New Plaza Lounge, which became a venue for exotic dancing and prostitution. (Kenton County Public Library.)

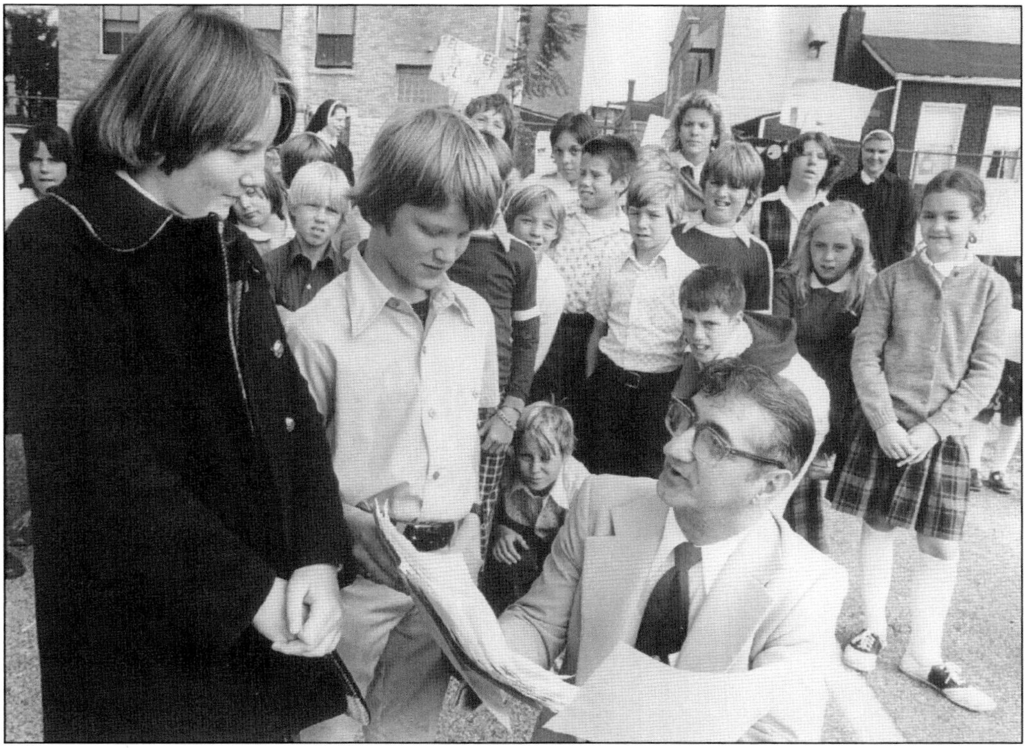

Johnny "TV" Peluso was mayor of Newport from 1964 to 1968 and again from 1976 to 1980. In 1977, the city created a zone for sexually oriented businesses. In this photograph, sixth-grade students from St. Stephen School present Mayor Peluso with a petition asking him to clean up the city by eliminating the seedy businesses in the vice district. The students collected 430 signatures. (Campbell County Historical Society.)

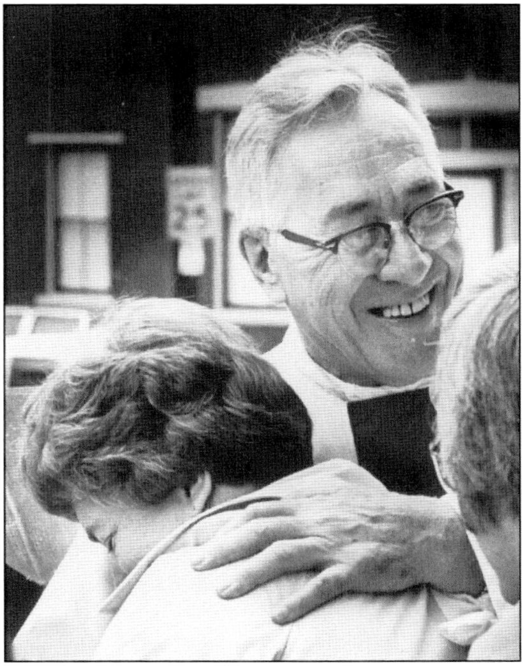

Rev. Anthony Deye was an activist who crusaded for civil rights. In 1965, he participated in the historic Selma-to-Montgomery March with the Reverend Martin Luther King. In the 1980s, Deye served as chairman of the Newport Ministerial Association and pastored at Corpus Christi Church in Newport from 1970 to 1982. Reverend Deye spearheaded the efforts to close the Cinema X theater and the Adult Bookstore in Newport. He pushed for reform to clean up the city. (Kenton County Public Library.)

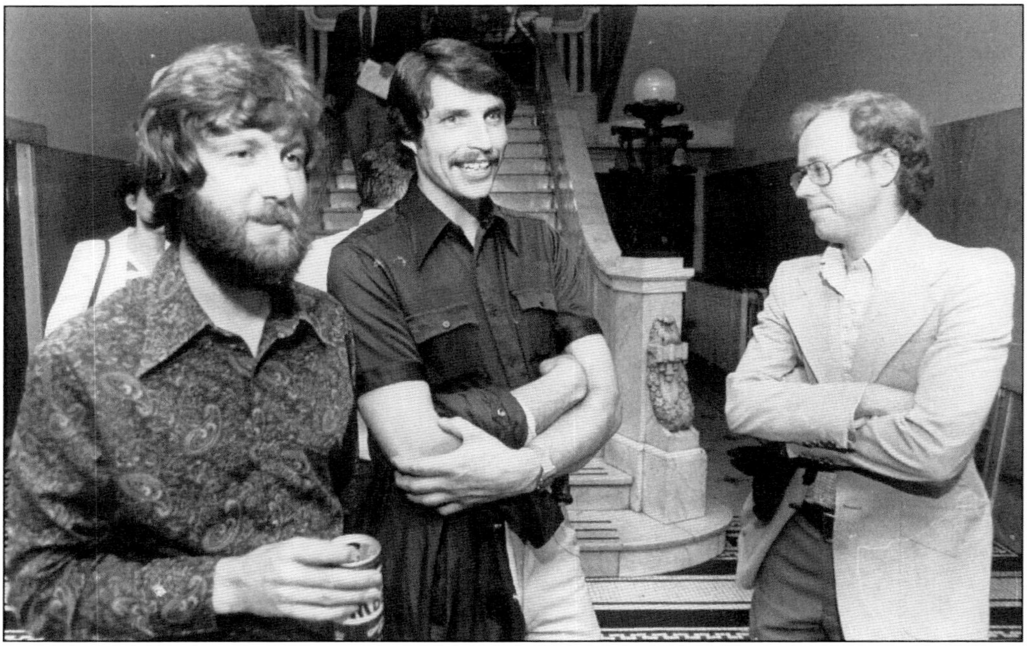

The Newport Political Action Committee was formed in the 1980s by concerned citizens who wanted to elect candidates to the city commission who were focused on eliminating prostitution and closing down strip clubs. The committee interviewed nominees and selected candidates to support for city commission. Pictured here, from left to right, are NEWPAC members Ian Bodd, Allen Dube, and Owen Cramer during a 1981 vote tally at the Campbell County Courthouse. (Kenton County Public Library.)

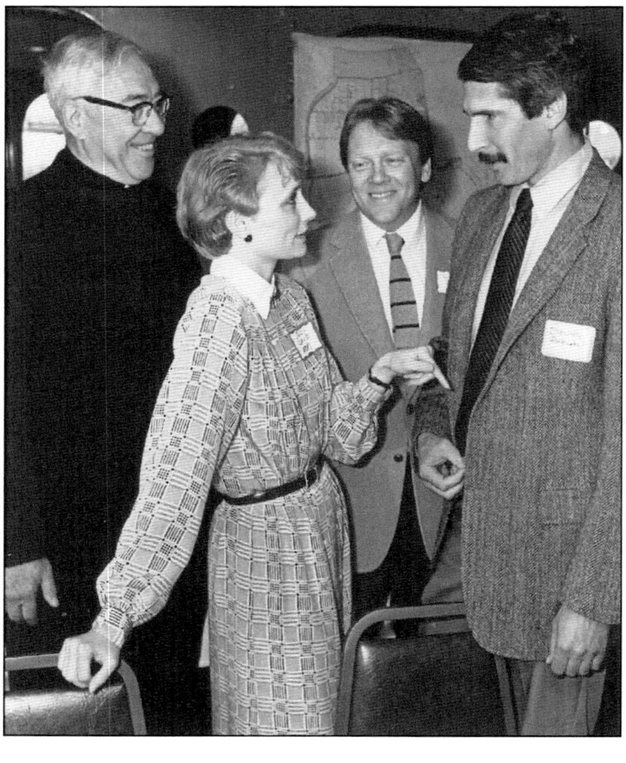

The Newport Citizen's Advisory Council (NCAC) was created to give citizens a voice in the city's decision-making process. Representatives from each neighborhood review issues of interest pertaining to their area and present those concerns to the board of commissioners. The NCAC encourages residents to participate in city government and promotes civic pride. Pictured at left, from left to right, are Rev. Anthony Deye, Judy Lloyd, Lee Ward, and former Newport city manager Dennis Phelan. (Campbell County Historical Society.)

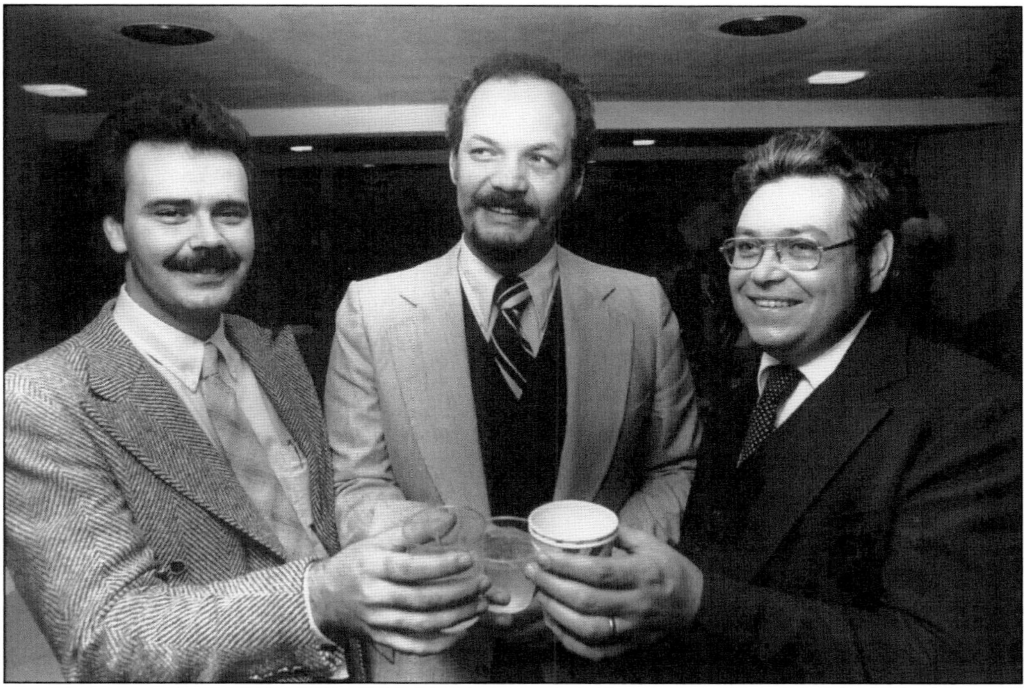

Reformers gained control of the city government in 1977 when Ken Mullikin (left), Steve Goetz (center), and Marty Due (right) were elected to the city commission. The new majority worked to improve conditions in Newport, but did not take immediate action against the adult entertainment venues because some aspects of pornography and nude dancing were protected by the First Amendment. The commission did create a zone for sexually oriented businesses and worked to prevent future salacious businesses from opening. (Kenton County Public Library.)

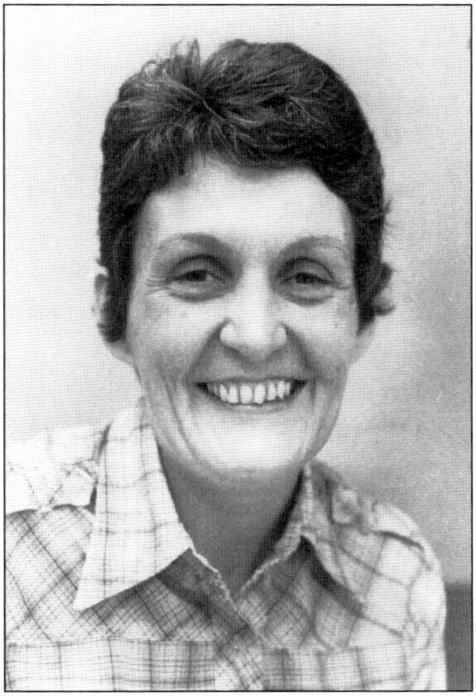

Newportian Irene Deaton was a wife and mother who longed to raise her children in a better environment. She urged city government to take action against the strip clubs and pornography venues that were degrading the city. She ran unsuccessfully as city commissioner in 1973 and won a seat on the commission in 1975. She became Newport's first female mayor and served in this position from 1980 to 1984. (Kenton County Public Library.)

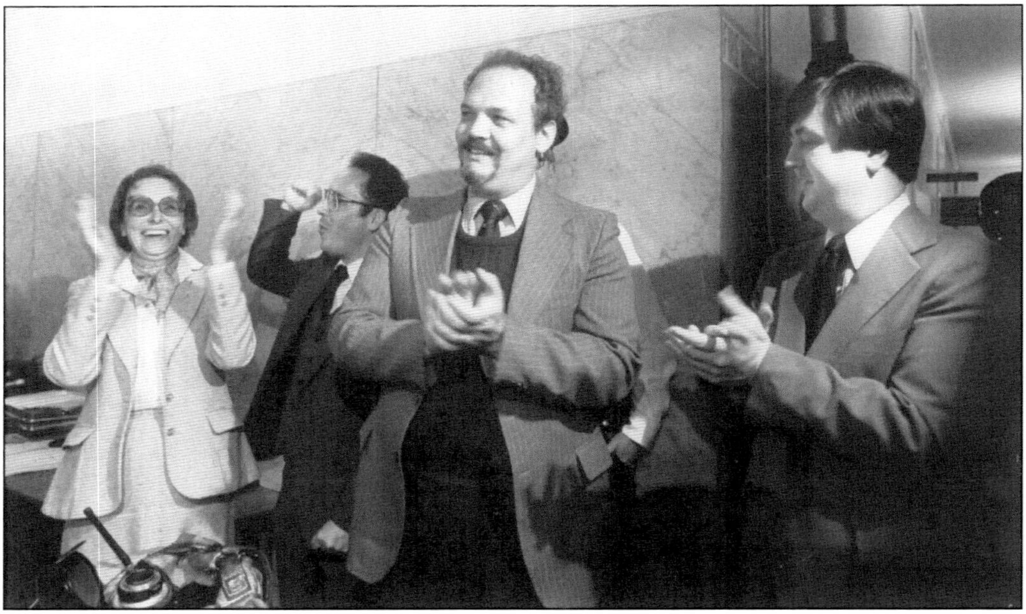

The 1981 commissioner's election was a pivotal turning point for Newport. The reform commission, made up of (pictured above from left to right) Laura Bradley, Tom Ferrara, Steve Goetz, and Fred Osburg, led a morals crusade and successfully brought an end to nude dancing and pornography in Newport. (Kenton County Public Library.)

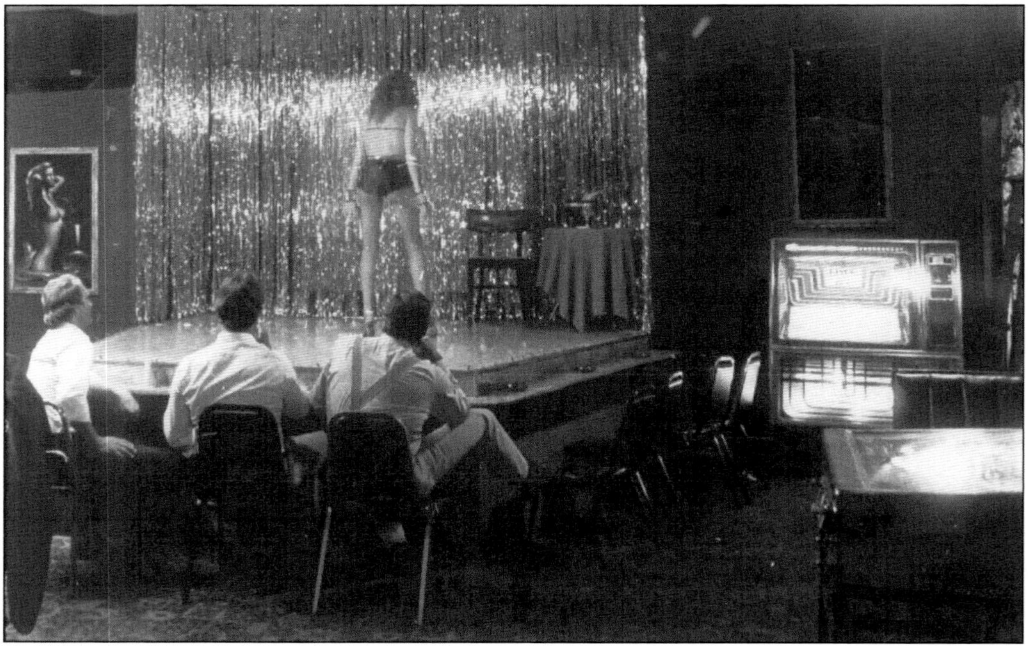

In 1982, the city passed Ordinance No. 0-82-85, prohibiting nude or nearly nude dancing in local establishments licensed to sell liquor. Many of the dancers and club owners challenged the ordinance, and the case went to the U.S. Supreme Court, who upheld Newport's edict by ruling that it was within the scope of powers delegated to the states by the 21st Amendment, which allowed each city to regulate the sale of liquor within its borders. Here an exotic dancer performs for spectators in a Newport strip club. (Kenton County Public Library.)

The Galaxie Club, located at 613 Monmouth Street, was a nude, exotic dancing venue. A large blaze broke out at the club on March 19, 1970, causing major damage to the building. The club was rebuilt and soon back in business. In April 1973, the Galaxie's manager, Richard Matrella, pled guilty to charges of aiding and abetting in prostitution. In this photograph from 1970, dancers employed by the club view the fire damage. The Brass Mule now sits on the site. (Kenton County Public Library.)

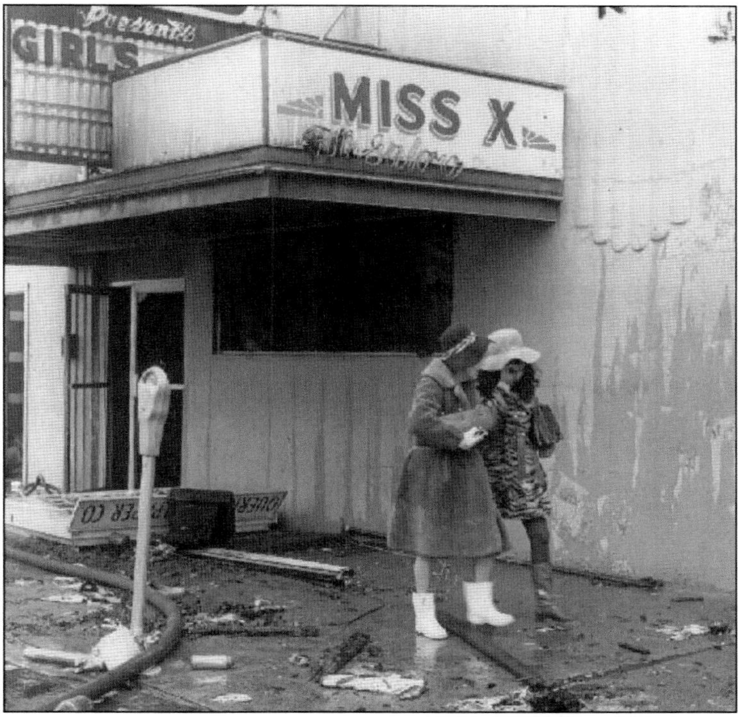

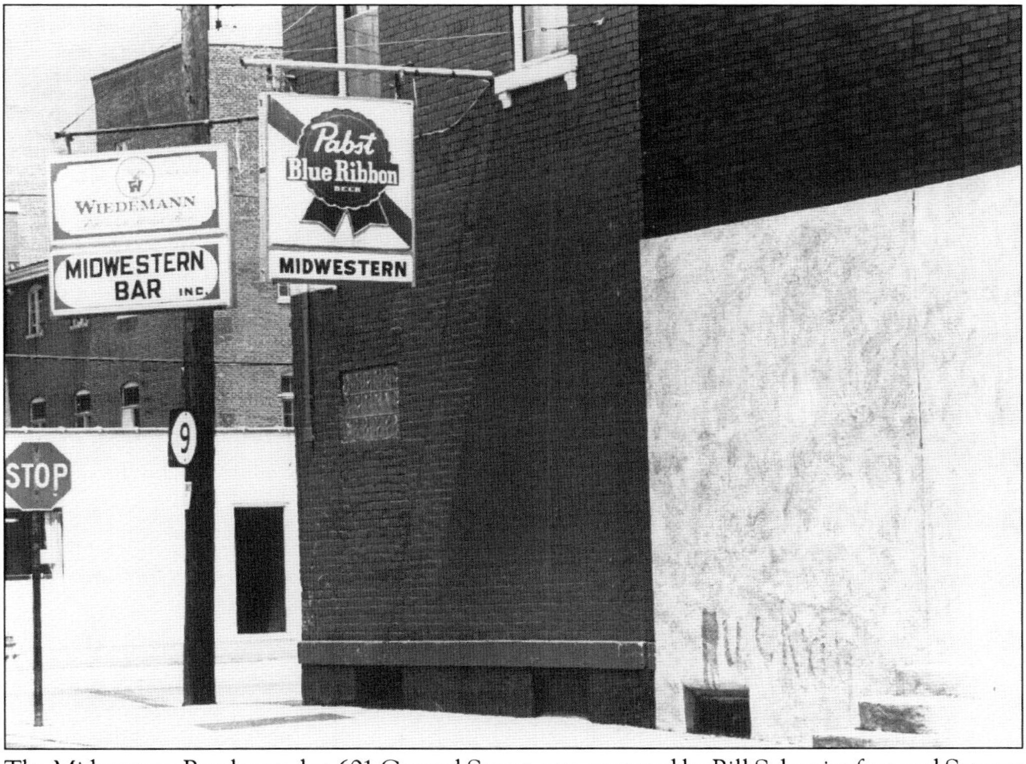

The Midwestern Bar, located at 601 Central Street, was operated by Bill Schweinefuss and Sammy Eisner. The club was the scene of the murder of Newport hoodlum, Clarence "Cue Ball" Thomas. The club was a well-known venue for prostitution. (Campbell County Historical Society.)

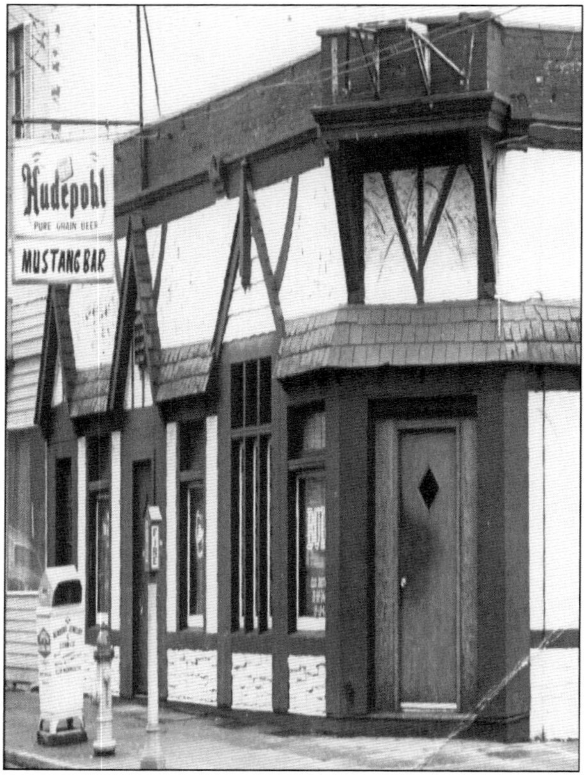

The Mustang Club was located at the corner of Sixth and Monmouth Streets. It was a strip club featuring nude go-go dancers. The club was easily recognized by a large statue of a mustang horse that sat on top of the building until a storm knocked it down and damaged it. The site was the location of previous nightclubs such as the Brick, the Frontier Bar, and the Davey Crockett Bar. (Campbell County Historical Society.)

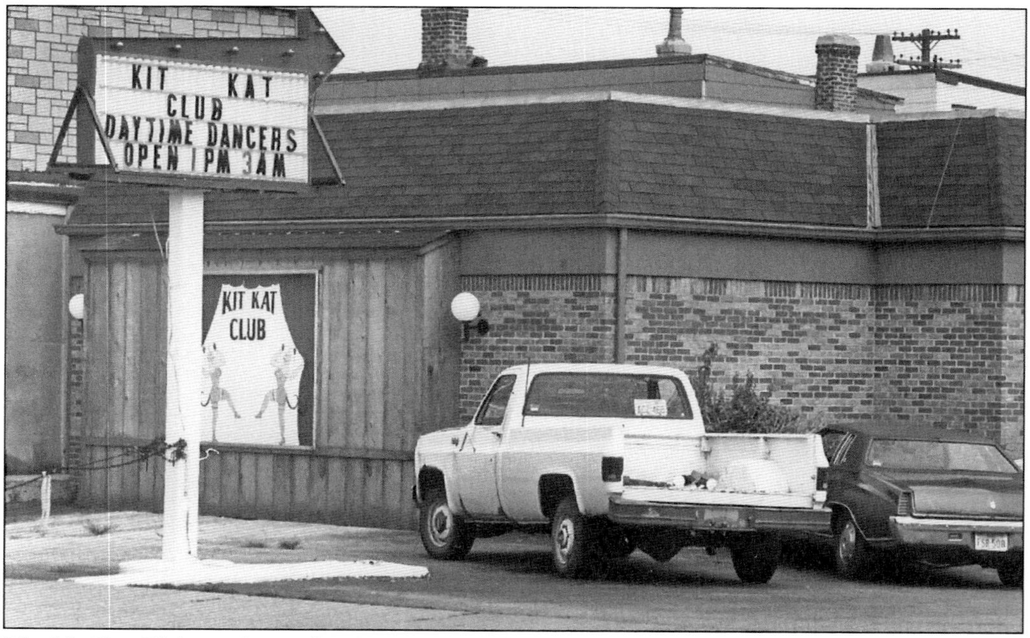

The Kit Kat Club was located at 711 Monmouth Street. It was a bar and nightclub that featured exotic, nude dancing. In March 1988, a 20-year-old exotic dancer employed by the club was shot and killed in the parking lot. A member of the Iron Horsemen Motorcycle Club was charged with her murder. In April 1986, the club was busted for promoting prostitution. Newport nightlife figure Tom Chambers owned the club. (Kenton County Public Library.)

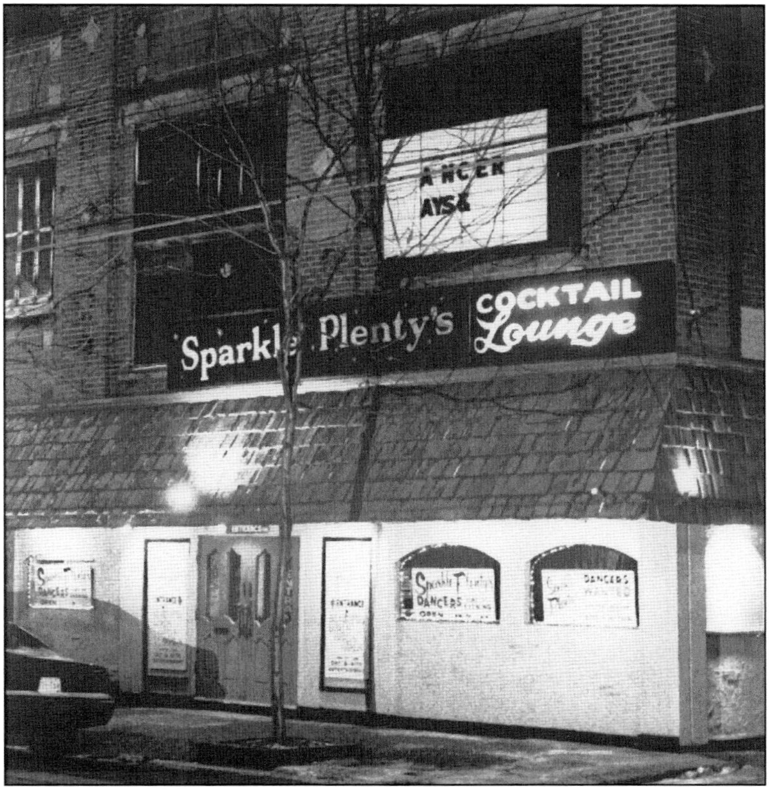

Sparkle Plenty's, located at 515 Monmouth Street, was owned by veteran nightclub operator Ben Kraft. It featured nude dancing until strict city ordinances forced the dancers to cover up and wear a bikini. In 1996, the club was transformed into a cabaret bar that catered to the gay community. Today Mammoth Coffee occupies the site. (Kenton County Public Library.)

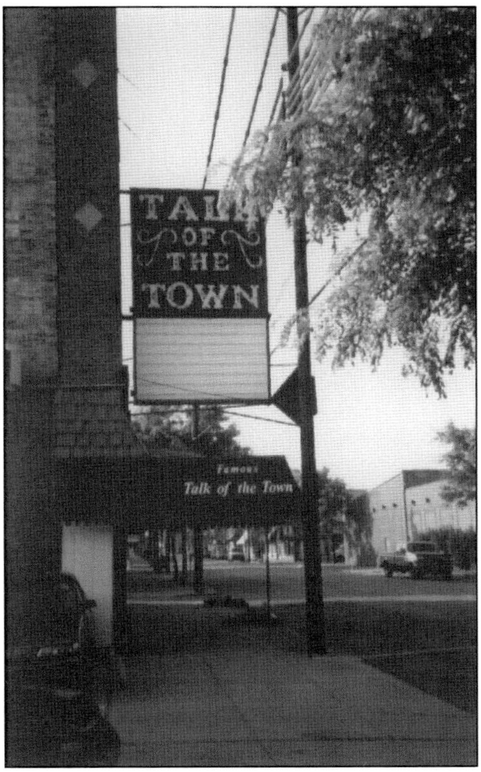

The Talk of the Town, at 513 Monmouth Street, was a strip club featuring nude, exotic dancing. It opened in the mid-1970s with an out-of-town revue of Broadway hits such as *Hello Dolly*. Strippers from New York, New Orleans, and Chicago displayed their talent upon the stage. In the 1980s, several dancers employed by the club were arrested for engaging in prostitution. (Kenton County Public Library.)

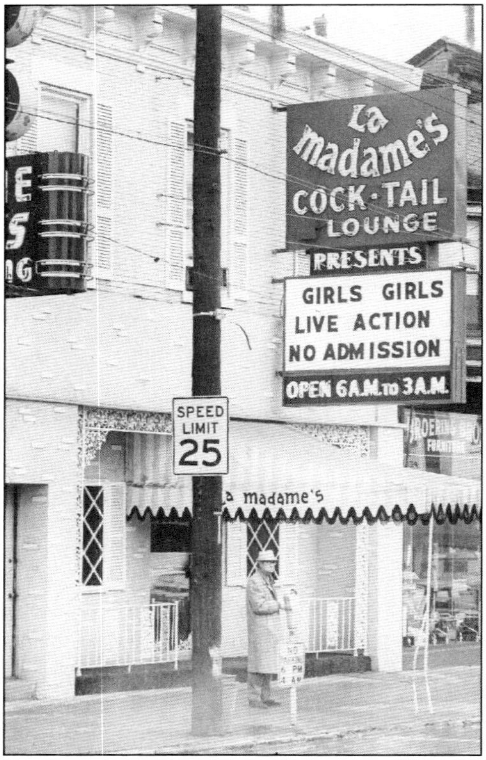

La Madame's, located at 636 Monmouth Street, was a nude, exotic dancing club owned and operated by Billy Ray Manning. Throughout the 1980s and 1990s, the club was shut down several times after numerous prostitution convictions. In March 1991, the club owner unsuccessfully tried to resurrect the bar on Madison Avenue in nearby Covington, but the city's zoning laws would not permit another go-go bar in the central business district. (Kenton County Public Library.)

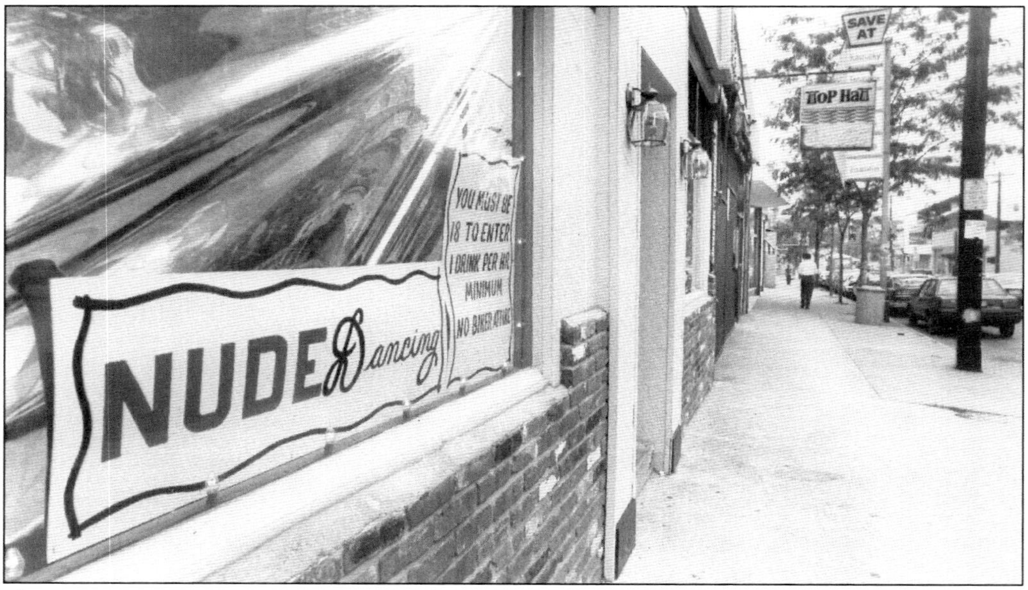

The Mousetrap Lounge was an exotic dancing locale at 924 Monmouth Street. It was popular for offering "couch dances" in lieu of lap dances. After Newport passed the nude dancing ban, which prohibited nude dancing at bars serving liquor, the Mousetrap Lounge allowed its liquor license to expire. The club exhibited totally nude dancers and served soft drinks and juice. In May 1985, the city declared the club a house of prostitution and shut it down for one year under the abatement law. In 1995, the club was demolished and replaced with a parking lot. (Kenton County Public Library.)

Striptease artist Morganna Roberts was displaying her talents in Newport as early as 1966 as "The Wild One." She packed the Galaxie Club along Monmouth Street for two and three shows per night. She also gained the reputation as baseball's "Kissing Bandit" by running onto the field to plant a kiss on the players. She was not above a good publicity stunt such a topless stroll from the clubs to the Travelodge Motel, where she stayed while in town. She eventually stopped stripping and branched out into pornographic films. (Kenton County Public Library.)

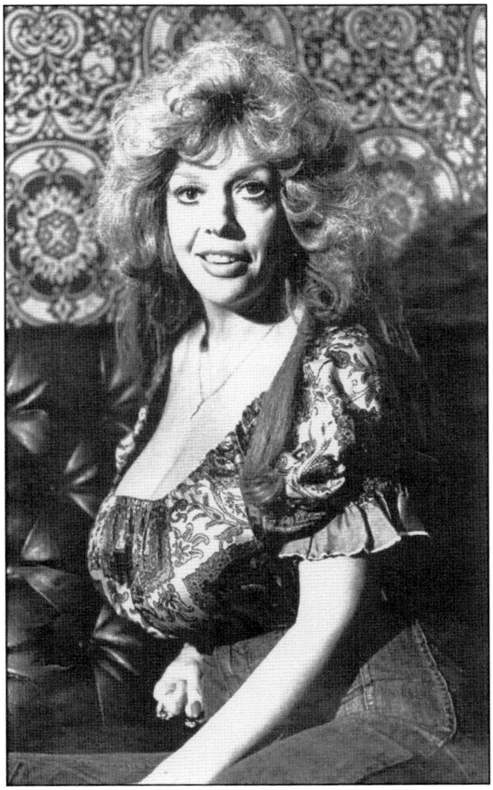

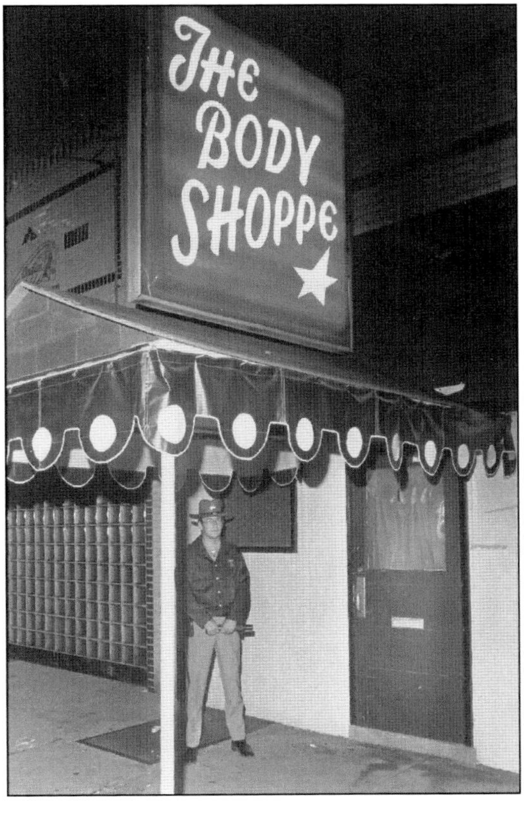

The Body Shoppe, located at 506 York Street, was a bar and lounge that featured nude, exotic dancing. In 1981, the Kentucky State Police raided several clubs on Monmouth and York Streets and found drugs and prostitution at the club. In 1982, the city revoked its occupational license. In this picture, a Kentucky State Trooper stands guard outside the club. (Kenton County Public Library.)

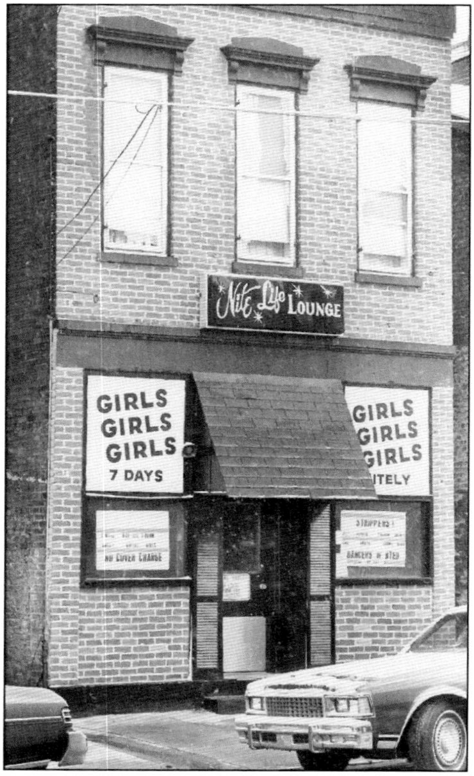

The Nite Life Lounge was a strip club located at 631 Monmouth Street. In 1983, the club was charged with violating the city's nude-dancing ban after dancers were caught using transparent tape to cover their areolas. In 1991, the club was busted for prostitution. (Kenton County Public Library.)

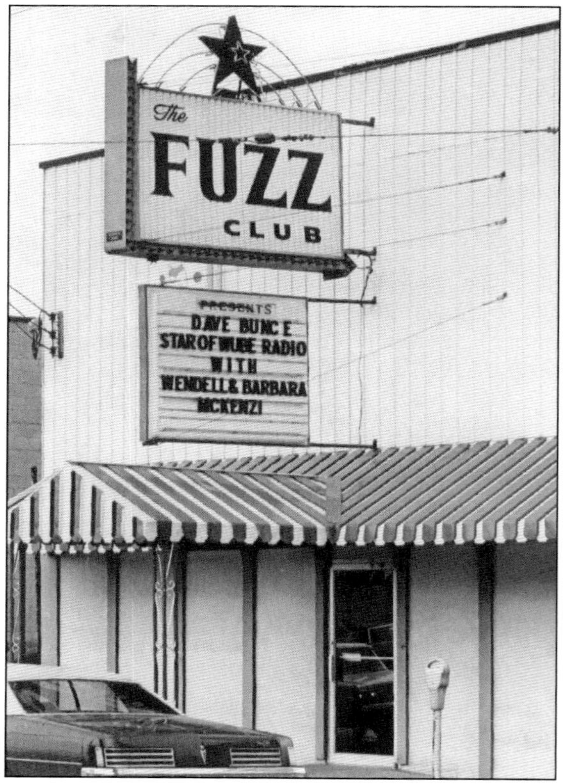

The Fuzz Club was a bar and strip club located at 1027 Monmouth Street. In 1980, several arrests were made at the club for prostitution. The club had its own swimming pool off to the side of the building that was used by the dancers. The club later became Club 55 and the Pure Social Club, a private swingers club. (Campbell County Historical Society.)

The Newport Health Club was located at 2 East Front Street. Operating as a massage parlor, the business was rumored to be a front for a prostitution outlet. Newport passed an ordinance to prevent illegitimate businesses from operating in the city. As a result, hours of operation are restricted and massage parlors must have nationally certified, disease-free masseuses who are required to obtain photo identification and to have their fingerprints on file. (Kenton County Public Library.)

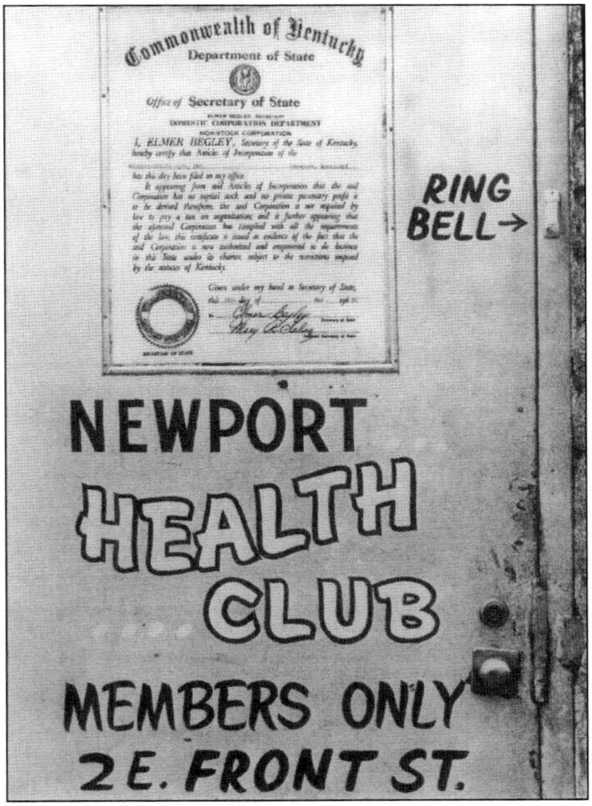

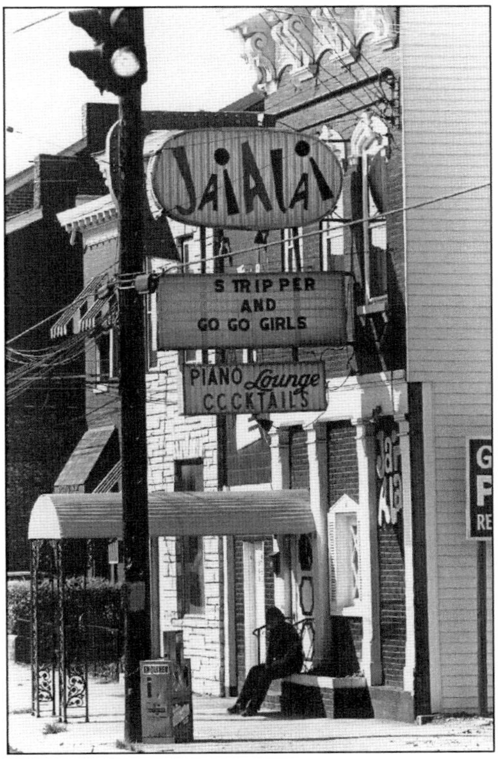

The Jai Alai Piano Lounge was located at 904 York Street. Operated by Big Jim Harris, it was a bar featuring exotic, nude dancing. On September 19, 1980, the club was raided by state police. Several dancers were arrested for engaging in prostitution, and Jim Harris was charged with promoting prostitution. The club mysteriously burned in February 1984. (Kenton County Public Library.)

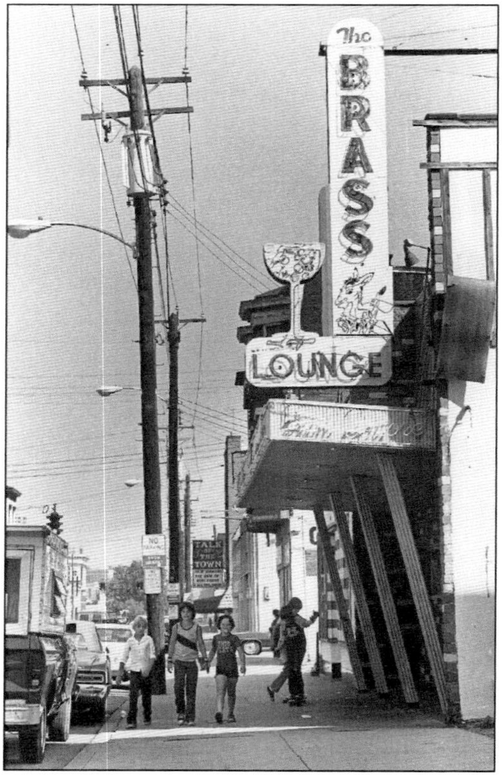

The Brass Mule, or the "Brass Ass," is located at 613 Monmouth Street. The club offered nude, exotic dancing and burlesque shows. The club was originally owned by Vance Raleigh, but after his murder, his sister Armina Lee Peterson gained ownership of the club and continues to run it. In 1991, Newport passed an ordinance banning all public nudity. (Kenton County Public Library.)

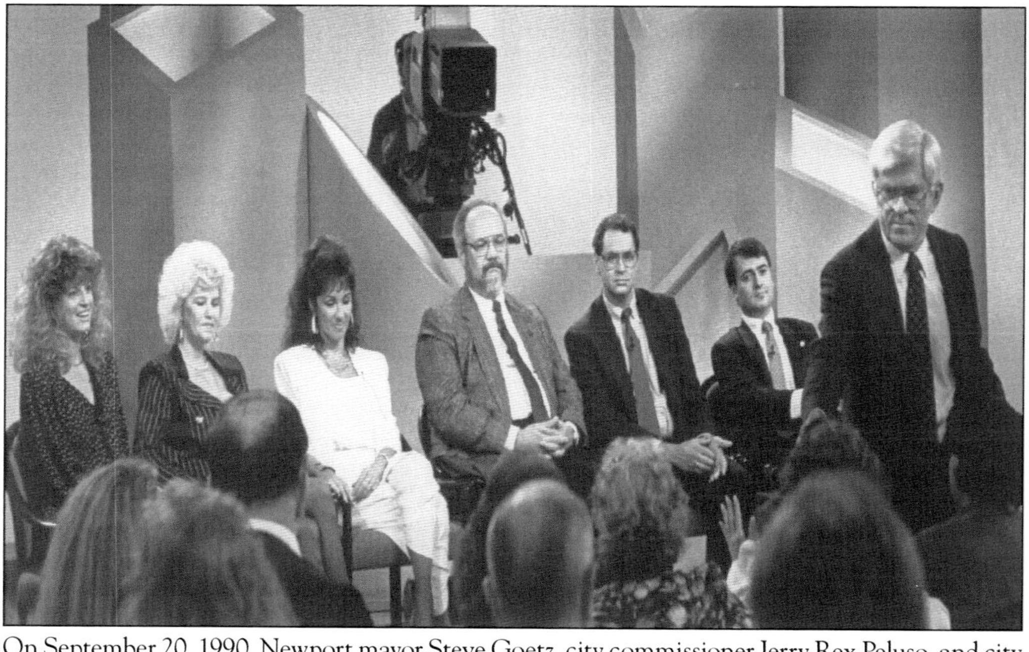

On September 20, 1990, Newport mayor Steve Goetz, city commissioner Jerry Rex Peluso, and city manager Jim Parsons (seated from left to right) were guests on a popular daytime talk show hosted by Phil Donahue (standing). They were joined by fellow Newport strippers, from left to right, Eelise LaShay, Sandi Summers, and Nikki Nielson, who battled over issues surrounding Newport's nude dancing laws. The show aired on October 1, 1990. (Kenton County Public Library.)

Steve Goetz was first elected to the Newport City Commission in 1977 on a reform ticket. He was elected mayor in 1983. Goetz made gallant efforts to clean up Newport's tawdry image. He was reelected in 1987 and in 1991. The Northern Kentucky Chamber of Commerce named Goetz Outstanding Local Official of the Year in 1991. In 1992, Goetz resigned after his involvement in a scandal involving unauthorized use of a city credit card. (Kenton County Public Library.)

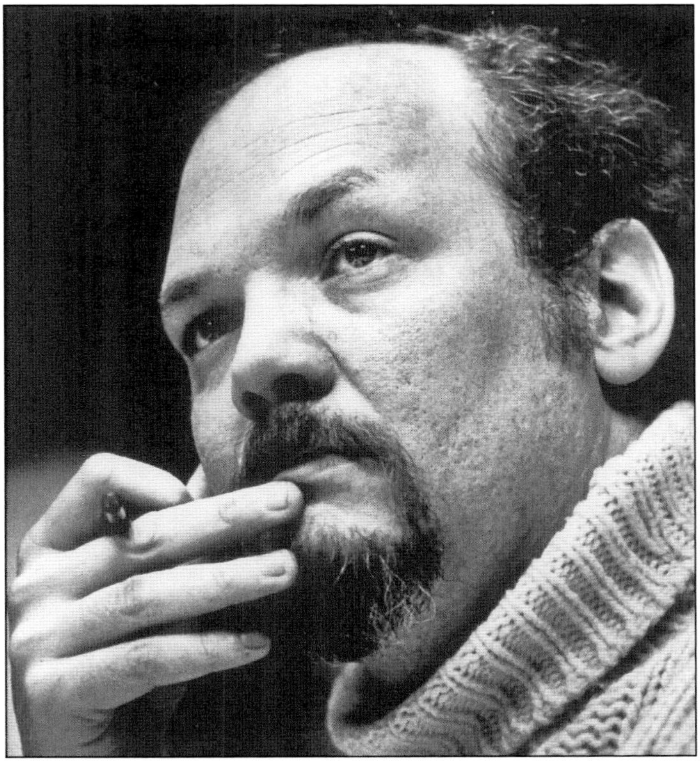

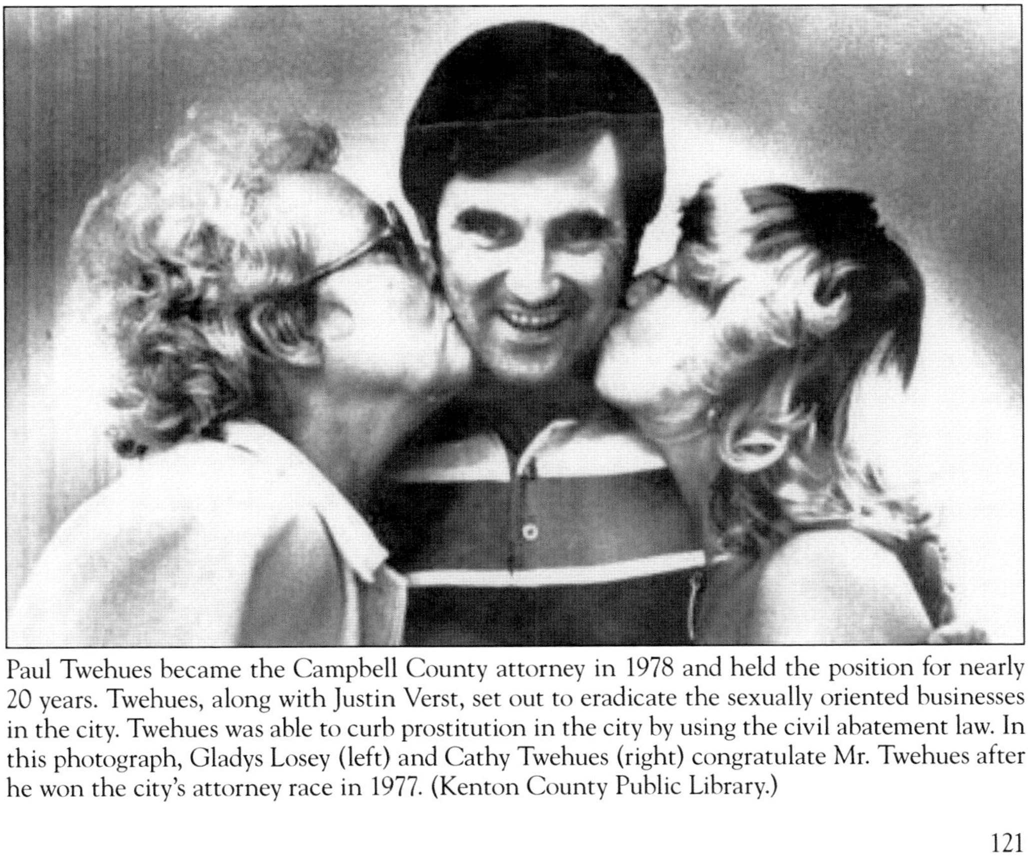

Paul Twehues became the Campbell County attorney in 1978 and held the position for nearly 20 years. Twehues, along with Justin Verst, set out to eradicate the sexually oriented businesses in the city. Twehues was able to curb prostitution in the city by using the civil abatement law. In this photograph, Gladys Losey (left) and Cathy Twehues (right) congratulate Mr. Twehues after he won the city's attorney race in 1977. (Kenton County Public Library.)

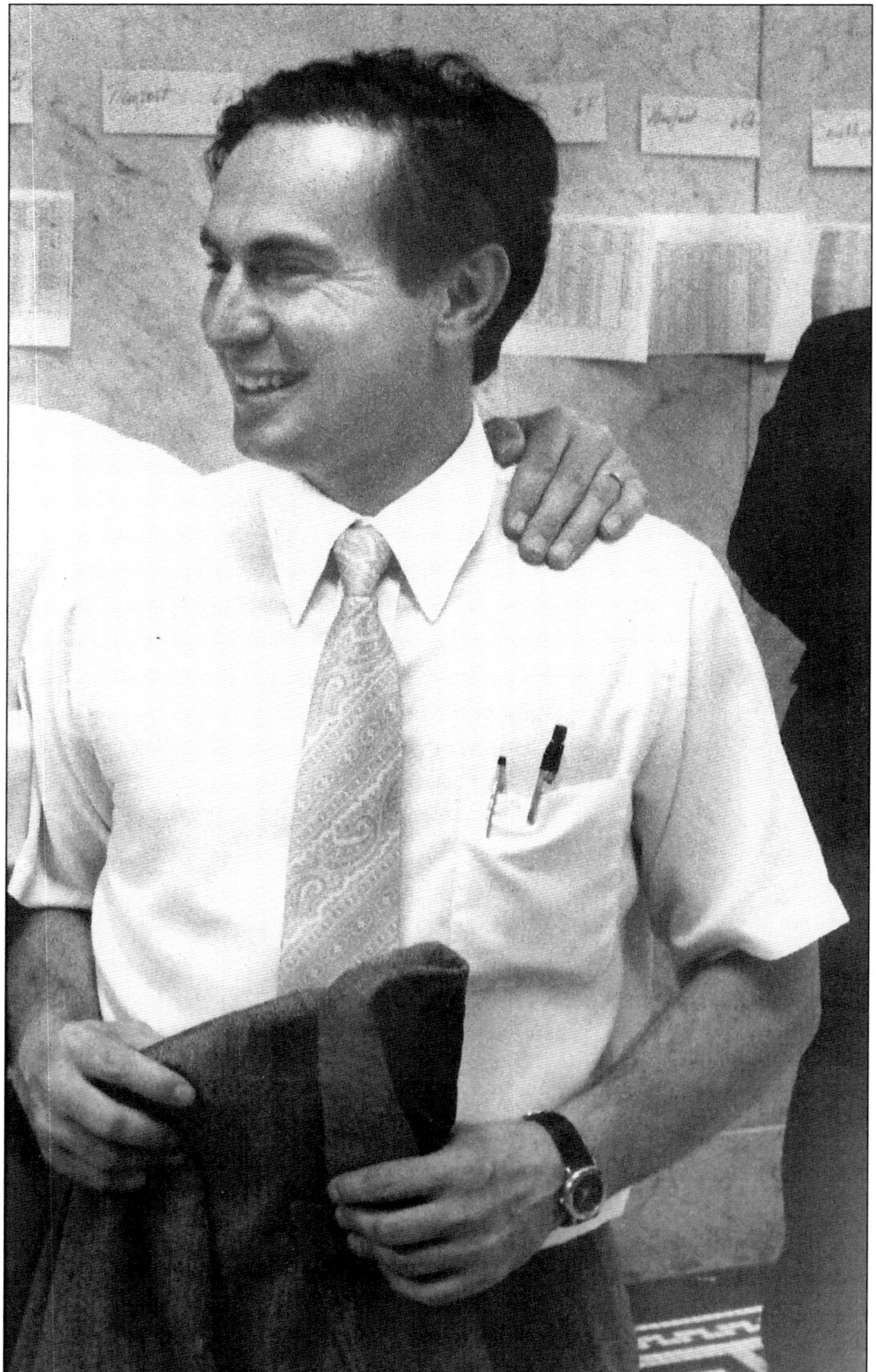

Thomas L. Guidugli was a Newport city commissioner who gained the title vice mayor because he was the top vote-getter during the 1989 and 1991 elections. He replaced mayor Steve Goetz, who resigned in 1992. In November 1993, Guidugli won a special election to serve the remaining two years of Goetz's unfinished term. He served as mayor until 2008. (Kenton County Public Library.)

Seven

A New Newport

The Department of Economic Development was created by the city commission to support and promote economic development by attracting new businesses and to aid in the redevelopment of existing businesses. Laura Long became the city's first economic development director in 1983. Long secured over $15 million in grants for the city's urban renewal projects. Recognizing the importance of Newport's historic districts, the city passed an ordinance to prohibit inappropriate modifications of building exteriors. Rehab-a-Rama was a program implemented to rehab historic houses that needed attention or sat vacant. Today Newport is the second largest historical district in Kentucky.

Waterfront development has stimulated the city's economy with the proliferation of Riverboat Row. What started out as a couple of floating restaurants later progressed into a shopping and entertainment complex that amplified city tax revenue, created jobs, increased property values, and stimulated tourism. The Newport Aquarium opened in 1999, followed by Newport on the Levee in 2001. Surrounding the Levee are other popular developments, such as the German-themed Hofbrauhaus. Opening in 2003, it is the first North American version of the world's best-known brew pub in Munich. The World Peace Bell was installed in 1999. Weighing in at 33 tons and measuring 12 feet high and 12 feet wide, it is the largest free-swinging bell in the world. The inscription on the bell reads, "The World Peace Bell is a symbol of freedom and peace honoring our past, celebrating our present and inspiring our future." A grant from the U.S. Department for Housing and Urban Development is helping to build and renovate subsidized housing units in the city. Million-dollar homes are being constructed on Wiedemann Hill. Currently under construction is the Newport Pavilion, an office and retail development in the former Cote Brilliante neighborhood. Newport has come a long way since its "Sin City" days. It has become the envy of the region where civic pride runs deep as we honor our past, celebrate our present, and inspire our future.

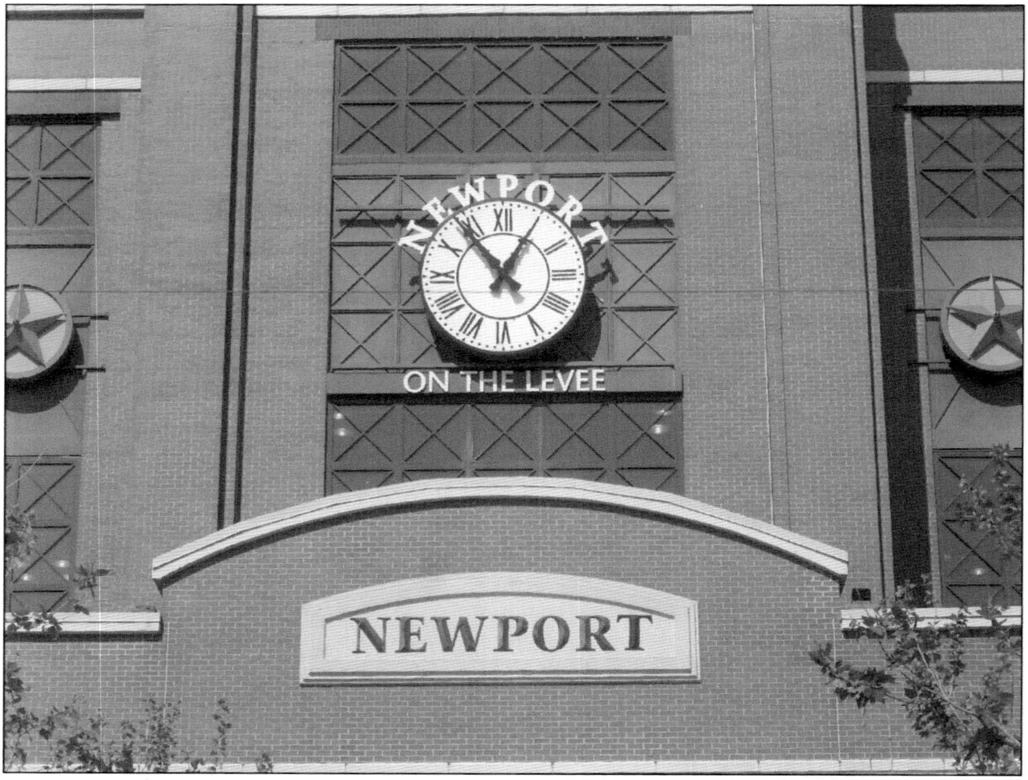

Newport on the Levee opened along the city's waterfront in 2001. It is an entertainment multiplex with shopping, dining, bars, dance clubs, gaming venues, a bookstore, an ice cream parlor, a candy shop, comedy clubs, and a 20-screen AMC movie theater. Anchored by the Newport Aquarium and adjacent to the Purple People Pedestrian Bridge, it is a popular attraction in the Greater Cincinnati and Northern Kentucky area. The Levee features a year-round schedule of special events and live music. In the Zagat Survey's 2004 U.S. Family Travel Guide, Newport Aquarium was named the number one aquarium in the Midwest and one of the 25 top-rated attractions in the country. Newport on the Levee topped the national list of malls and shopping centers. (Photograph by Cody Short.)

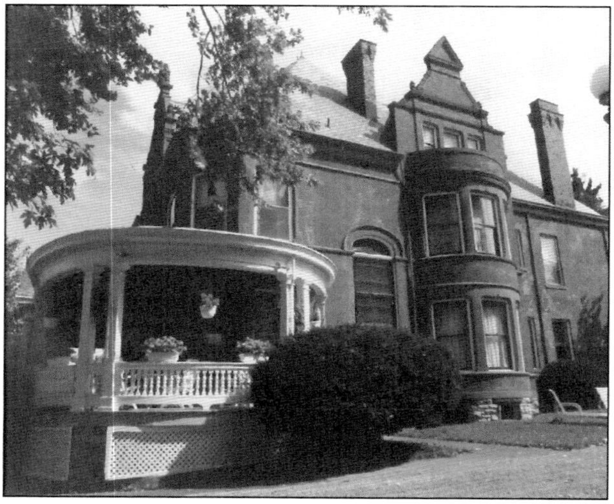

Newport has the second largest local historical district in Kentucky. In 1993, Newport devised a program known as "Rehab-a-Rama." The city arranged for local developers and contractors to secure low-interest loans to purchase historic properties for rehabilitation. The city set design standards to ensure the properties kept their original 19th-entury charm. Many, like the Charles Wiedemann Mansion located at 1102 Park Avenue, have been restored to their original beauty. (Kenton County Public Library.)

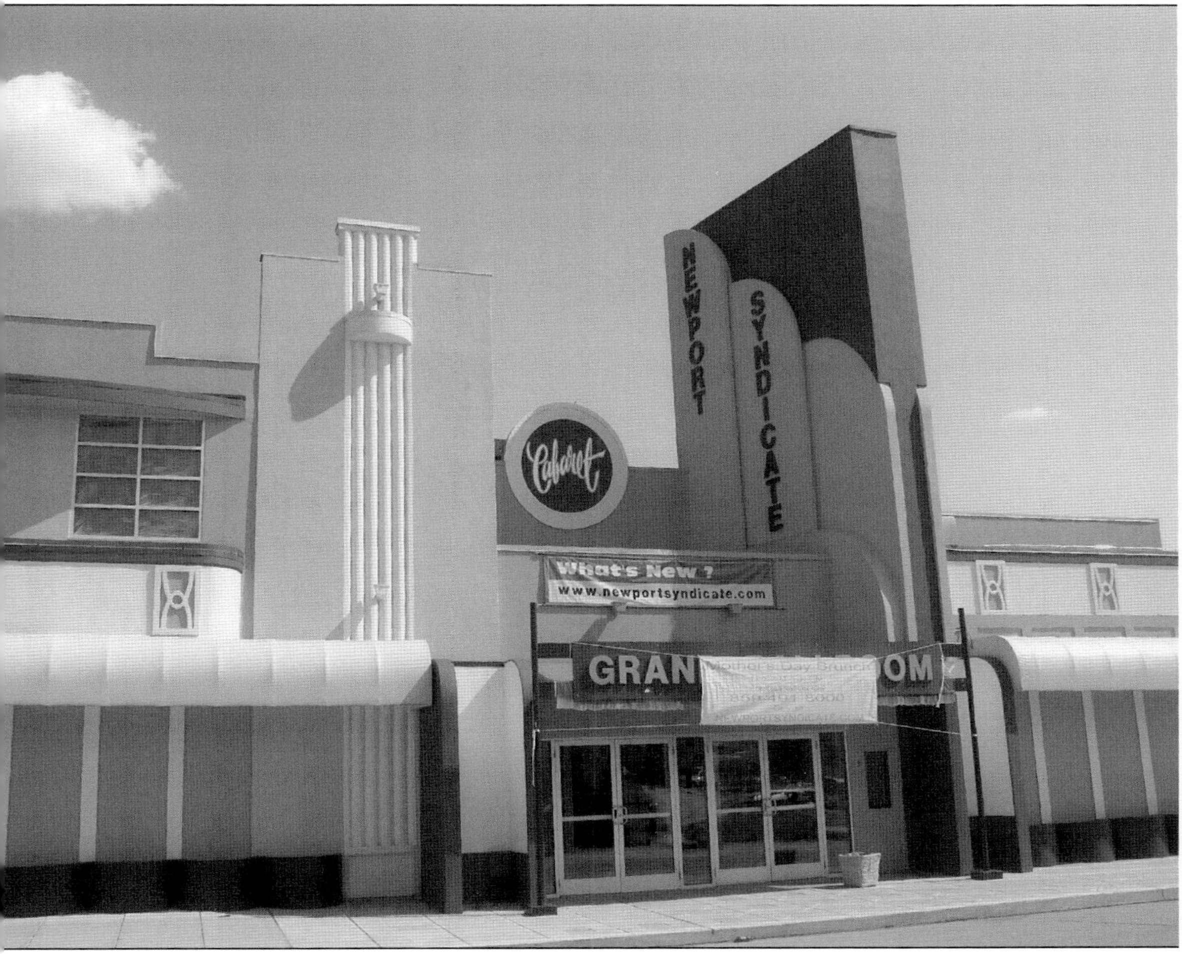

Several businesses in the city pay tribute to Newport's colorful past. The Syndicate Restaurant is an upscale supper club located at 18 East Fifth Street in the former Glenn Schmidt's Playtorium. Wayne Carlisle and David Hosea opened the restaurant in 1995. During renovation of the building, contractors found several secret passageways and bullet holes throughout the building. The interior of the supper club carried a gangster theme. The Syndicate opened with two 1930s-era cars on display in front of the building. In 2003, the restaurant underwent a transformation and was renamed the Coconut Grove. After several years, the restaurant was restored to its original décor and is once again known as the Syndicate. (Photograph by Cody Short.)

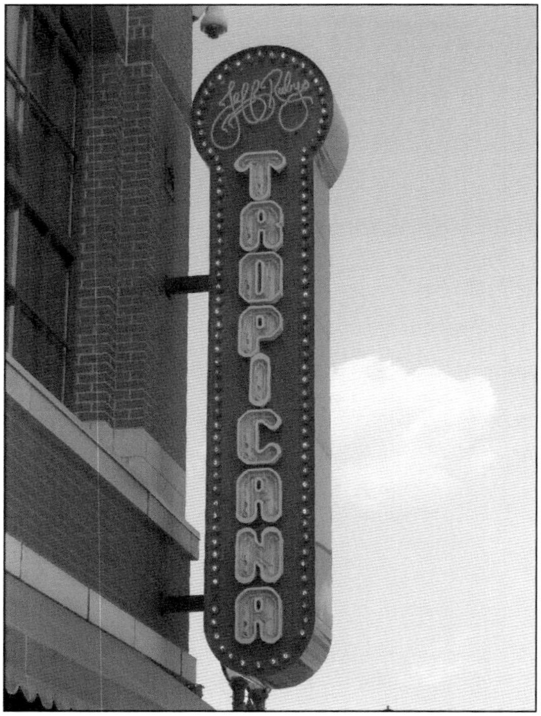

The Tropicana Nightclub is another salute to Newport's past. Named after the famous nightclub on Monmouth Street, the Tropicana is an upscale bar and restaurant located in the Newport on the Levee complex. Jeff Ruby, owner, opened the Tropicana in 2002. The restaurant's decor, which includes a blackjack table, pays homage to Newport's past gambling clubs. Former police chief Pat Ciafardini and former mob associate Tito Carinci attended the Tropicana's grand opening. (Photograph by Cody Short.)

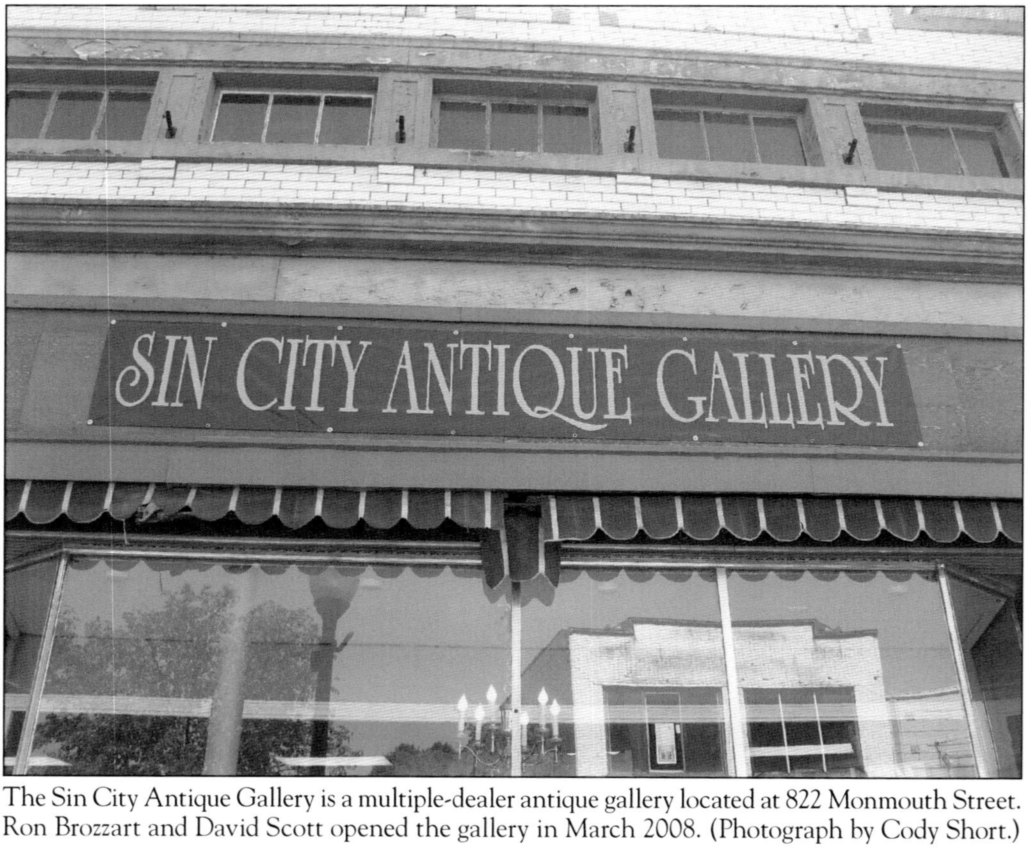

The Sin City Antique Gallery is a multiple-dealer antique gallery located at 822 Monmouth Street. Ron Brozzart and David Scott opened the gallery in March 2008. (Photograph by Cody Short.)

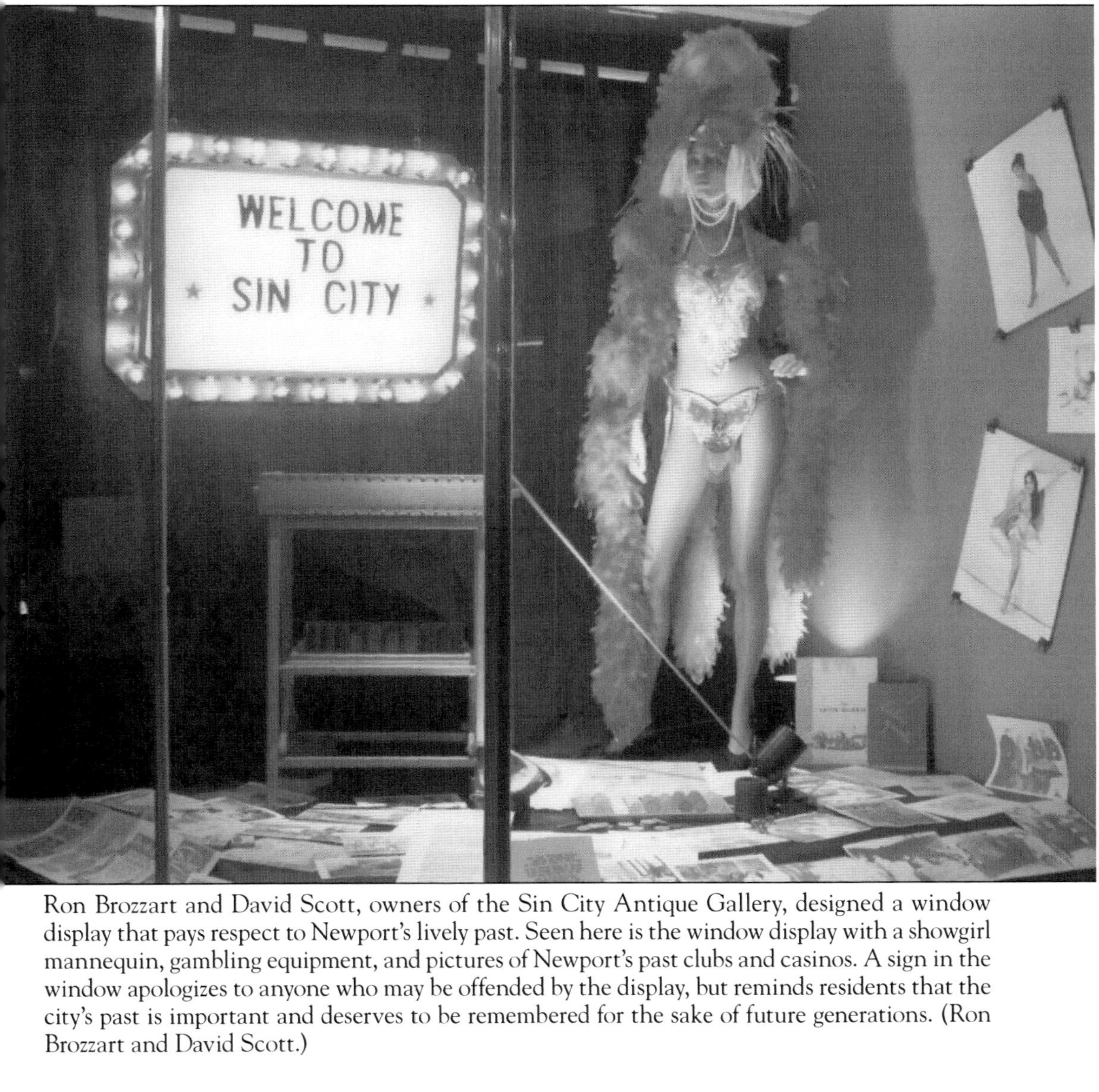

Ron Brozzart and David Scott, owners of the Sin City Antique Gallery, designed a window display that pays respect to Newport's lively past. Seen here is the window display with a showgirl mannequin, gambling equipment, and pictures of Newport's past clubs and casinos. A sign in the window apologizes to anyone who may be offended by the display, but reminds residents that the city's past is important and deserves to be remembered for the sake of future generations. (Ron Brozzart and David Scott.)